BENJAMIN FRANKLIN
AND PENNSYLVANIA POLITICS

BENJAMIN FRANKLIN
AND PENNSYLVANIA POLITICS

William S. Hanna

1964
STANFORD UNIVERSITY PRESS
STANFORD   CALIFORNIA

For my Parents

PREFACE

The pre-Revolutionary political history of Pennsylvania has been understood chiefly as an expression of Franklin and Quaker themes, around which other men and events have been ordered and judged. Both Franklin and the Quakers have become historical determinants because they long ago achieved a special place in American mythology as symbolic representatives of certain qualities popularly believed to lie deep in the national character. Franklin, for instance, immediately suggests a distinctive—some would say a peculiarly American—blend of enlightenment and reason, hard-headed practicality graced with tolerance and a liberal spirit, and a native wit and wisdom joined with a many-faceted genius successfully applied. In short, he exemplifies colonial Americans and especially colonial Pennsylvanians at their best.

Whatever the validity of these associations for Franklin's life as a whole or for the essential meaning of American history, they have stamped a misleading interpretation upon one of his major occupations and forced the political history of his province into an arbitrary mold. This distortion is supported, on different grounds, by Quaker-inspired accounts. As a group, the Quakers are almost equally freighted with praiseworthy qualities and larger significances and, like Franklin, have been elevated to the status of symbols. Standing for tolerance, liberality, and virtuous simplicity, the Quakers undertook a "Holy Experiment" in the wilderness and thereby created a model for America's subsequent welcome to all persecuted minorities.

Franklin and the Quakers together provide an interpretative framework that rests upon the application of Quaker religious ideals and Franklinian rationality to politics. In broad outlines, this view presents politics in Pennsylvania as a conflict between good and, if not evil, at least retarding forces. In the beginning, William Penn and his fellow Quakers established a liberal and rapidly prospering society in Pennsylvania, founded upon advanced social, religious and political principles. Yet, however benevolent William Penn may have been, the fact that he was a Proprietor inevitably meant that he was an obstacle to the full development of the colony's auspicious beginning. It therefore fell to the Quakers in Pennsylvania to battle for additional rights and liberties and the preservation of the founder's ideals. This contest—part of a similar struggle going on all over Colonial America—began against William Penn, but reached its greatest intensity under the misrule of the later proprietaries. Thus, after 1718, proprietary government is portrayed as increasingly inept, a distant, illiberal, feudal anachronism whose main object was to exploit the province for revenue. Dual proprietary functions—in government and in land management—led to a conflict of interests that threatened the welfare and liberties of the inhabitants. And, repeatedly provoked beyond endurance, the Quakers in the legislature were driven to a strenuous resistance to arbitrary, selfish executive misgovernment.

Until 1756 this contest was the fundamental order of politics. Then, suddenly, the Quakers faced a war crisis that, for various reasons, they could not meet. Sadly recognizing the impossibility of their position, they surrendered their ancient political power and responsibility and withdrew. The mantle of power and leadership went to Franklin, who, with the help of some Quakers willing to support war measures, continued the well-established lines of politics, now based, however, upon secular rather than religious considerations. Franklinian reason demanded, of course, continued warfare against proprietary rule. For the next decade, Franklin's work in behalf of local rights and interests and against executive power prepared him and Pennsylvania for a larger threat in 1765 to American liberties. His efforts on behalf of reform in government, good laws, and progress toward democracy, which he exerted in Pennsylvania and in imperial affairs, represented a fulfillment of his principles and the Quaker inheritance. Thus for Franklin and for Pennsylvania, 1776 marked the culmination of the long struggle for local, popular rule that began with the founding of the colony.

An examination of politics in Pennsylvania and of Franklin's part in provincial affairs will show, I believe, that a whiggish interpretation—progressive versus backward forces, a sustained democratic impulse, and Franklinian liberalism in politics—cannot be maintained. There is little evidence of any inner direction in provincial politics that responded to fundamental principles. Nor do colonials, at least in Pennsylvania, show evidence of increasing political maturity and sophistication. Rather, they appear preoccupied with immediate concerns, less interested in principles and theories than in power and advantage—hence probably no better or worse than politicians in any age. Whatever their apparent differences and labels—legislative or executive, Quaker or Presbyterian—the men who dominated government and politics in the quarter century before the Revolution were much alike. And in the occupation of politician, Franklin was much like his contemporaries. He was not a symbolic historical figure but a very human Philadelphian engaged in a passionate, often dirty business that elicited from the combatants more hot temper than cool reason.

This study has been generously assisted by fellowship grants from the University of California (Berkeley) and the Horace H. Rackham School of Graduate Studies of the University of Michigan. I also appreciate the valuable assistance I have received from the staffs of the Historical Society of Pennsylvania, the American Philosophical Society, the Library Company of Philadelphia, and the University of Pennsylvania Library. My task was made much easier by the availability of many new materials of and about Franklin in the Papers of Benjamin Franklin at Yale University, where I also found the efficient help of Leonard Labaree and his colleagues. Indeed, all of these institutions made their superb manuscript collections readily available, and I warmly appreciate their generosity. To Nicholas B. Wainwright of the Historical Society of Pennsylvania go my thanks for his counsel and friendly interest in my work. And most of all I have drawn heavily upon the inspiration and guidance of Professor and Mrs. Carl Bridenbaugh, whose friendship has meant so much.

W. S. H.

Ann Arbor, Michigan
1963

CONTENTS

BENJAMIN FRANKLIN
AND PENNSYLVANIA POLITICS

I

THE POLITICAL ORDER

Only 70 years after its founding, Pennsylvania could fairly claim to be the most successful colony in English America. No other colony had a higher rate of growth or a greater accumulation of wealth. By 1750 close to 250,000 people had settled within its boundaries, which extended from the Delaware River on the east to the foothills of the Appalachian Mountains on the west. Land—rich, abundant, and amply rewarding to the labors of ambitious men and their families—lured the immigrants. They took it up, legally by patent or illegally by squatting, to establish family farms, which depended upon their own or indentured labor rather than slave labor, and on many products instead of a single staple. The settlers of Pennsylvania had thus quickly built a prosperous agricultural society upon which the port city of Philadelphia also flourished.

Proof of the colony's economic opportunity and the well-publicized liberality of the Quaker founders in religious and political matters attracted a high proportion of immigrants from Western Europe. A mixture of English, Welsh, Scots and Scotch-Irish, and Germans of assorted varieties, seasoned with French, Swiss, and Scandinavians, created a diverse but unstable society that was fragmented by sharp differences in language, culture, religion, and experience with social institutions and government. Pennsylvania's welcome to this diverse assortment of people, which set a pattern for America's future, was part of its proud record and a major reason for its rapid growth. Yet it also brought to the colony a population divided by Old World hatreds, fears, and rivalries, and unfamiliar with the prevailing English culture and political institutions.[1]

In 1750, many Pennsylvanians were first generation, engaged in adapting to the strangeness and loneliness of their new environment. Most of their energies were directed toward the immediate problems of supporting themselves and living in a foreign land among a confusing—and, for some, an alarming—number and variety of foreigners. Busy with their farms and crafts, dispersed in a rural society, and further isolated by neighbors of different backgrounds—who might have been their enemies back in Europe —uninterested or uneducated in government, these people were not yet capable of concerning themselves much with the remote affairs of provincial politics. Their interests in government were simple and essentially negative: they did not want war or high taxes or difficulties in getting land. They did not want to serve in armies or be threatened by armies. They wished no established church or restrictions upon the practice of their faiths. They wanted a minimum of government interference and expense. If government satisfied these requirements, most of the people were willing to let those in power continue in power.

Pennsylvania's government had generally met these requirements. Hence it was, by this standard, good government—better, perhaps, than that of any of its contemporaries. Peace had been maintained. There was no army. Taxes were low, and the policies of religious toleration and liberal forms of local government established by the founders remained in force. Peace, prosperity, and easy government produced apathy as well as contentment; hence the colonists had little reason to challenge the existing order.

The high quality of Pennsylvania's record and the lack of challenge to government cannot conceal the fact that the colony was ruled by a narrow, privileged minority whose power and policies were maintained in a political structure that had changed little since 1701. The proprietary executive was of course not representative of the people; but, in a number of important aspects, neither was the Pennsylvania Assembly. Although many men could meet the property qualification for voting, the size of the electorate had little bearing upon the actual conduct of government and politics. Whether because most people failed to take an interest or because they were prevented from interfering in its business, the Pennsylvania Assembly was insulated against the effective influence of major parts of society. Before 1764, for instance, it was rare for a German to sit in the Assembly, even though the Germans made up approximately a third of the population. The same held true for the Scotch-Irish. Reputed to be lawless and shiftless, they were regarded as an element to be kept out of politics. Those few who had risen to the upper social levels—usually Philadelphians or clients of Philadelphians—dissociated themselves from the newer arrivals from Ireland.

In class terms both the active electorate and the membership of the Assembly were drawn chiefly from the upper and upper-middle social levels. Excluded were most of the laborers, indentured servants, frontiersmen, and even many of the rural middle class who legally could vote but were "discouraged" from exercising the franchise. Representation was also established upon a system of sectional discrimination. The three eastern counties, Bucks, Chester, and Philadelphia, had eight seats each in the Assembly (out of some thirty-six), whereas all the rest had from one to four. Although this inequity could be justified on the grounds that these counties paid the largest share of the taxes, the result was that any political group able to dominate these counties had absolute control of the legislature.

The real rulers of Pennsylvania were the heads of the political factions. These men, who were often linked together by marriage, business, and religious ties, dominated politics through their ability to command a following of family, friends, clients, and others who were disposed to attach themselves to the faction. Politics was, regardless of the issues involved, essentially a rivalry between these personal organizations and their leaders. This was government and politics by a Philadelphia-centered oligarchy. Although the composition of the factions and the relative power of one group or another within the oligarchy might change from time to time, this narrow, centralized rule was the political order until the Revolution.

The leaders of the major factions were well aware that perpetuation of this minority rule depended upon a continuation of the divisions within society. In order to keep the citizenry politically impotent, they encouraged intra-group conflicts and the ignorance and fears sustaining them. But at the same time, they knew that the struggle for power must not become so intense that political stability and the necessary government functions would be imperiled. The great question in these years before 1776 was whether the traditional competitors for power could dispute among themselves about the imbalance between the executive and the legislature, defense and Indian relations, the role of a religious society in politics, or the intervention of England in provincial affairs without upsetting the political order. In the 1750's, interfaction rivalry came perilously close to upsetting this order. Faced with a number of internal and external challenges demanding an energetic, forceful leadership, the old regime sacrificed the responsibility that went with power to maintain its private quarrel.

Conflict in Pennsylvania was most often expressed in terms of the rival claims of the executive and legislative parts of government. And around these two positions ranged the major political groupings. While this dispute was important in itself, it always involved a much larger area of social, religious, personal, sectional, and ethnic relationships and rivalries. Although these factors were often masked by the noise and fury of the never-ending constitutional struggle, they underlay the actions and reactions of the politicians. But the politicians knew that any decision affecting the relative power of the proprietary and the Assembly would have a direct influence upon these broader questions. Hence they gave their first attention to a resolution of the constitutional conflict.

The problem in Pennsylvania was not unlike that in other colonies—executive versus legislature and local versus overseas control. Indeed, Pennsylvania profited from earlier disputes over these questions in other colonies. At its beginning, late in the seventeenth century, William Penn recognized many of the gains achieved elsewhere. Penn's liberal policies plus his quickly discovered tendency to give way under pressure encouraged local leaders in the colony to advance their interests, through the Assembly, at his expense. In the Charter of 1701, the last in a series of modifications in the frame of government, Penn sacrificed a great deal. He allowed the Assembly to rid itself of the rival upper house and become a unicameral, elected legislature, and thus a greater menace to the executive. While upper houses or councils did not necessarily help governors curb lower-house aggressiveness, they might. Astute governors in other colonies had the opportunity to split the local leadership, playing one faction against another by offering "well-disposed" gentlemen seats in the council, and thus rewarding them with prestige and patronage and the opportunity to exercise real legislative power. Through his council the governor could build a party to compete with lower-house opposition. But he had no such opportunity in Pennsylvania; there he was exposed to the full force of legislative attack without any upper-house buffer. His vulnerability was further increased by the failure of William Penn and his successors to defend themselves and their deputies against legislative assault.

Penn spent most of the last years of his life making unsuccessful attempts to thwart the plots of his enemies in England and Pennsylvania. Harassed and defeated on both sides of the Atlantic, he left, at his death, a nearly bankrupt estate and a government whose powers were rapidly undermined by ambitious Pennsylvania politicians. His heirs were too busy trying to escape bankruptcy and lawsuits to give adequate attention to the affairs of the province. For over thirty years—until the late 1740's—the Assembly was able to take over ill-used or inadequately defended proprietary functions and prerogatives. In some cases the acquisition was necessary, but in others it was a simple case of theft. By 1750 the Assembly had emerged as the most powerful part of the government, and a much weakened executive was still under attack.

Proprietary weakness allowed the local legislators to gain an almost independent authority in provincial finance. The Assembly claimed that the Governor could not amend money bills, and gave him the choice of money on legislative terms or none at all. If he resisted, he faced a crippled government. During the 1730's the Assembly also assumed authority over paper money, which gave it a virtually unchecked command over finance. Its influence in this area was matched by its assumption of power in Indian relations, the colonial equivalent of foreign affairs and an activity properly directed by the Governor.[2]

The peaceful policy of Pennsylvania toward the Indian depended as much on the regular payment of presents to the various tribes as on fair dealing and respect for treaties. There had been little conflict between William Penn and the Assembly over this policy, but after Penn's death proprietary poverty and inattention to Indian problems gave the Assembly an opportunity to assume this neglected power. Because it provided the money for presents, the Assembly claimed that it was entitled to direct conferences and treaties with the Indians. The impoverished Proprietors were agreeable to this as long as they got an occasional land purchase from the Indians. What began as a necessary legislative cooperation in Indian relations came to be regarded as an exclusive legislative right. While this worked reasonably well before the outbreak of the French and Indian War, it was nonetheless a usurpation of proprietary prerogatives.

Peace in Pennsylvania, whether the result of Quaker principles or presents to the Indians, was a noble achievement, but the policy of pacifism had an adverse effect on the position of the Governor. In more conventional colonies, periodic threats of war and the subsequent need for defense gave meaning to the Governor's title of Captain General. Any serious military crisis provided the Governor with a powerful lever to pry concessions and money from the legislature (legislatures tried to use such crises to the opposite effect), but once money was voted for defense the Governor got the means to reward his friends. He could appoint officers, let contracts for military supplies to the "right" people, and gain the prestige of directing the military operations of his colony. The Governor of Pennsylvania, of course, had no such advantages: Quaker pacificism and Quaker politicians blocked any military embellishments to his power.

The Assembly also limited the executive in other ways. A portion of the Governor's support and some of the money the Proprietor received from the colony came from fees and perquisites granted by the Crown to William Penn. These items of revenue included escheats, fines, license fees, and quit rents. Together they comprised a sum of money sufficient to hamper the Assembly's absolute control over finance. William Penn had opened the door to legislative interference with these perquisites when he allowed the Assembly to regulate tolls and fines in Pennsylvania and to apply the proceeds locally. Thus encouraged, the Assembly persisted in its attempts to supervise all proprietary incomes. Where it failed to regulate or appropriate these revenues for its own purposes, it made their collection as difficult as possible.

Penn's charter gave him the right to establish courts and appoint judges. This particular power had long been the object of legislative jealousy. Whenever a Governor proposed an expansion of the court system and the appointment of new judges, the Assembly's traditional response was obstructionism. Assemblymen declared that justice was impossible where the Proprietor had any share of influence, and asserted that new courts were nothing more than instruments of proprietary despotism. To prevent the establishment of any such tyranny, the Assembly demanded the right to regulate the courts and review the conduct of judges, who should be appointed by the Governor and continued in office during good behavior. Legislative opposition was directed in particular at plans to create chancery courts. By 1750, the Assembly had so successfully frustrated the expansion of courts that a desperate Proprietor agreed to legislative regulation of the courts and fines, and was willing to modify the terms by which judges were appointed if the Assembly would provide them with permanent support.[3] With these advantages giving it near supremacy in finance, Indian relations, and defense, and an effective limitation upon the judicial and executive functions in government, the Assembly had emerged a uniquely powerful body, unaccustomed to any serious challenge from inside or outside Pennsylvania.[4]

The imbalance between the two principal parts of government was not the only reason for the distinctively violent nature of politics. Another reason, unique to Pennsylvania, was that the legislative branch was a wholly controlled subsidiary of a religious denomination. The Quakers, directed by the heads of their leading families, ruled the Assembly. It was therefore a bastion of defense for a religious and social minority representing one section of the colony—a privileged group of people, admittedly responsible for a generally good record, but also determined to prevent any other portion of the population from sharing its power.

As the colony's original settlers, the Quakers had, from the first, quite naturally taken control over local government, warring on their political enemy but fellow Quaker William Penn in order to establish their power. Some of them may have had guilty consciences about this cavalier treatment of Penn, but his death removed that slight inhibition and left the Quakers in command of the colony's future and on guard over its inheritance and founding principles. Inevitably, they came to consider local government their private possession. Proud of the colony's growth and its liberal, peaceful development, they saw this record as a distinctively Quaker accomplishment. Responsibility for the Charter of 1701, the Indian policy, the rights claimed and obtained for local government, and, above all, the Assembly, could not be entrusted to any other hands. Their leaders repeatedly warned that to tamper with the traditional political order was to threaten the advantages and liberties of all Pennsylvanians. If the Quakers were displaced, the colony would be thrown into Indian wars, and militia and defense measures would lead to a military tyranny and confiscation of property. If the Proprietor grew strong or if some non-Quaker group took over the legislature, no political or religious rights would be safe. These and similar claims represented a desperate attempt to justify a minority's continued rule in Pennsylvania. The Quakers were responsible for past accomplishments; they believed that they alone were—almost by divine right—capable of protecting the future.

The constitutional dispute with the executive therefore implied more than a simple resolution of conflicts over the Governor's right to a share in the appropriation of money, the Proprietor's right to appoint judges, the legislature's determination to supervise Indian affairs, or any of the other quarrels that appear in retrospect to be bad-tempered quibbling over trivia. Because the Quakers identified the secular problems of government with the ideas, policies, and future position of a religious society, they made the constitutional dispute a religious one as well. Any attempts to change the political order were regarded as threats to the security of the Quaker minority and thus to the best interests of the colony. To the Quakers the Assembly was more than a legislative body; it was part of the Holy Experiment. It was as unthinkable that the Assembly should fall into the hands of unbelievers as that the Yearly Meeting of the Society should take orders from the Bishop of Rome. No political question conceivably affecting this close-linked religio-political power could be judged simply on its merits. Politics was endowed with all the passion of a religious war, both to the defenders and—under the terms laid down by the Quakers—to their opponents as well.

To preserve their privileged position in Pennsylvania, the Quakers had organized themselves into a strong political party. Well disciplined and ably led, they were guided by past achievement, a number of clear political principles and objectives buttressed by religious sanctions, and the most compelling stimulus of all—fear. Decisions on political and religious policies were reached in the pious but pragmatic atmosphere of the Yearly Meeting of the Society, which served as both a convocation and a caucus.[5] By the middle of the eighteenth century, the Yearly Meeting was directed and closely controlled by the heads of the leading Quaker families, who usually resided in Philadelphia. Heading this oligarchy in the 1750's were two commanders: Israel Pemberton, scion of the great Pemberton clan and, as Clerk of the Yearly Meeting, the high inquisitor of the faith and guardian of unity; and Isaac Norris, a member of an equally illustrious family, who managed the political interests of the Society as Speaker of the Assembly. With representatives of other important families such as the Whartons and the Logans, the Society's directors defined the Quaker stand on political issues and chose acceptable candidates for election to the Assembly. Confident of the support of the faithful, the leadership of the Old

Party—as the Quaker political group was called—knew that the concentration of Quakers in the three eastern counties ensured election success there. In these counties the long-established political organization, responding to the direction of the City leaders, had traditionally been able to win most of the 24 seats for the Party, and thus an overwhelming majority in the House.[6]

Party discipline and the obedience of its members to the dictates of the oligarchy were preserved by the fear that disunity would topple the Quakers from power. Any breach in the united front or failure to sustain the decisions of the leaders was regarded as an invitation to religious and political enemies to rise up and take over. Discipline and unity were valuable enough, but emphasis on these and upon a fear of outsiders made the Party inflexible and defensive. Because they were long in command of the political order, the Quakers tended to grow conservative and rigid in their response to new conditions. Old formulas and answers to such political problems as defense took on the sanctity of dogma, invoked automatically and without question. As they faced an ever-expanding non-Quaker population, the Quakers turned in on themselves, ceased proselyting, and guarded their own behind walls of orthodoxy and conformity. The defense was often expertly directed, but expediency came to serve in place of a dynamic strategy that comprehended the forces affecting Pennsylvania from within and without. The Old Party was nevertheless vastly stronger than any of its potential rivals. Despite its conservatism, it might have weathered the crises of the 1750's and beyond, had its unity been as firm as outward appearances suggested. Actually, it was suffering from serious internal weaknesses, covered over before 1756, that threatened to bring the division and disorganization the leaders feared. Awareness of these weaknesses made the leaders all the more desperate to ward off political issues and challenges that might split the Party.

One of the problems confronting them developed from Quaker

economic success. Increasing wealth weakened the faith's foundation of plain living and simple virtue. Some of the prosperous Friends shed the external forms of dress and address, or kept these but lost the inner light. This loss was grave, for it made the Quaker susceptible to outside political and social contagion. A small but growing number gave up altogether and surrendered to the Anglican form of worship, finding in the Church of England pomp and prestige without troubled consciences. Though few in number, these apostates were often among the richest and most highly placed Friends, and their defection set an alarming example.

Division at the top was matched by restlessness in other ranks. Young City Quakers, many of them artisans, mechanics, small merchants, and rising members of the professions, were not easy under the near-hereditary domination of the privileged old families. These younger men wanted to share power in the Society, and did not relish paying religious, political, or financial deference to old or young Logans, Norrises, and Pembertons. In many respects these ambitious City men had more in common with their counterparts among the Presbyterians, Anglicans, and Lutherans than with the oligarchs of their own faith. A few rebelled and left the Society, but most remained outwardly submissive to the leadership, awaiting an opportunity to exert themselves. They were kept in line by powerful bonds, not the least of which was their religion, but if they could not achieve a share in power without breaking from the Quaker allegiance, a substantial division in the Party might result.

Many rural Quakers were also restless and dissatisfied. Living chiefly in the three eastern counties, they were numerically the most important part of the denomination. But despite their numbers, they were also commanded at the Yearly Meeting by the Philadelphia gentlemen. Bowing to this direction in religious and political affairs, the county Quakers nevertheless held the key to party power. Like the City Quakers, they could find economic, social, sectional, and even political interests that differed from those of the City leaders. Yet the arguments for unity had an imminent significance in the counties where, as defenders of the Quaker frontiers, they could readily see the rising flood of Germans and Scotch-Irish moving in on them. With most of the Party's voting strength in their hands, the rural Quakers had a great responsibility; if they split their "interest," only the enemies of the Society would profit.

For many years James Logan, Philadelphia's greatest Quaker grandee, had led a minority faction in the Party. He took a rational, practical attitude toward the defense issue, advocating that, for the ultimate welfare of the Society (to say nothing of the colony), it would be well to compromise strict religious principles to preserve the essentials of Quaker political and religious strength. As trustees of the political power in Pennsylvania, the Quakers could not afford to ignore their responsibilities to the rest of the people. If they did, they would ultimately lose everything.

Logan was rebuffed by the traditionalists in the Society. For a time, the need for unity and the explanation that Logan's high place in the Proprietor's government made his attitude understandable suppressed the appeal of his argument. But his logical, flexible attitude was in harmony with the practice of the Quakers in England. It would soon attract many in Pennsylvania who valued their political interests at least as much as their religious beliefs.

Internal party difficulties were partly balanced by some external resources. The Quaker organization could usually handle the political task in Pennsylvania by itself. But, if necessary, it could call upon reserve forces—allies not normally active in provincial politics but useful when needed. The Quakers had cultivated a long-standing alliance with the German immigrants in

Pennsylvania. Among these immigrants were some Pietists, whose beliefs were similar to the Quakers'. Though relatively few in number, these Pietists carried the Quaker message, in the German language, to later settlers of other faiths. They helped to convince the Germans that they owed most of their rights and opportunities to the benevolence and government of the Old Party. Handicapped by ignorance of the English language and English methods of government, most Germans, if they acted in politics at all, placed their faith and votes in the hands of Quaker politicians. Because the Germans had not forgotten their experiences in the homeland, it was easy for Old Party leaders to frighten them with warnings about dangers to their liberties. They told the Germans that if they failed to support the Old Party, they might lose their religious freedom, be required to till the Proprietor's manors as serfs, pay high taxes, and fight in a militia, or have their goods confiscated by an army, which was likely to be an instrument of proprietary tyranny. These warnings were almost always effective when the Quakers wanted German support.

Quaker leaders did not encourage the development of an active German political party. They wanted passive support, not a rival organization with its own leaders. Like other members of Pennsylvania's upper class, they feared any unruly, lower-class political activity independent of proper supervision. Although there was a risk in using German support—they might get out of control and act on their own—the Quakers found that the Germans were not troublesome. All they wanted was a continuation of cheap, remote, peaceful government, prosperity, and ready land.

Across the Atlantic, the English branch of the Society of Friends served the political interests of their American co-religionists. Unlike the Pennsylvania Quakers, the English Friends did not live atop the political heap, but down among the mass of contending and competing factions in English society. Their struggle for political favor and for security of their rights had been continuous. The difficulty of their situation had long since forced them to compromise principles for survival; they paid taxes for war, armed their ships, and played the political game with a finesse that shocked their conservative and secure American brethren.

The English Quakers displayed an urbanity and sophistication about the affairs of the world that was not always evident in Pennsylvania. They held a prominent place in the merchant and commercial life of England, particularly in London, where they developed influential connections in government. Respected for their social and economic power, they formed a powerful lobby for Pennsylvania and Quaker interests. With their knowledge of English men and affairs, they advised and helped the Pennsylvanians on various personal and business matters and on matters affecting the welfare of the Society. During the 1740's, the London Friends had succeeded in mitigating the English government's displeasure over the failure of the Pennsylvania Assembly to support the war effort properly and obediently. They helped to block ministerial and Parliamentary action that would have damaged the position of the Quakers in the colony, and urged the Pennsylvanians to adopt a policy of compromise, flexibility, and prudence. Too often the Philadelphia oligarchs accepted the assistance but ignored the advice. Though exasperated at times by the intransigence and blindness of the leaders in Pennsylvania, the English Quakers worked steadily in their behalf.[7]

Confusion, distraction, and poverty were the hallmarks of the proprietary family after the death of William Penn. None of the Founder's heirs took command of the situation until Thomas Penn inherited enough shares from his brothers to assume the active management of proprietary affairs in Pennsylvania. In 1746, Thomas Penn became the leading Proprietor, acting as head of the family and chief executive authority for the province.[8] It is one of the ironies of Pennsylvania history that he, by far the ablest of the Penns, experienced the greatest difficulty with the colony. Penn was an honest, capable, conscientious, and informed man whose papers and letters reveal the care and attention he devoted to the colony and its welfare. No one in England was more intimately aware or more accurately informed of the conditions, interests, and peculiarities of the colony. But no matter how detailed his knowledge, he could not know everything that went on in the colony, and his inclination to assume that he did often led him to attempt to manage everything relevant to his interests. Immersed in the minutiae of government and land problems, he sometimes lost sight of the larger implications of policy and the changing character of his province.[9]

Many people in Pennsylvania and in England believed that the proprietary family reaped great wealth from the colony. Actually, in 1750, it cost the Proprietors more to govern Pennsylvania than the revenues brought in. To reverse this situation, Thomas Penn was determined to collect every revenue he could legitimately claim. Reforms in the land offices and surveys and the eviction of squatters were obvious measures. He also saw that the flaws— and, from his viewpoint, the illegalities—in the colony's government would have to be corrected.[10]

Penn's position as both landlord and Governor was an obstacle to satisfactory government in Pennsylvania. His difficulties in governing a colony from England were compounded by his interests in collecting rents, selling and buying land for profit, and prosecuting offenders against his properties. These activities left him open to the charge of greed at the expense of the people and their liberties, and his dual and sometimes conflicting functions permitted his enemies in both England and Pennsylvania to plot the destruction of his personal empire. His authority as landlord was undoubtedly more complex and more annoying to the colonists than his authority as Governor. Yet it was not this power, archaic and frustrating for those who had to deal with it, that evoked the attacks of Penn's enemies in Pennsylvania. Until well into the 1750's, the Assembly avoided any direct interference with proprietary lands, and when it did interfere it was more concerned with the appropriation of revenues arising from the land than with the nature of the power and the source of the revenues. Carefully attempting to separate the Proprietor as Governor from the Proprietor as land officer, a distinction Penn hotly refused to recognize, the Assembly contested his government and ignored his private properties except where their rents might be useful to the legislature or dangerous to it if retained in his hands.[11]

In an attempt to justify its usurpation of power, the Assembly had made much of the undeniable conflict of interest in the colony's government. However, political conflicts did not center around ownership of land, but around government powers that were not seriously compromised by proprietary land management. Though many small farmers might have considered the payment of rents or the delay in obtaining land titles the great objections to proprietary government, the Assembly did not. Its leaders were much more intent upon obtaining power in the colony than upon disturbing private property, even if it was managed badly.

Certainly Penn entertained no tyrannical designs on Pennsylvania; he was sincerely interested in its welfare and believed that his policies were in its best interests. Proud of Pennsylvania's prosperity and accomplishments, he wished to be generous in supporting the various projects intended to improve its culture and well-being. He was an enlightened gentleman with a deep respect for representative government and the political institutions and rights accepted by most Englishmen of the eighteenth century. He believed that the legislature should have a proper share in government, but so too should the executive. Time after time, he wrote that what he desired was a balanced government—one that represented a balance of interests in all the important areas where the executive and legislative power touched. To make such a government work, he expected that the local aristocracy would provide a natural leadership, without factions or party spirit. And in such an aristocratic government, he fully accepted the Quaker leaders as rightful participants, but not as exclusive ones. In essence, he hoped to achieve something approaching the English form of government. He saw himself in a quasi-royal role, acting as an arbiter of disputes and guardian of prerogatives given him by the King.

Penn's intentions were good, and he expressed the prevailing legal and theoretical sense of what government should be. On most occasions he had law and precedent on his side in his disputes with the legislature. But knowing this, he came to depend primarily upon legal opinion for his actions. Tidy and precise of mind, Penn could be stiff-backed and cold when he suspected some slight to his honor or a thrust at his legal rights. Sparing in his thanks for the services of his friends in the province, Penn regarded whatever they did in support of his policies as merely their proper duty. Hence he was not the sort of leader to stir men to enthusiastic allegiance to his cause.[12]

Unlike the Quaker Party, the proprietary association was a loose, very informal congeries of men, interests, and factions that rarely worked together in harmony or for a common purpose. Similar to an English political group, it was formed out of a collection of independent interests directed by some great man or aristocratic clique desiring power. The Proprietary Party in Pennsylvania was led by a number of highly independent gentlemen.

The "better sort" who adhered to a proprietary faction were moved by a variety of motives. Their real interest was not so much enthusiasm for the Proprietor as ambition to displace the Quakers from power. Their degree of allegiance to Penn usually depended upon their assessment of how much the allegiance was worth or how much the Quakers offended their aspirations. They might be inclined to support him in exchange for a land grant on favorable terms or a post in his government. A few of them, such as Richard Hockley, Richard Peters, and the Governors, were Penn's agents in the colony. The rest were Pennsylvanians who often considered themselves the Proprietor's social and financial equals, and thus needed little from him. In any contest with the Quakers or the Assembly, Penn had difficulty persuading his allies to work together or to go beyond their limited objectives. At election time some refused to solicit votes or sulked at home, annoyed by some personal slight or point of dispute with another gentleman.

Most shocking to the Proprietor was the sad realization that many of the men of "better sense" were not in sympathy with his plans for a reformed government in the colony. As local aristocrats, they often joined with the Quaker oligarchs in the belief that the Pennsylvania legislature was better able to manage the affairs of the province than a Proprietor three thousand miles away. In response to Penn's claims and his intention to reassert his place in the government, they were frequently critical only of Quaker control of the Assembly rather than of the nature of the Assembly's power.

The proprietary alliance bore a similarity to the Quaker party in two respects. Both were led by powerful members of the Pennsylvania aristocracy, whose family and business ties linked them together to form the nucleus of their following: the Allen-Hamilton-Shippen connection represented for the Proprietary Party a leadership comparable to that of the Pemberton-Logan-Norris combination of the Quakers, though the former exhibited less unity and effectiveness in politics. In addition, the proprietary factions were directed, like the Quakers, from Philadelphia. However, this leadership was neither as consistent nor as well executed as that of the Yearly Meeting. The Proprietor's agents in Pennsylvania carried out his policy and formed the core of his following, but he never solved the problem of how to attract able men to fill posts in the government. Men of first rank did not seek the

Governorship, because the pay was not large and difficulties with the Assembly had given it a bad reputation in England. In addition, the Governor in Pennsylvania lacked many of the advantages possessed by royal governors; he had no powerful council to bolster his authority and smooth his way into the society of the colony. Indeed, he was denied the social leadership of Philadelphia or the province—the Quakers had their own exclusive society and did not need his. Lacking the authority and prestige that came from being the King's representative in America, the Pennsylvania executives found that sifting the King's powers through the sieve of proprietary delegation took away much of their force. Neither a social leader nor a regal deputy, Penn's Governor was sometimes ill-equipped by training, ability, or interest to master the difficult political conditions in the colony. Finally, the Governor lacked ample patronage funds and places for potential candidates to the proprietary cause. This scarcity of rewards for the Governor's use, which was nearly fatal to the establishment of a political party, also stemmed from the inadequacy of proprietary revenues in Pennsylvania. Not until after the end of the French and Indian War did Penn reap the full benefits of his possessions, and until that time his political organization languished.

Other officers of the government, who owed their positions to proprietary grace and favor, were chiefly those concerned with land management and the judiciary. Never numerous enough to constitute a sizable political organization, these men were more inclined to quarrel with Penn over their poor pay than to be grateful for their places. A few did gain wealth from their positions. The most important of these officials was Richard Peters, the Secretary of the Governor's advisory Council. This clever, hardworking, ambitious, sometime-cleric of the Church of England was able to influence the Proprietor as no other person in Pennsylvania could. Unfortunately for the peace of the colony and the harmony of the Proprietary Party, Peters was a gossip, and his sharp tongue and special prejudices set him, and eventually Penn, against some of the colony's cherished interests. Hardly less damaging was Peters's tattling to Penn about the misdeeds, actual or imagined, of proprietary friends in Pennsylvania. The Secretary was jealous of his close relationship with Penn, and cut down those who seemed to grow too large in his favor. This failing aside, Peters was a valuable worker for the party and the man most responsible for its election campaigns.[13]

Peters's most urgent task was to find some way to increase the small and unstable support for the government. He tried to gain seats for anti-Quaker candidates in the Assembly, but encountered not only Quaker resistance but such divisions among those responsible for election tickets that many of the seats were not contested by the proprietary forces.[14] The great merchant princes and the owners of large estates could gain very little from Penn; they could not be coerced, and they were very sensitive to criticism or lack of appreciation for their exertions on behalf of proprietary interests. Some were especially upset by Penn's tight-fisted hold on choice lands, believing that he should award them grants in return for their political support.[15]

Both Penn and Peters realized that they must somehow increase their following from among the less aristocratic portion of society. Although Penn did not intend to undertake anything smacking of a democratic or popular appeal, he was increasingly aware of the attitude of "the people." By "the people" he meant those property holders who were qualified to vote but did not, or, worse, joined the Quakers. Completely in agreement with the aristocratic concept of government held by the leaders of Pennsylvania society, the Proprietor wanted no real extension of the franchise or increased participation of the "lower sorts"; such new men as might strengthen his political following would be those who rose to meet the voting and property qualifications requisite to active political participation in Pennsylvania. These voters would, of course, take their direction from the gentlemen.

Had Penn seriously tried to build the party before 1750, his chances of success would have been poor. Quaker election arguments held the Germans fast to the alliance. In addition, the small number of politically active Scotch-Irish were receptive to the same arguments. The Scotch-Irish had no reason to think warmly of proprietary government, because they saw it in the form of magistrates, land surveyors, and rent collectors. Furthermore, they were a dispersed and badly divided people, still conducting an intracongregational warfare to determine the "true" Presbyterian form of worship. They were too absorbed in this New Side–Old Side contest to bother much with provincial politics. And the defense question did not move them to side with Penn, since they were scarcely more impressed by the zeal of the Philadelphia Proprietary Party for the protection of frontier settlements than by the zeal of the Quaker Assembly.[16]

Beyond the major political factions, the rest of the Pennsylvanians were neither organized nor mature enough to participate effectively or consistently in provincial politics. The diversities and divisions of the population, especially among the newer arrivals in Pennsylvania, who were outside the normal range of provincial politics, left the field to those already in power.

The political order in Pennsylvania was in precarious balance. The Quakers, supreme in the Assembly, continued almost as a matter of habit to attack the executive. The Proprietor, on the other hand, was determined to lose nothing more; indeed, he was planning to recoup as many of his lost powers as possible. All this meant political warfare, intense and prolonged, wherein the Quakers were certain to retaliate with all the weapons at their command. The risks for both contenders were great. Fighting at the top might open the door to an internal political upheaval— something that neither side really wanted. A number of unknown factors inside and outside the colony might affect the outcome. One of the unknown ingredients about to be added to the conflict was Benjamin Franklin.

ＡN INDEPENDENT

Had Benjamin Franklin died before 1750, he might have merited a few lines in American history as a minor worthy of the eighteenth century, but little more. Still an obscure, provincial Philadelphian, very successful in the City but hardly known beyond, he was exactly what he later put at the head of his proposed epitaph: a printer. If Franklin was scarcely more significant than one or another of his able contemporaries in 1750, he was about to burst forth with the dazzling accomplishments that would raise him to historical greatness and earn him first place among America's early heroes. And oddly enough, this was the achievement of retirement, or—as he thought—of the declining years of middle age.[1]

The first half of his life was not without indications of his future; yet Philadelphians had no reason to be awed by him or to imagine that they lived in the Age of Franklin. Nor could they guess that the future would regard them chiefly as props and scenery for the unfolding epic of his career. To his contemporaries, he was a successful and prosperous tradesman, a popular and respected member of society, undoubtedly talented and ingenious, and certainly a genial friend and associate. He was also one of the best-known men in the City—but a popular writer with his own press, newspaper, almanac, and bookstore was likely to be well known in any case. He was recognized as a public figure busily engaged in civic good works, a joiner and organizer full of interesting ideas and projects. As a token of their recognition and esteem, his fellow Philadelphians urged him to run for public office. When Franklin decided to run, neither he nor his fellow citizens suspected that his almost casual election to the Assembly in 1751 was the beginning of an extraordinary political career and an exceedingly turbulent period in Pennsylvania history. For politics did become his chief occupation, propelling him to the top in the Assembly, sending him to England for most of the years between 1757 and 1775, and then making him, in succession, an Imperial statesman, a Revolutionary, and a Founding Father.

All Franklin expected after he retired from active business in 1748 was the "Leisure to read, study, make Experiments, and converse at large with such ingenious and worthy Men as are pleas'd to honour me with their Friendship or Acquaintance, on such Points as may produce something for the common Benefit of Mankind."[2] But once in the Assembly he found that politics, in one form or another, demanded most of his time, talent, and energy. And he proved to be unprepared for the demands of the occupation, refusing to admit at first that he was deeply involved, and then failing to perceive the nature of the problems facing him and Pennsylvania.

Both his business and his political careers began with a period of apprenticeship. It is significant that although he wrote a great deal about his efforts to be a successful printer, he virtually ignored his beginnings in politics. Before 1751 he had carefully remained outside the political order, letting others have the power and the responsibility of managing provincial affairs. Yet Franklin was Pennsylvania's most socially engaged citizen, its chief instrument of public progress, a preacher and practitioner of public virtue and service to society. How could he have ignored for over twenty years the most obvious instruments of influence and leadership? This paradox is not resolved by searching for Franklin's theories of government in his writings from the 1730's and 1740's. They reveal no serious speculation about political matters or problems of government and no analysis of or suggestions for improving local conditions. It was almost as if the institutions of government and the political structure had not existed. Even when he took a place as Clerk of the Assembly—a position he assumed in 1736 and held for 15 years—he gave no sign of interest in legislative proceedings. Despite the opportunity for a first-hand education, the only legacy Franklin left from the experience was his famous "magic squares"—the doodlings of boredom designed to pass the time while he sat in the House. Franklin's untypical reaction to something that occupied a fair amount of his time cannot be dismissed as a simple lack of interest or a dislike for the Byzantine character of local politics, for he was a politician even if he denied both the fact and the interest.

Whether it prepared him for a political career or not, Franklin's experience in Philadelphia before 1751 gave him a number of attitudes—almost theories—about his role in society, together with some personal objectives, techniques, and resources that he came to use habitually. These were, however, developed outside of the political order, and, in a way, expressed his criticism of government and of the squabbling, time-consuming proclivities and scanty accomplishments of the politicians. Franklin thought he had better ways of doing things, and spent more than twenty years perfecting alternatives to direct political action. Consequently, he was an outsider, a maverick, little understood by the leading politicians and later causing them considerable puzzlement and alarm.

When Franklin arrived in Philadelphia, he was a poor printer from Boston without influential connections. His first task was to establish himself in his trade; then he would develop a printing business and a newspaper. The highly vulnerable nature of his trade made his task far from easy. Successful printing and, above

all, publishing required wide public acceptance, and it was easy to
make enemies if the product served political interests. Franklin
needed no reminder of the hazards of business. Political partisanship had nearly ruined his brother's paper in Boston, and politics
was taken just as seriously in Philadelphia. Franklin quickly realized that any political activity on his part might incur the wrath
of the Quaker or the proprietary leaders. Unable to afford to engage in local feuds or to identfy with any faction, he maintained
a policy of strict neutrality in issues that might touch the sensitivity of the leaders. When he felt compelled to express his true
feelings in his newspaper, he concealed his identity with a pseudonym. The reward for such wise behavior was just what he
wanted: the bipartisan friendship of the gentlemen and their patronage for himself and his business. In 1736, the Assembly and
its Quaker leaders thought well enough of him to reward him
with the colony's printing and the Clerkship of the House.

Avoidance of issues and concealment behind a pseudonym may
not have been examples of editorial courage, but the strategy was
prudent and it suited Franklin's first objective, the achievement
of financial security as a prerequisite for his larger ambitions. In
the 1730's, Franklin was unable and unwilling to compete with
the gentlemen who ruled the City. These men did not welcome a
challenge to their prerogatives and were quite capable of punish-
ing an upstart. Because he could not risk direct action, he was
forced to devise other ways of exerting his influence and accomplishing his social objectives. These substitutes for public position
and power were remarkably successful. Beginning with the Junto
Club in the 1730's and extending to the Association of 1747,
Franklin managed a personal system of power that operated outside the structure, permitting him to do what he wanted without
bothering much with political factions or issues.

One of Franklin's most valuable tools was a pleasing personality. He has left full accounts of his self-examination and of the

deliberate effort he made to correct or disguise what he thought were flaws in his personality and to strengthen his strong points. He worked hard to fashion an influential personal instrument especially suited to the small, intimate society of Philadelphia in the 1730's. The physical size of the City and the small number of men who counted in its life made it a congenial place for one who practiced social leadership by personal charm. He took great pleasure in deliberately applying the most suitable personal technique to gain a particular objective. Especially anxious to win the approval and favor of the leading gentlemen, he carefully cultivated a reputation for thrift and industry, and to impress the learned and powerful James Logan he asked to borrow books from that great man's library. By applying such appropriate psychology, Franklin soon ingratiated himself with the Logans, Pembertons, Hamiltons, and other influential Philadelphians.

From a strong base of personal relationships and friendships Franklin sought to increase his effectiveness by developing special organizations designed to extend his influence and gain support for his projects. He formed or belonged to a proliferation of organizations, which enlisted virtually every man in the City with the time, talent, or money to contribute. The extent of his participation in such enterprises was greater than that of any other man in Philadelphia and concentrated a unique power in the hands of one man. By acting alone or as a member of a group, he achieved by mid-century a virtual monopoly of public and private welfare projects in the City. Indeed, some claimed that almost no public undertaking of this sort could be considered without his advice and support.

In the hands of a less skilled and less astute manipulator, this zeal for improvement and ability to organize might have aroused the jealousy and suspicion of the upper-class leaders. No matter how obviously useful they might be, such projects as academies or libraries were not usually promoted by the kind of publicity

and appeals for popular participation Franklin used. Sponsoring
and managing civic projects were prerogatives of the upper class,
but like many gentle customs they were sometimes practiced in
too leisurely a fashion to suit Franklin. He could not afford, however, to appear presumptuous or to threaten the prerogatives of
the gentry. To protect himself and the success of his plans, he
worked with prominent men, put them in sponsoring positions,
and generously shared any credit for good results. In this way he
enlisted their support without letting them suspect that he was
interested in personal gain.

His attitude toward the aristocracy was not, however, cynical
or hypocritical. Although he did use and manipulate his social
superiors, he was primarily interested in results. He believed
fully in the natural and rightful leadership of the men whose
wealth, social position, education, and ability could do so much
to advance the public welfare. Democratization and leveling were
not his aims; rather, he desired that the established social con-
ventions and customs be more effectively applied to benefit the
aristocracy as well as the rest of the populace. Even after Franklin
became an acknowledged leader in Philadelphia and might have
dispensed with social proprieties and relied upon his own power
and popularity to win his way, he continued to encourage the
aristocracy to fulfill its proper function.

High performance in life was an important criterion in Franklin's concept of a genuine aristocracy, but he did not discount the
value of wealth and social position. Those fortunate enough to
possess such advantages would use them, he believed, to lead society. Only when the gentry failed to match its social privileges
with responsible social action did he criticize. Prior to 1750, the
members of Philadelphia's remarkably able upper class per-
formed, with some prodding, generally to his satisfaction. He
therefore had little reason to question their place and power.

In many ways Franklin's social attitude was that of an aristocrat. Fully aware of his own achievements and abilities, he knew he was superior to the common run of men and tended to regard the failings of others from a rather lofty perspective. Believing in the efficacy of enlightened virtue and self-improvement, he reached down to offer his advice and experience to those less favored than he or less conscious of their inadequacies. He disguised his didactic purpose and made it palatable by adopting a genial, felicitous style of writing and by making the point at his own expense. To this extent his writings for public consumption were triumphs of literary deception. They suggested a humble, amusing—and sometimes bemused—common man, trying to meet the difficulties of life and modestly offering wise suggestions from his experience. But in his private letters to men he considered his equals, Franklin displayed a sharply critical attitude toward the "lower sorts" who did not diligently strive to measure up to his standards. Behind the façade of geniality was little real tolerance for or understanding of the obstacles that might prevent most of the people from achieving successes similar to his own.

Perfected and polished and very flexible, Franklin's personality served as his primary instrument for social action. In time, his repeated success in Philadelphia convinced him that he had found the most appropriate methods of handling any situation, political or otherwise. Many of his early writings were devoted to discussing how the individual can improve society and what tools he must possess to do so. Some of his beliefs are expressed in the personal maxims, the ways to wealth, and the hints on self-improvement that seem to form his philosophy of the successful life and are the despair of those who seek in his writings some philosophical profundity comparable to that of his great contemporary Jonathan Edwards. While these simplistic, "Poor Richard" formulas appear shallow and superficial, they were in fact only means he devised in an attempt to reach the higher goals of service to mankind, the increase and dissemination of knowledge, and the improvement of the physical and moral conditions in society. These methods reflect Franklin's belief that the superior individual, improved and perfected by every means available, must direct social progress. In this brand of individualism, established social forms and institutions were not especially important, and required modification only if they seriously hampered the work of the enlightened leader. This theory fitted Franklin's estimation of his own resources and his belief that he could lead most effectively if he remained independent from the limitations of conventional social categories.

If Franklin had developed a highly personal view and manner of dealing with his society, he had also separated himself from some of its other aspects and standards of measurement. In part, this separation owed much to the fact that he was Franklin, with all the extraordinary ability and unconventional quality of mind that were his genius. But it also resulted from his activities and special interests.

In a society defined by a clear though not rigid class structure, he was virtually a classless man. Middle-class in origin and trade and lacking a formal education and an advantageous marriage, he nevertheless came to possess the advantages of a member of the upper class—fortune, prestige, public acclaim, influence, high-placed connections, and power. Good works, political neutrality, and the capacity to make friends permitted him to move across class lines in his private and public associations. To some of his contemporaries in 1748 he was a gentleman; to others he was still a printer with an apron and ink-stained hands.

His freedom to move easily in the middle and upper levels of Philadelphia society was paralleled by his relationship with various religious denominations. Religious association provided an important measure of a man's place in Pennsylvania, giving the communicant a social, ethnic, and often a political—as well as a doctrinal—identification. Franklin accepted religion's utility as a moral, stabilizing force in society and encouraged its general principles, but rejected what he considered sectarian excesses and prejudices. Heterodox, rational, and inclining to deism, he found little of value in interdenominational disputes and the fine points of theological differences, which preoccupied so many Pennsylvanians. While members of the several denominations might despair of the ultimate safety of his soul, they could find little cause to fear that he would give partisan aid to a rival sect. This was an advantage. But Franklin's freedom from identification with traditional orthodoxies and their particular interests also meant that he did not share their particular aspirations.

While politics was an intense, inward-turning concern in Pennsylvania, Franklin's attention turned increasingly outward, to other colonies and to England and Europe. This had begun early in his career. Printing and publishing not only provided an income and a means of influencing his fellow citizens but gave him an unequaled access to information. Through his print shop and bookstore passed the news and ideas that comprised the recorded culture of the contemporary Atlantic civilization, and his mind absorbed something from everything that came to his notice. This constant supply of information was quite as much a part of his trade as ink and type.

He was educated by his trade to look beyond his city, and especially in the direction of England and Europe. It is significant that his *Pennsylvania Gazette* contained more news about Philadelphia, England, Europe, and other colonies than about the rest of Pennsylvania. Because of this, Franklin was undoubtedly better informed about affairs in London or in Boston than he was about those fifty miles west of Philadelphia. Publishing gave him an eastern orientation and correspondingly less knowledge of or interest in the interior of the province. Always a Philadelphian and later a man of the world, he was not as thoroughly a Pennsylvanian.

Scientific investigation likewise reinforced the outward direction of Franklin's mind. His experiments soon surpassed the work of the best-educated men in Philadelphia, and, as they did, he sought ingenious men beyond the City with whom to share his interest. His correspondence and associations outside Pennsylvania greatly expanded his scientific vision and eventually brought him international fame and recognition. Hence while he was busy with local politics in the 1750's, part of his attention was elsewhere— in the scientific community of learned men spanning the Atlantic. The realization that he was engaged in this exciting world where he was recognized and acclaimed also strengthened his sense of social independence. For his scientific work and its acceptance did not depend upon local considerations; he had already gone far beyond these. Yet the politics of Pennsylvania responded to just such considerations from which he was increasingly removed.

Just before Franklin retired from active business, he got an opportunity to test his political theories and techniques in the colonial defense crisis that arose during "King George's War" (War of the Austrian Succession). In an atmosphere of passion and deadlock, he undertook to interpose himself between the feuding politicians with a brilliantly conceived solution to a problem that had hitherto been all but insoluble. With the publication of *Plain Truth* and the formation of the Association in 1747, he abandoned his political aloofness and stepped into the rivalries and issues of politics.[3]

The deadlock between the Quaker-controlled Assembly and the proprietary executive over providing defense had virtually paralyzed the government and brought down English censure on the colony. Pennsylvania was defenseless and was making little contribution to the larger war effort. This alarming political and military situation suggested to Franklin the possibilities for a rational compromise. In *Plain Truth* he proposed a voluntary association of citizens in a militia to defend the colony. Impartially criticizing the stubbornness of the two major parties, he appealed to all public-spirited men for assistance and urged the leaders of the political factions to give up their political or religious objections for the common welfare. Franklin offered them inducements to join in his scheme. By making the Association voluntary, he permitted the Quakers to remain outside if they chose. The Governor got some sort of a military force, even if it was not quite legal, and a sufficient defense effort to answer English criticism.

The popular response to Franklin's proposal was enthusiastic. Some contributed money; others enlisted in the militia. Swept along by the force of Franklin's campaign, the political leaders who had hitherto been cool to the proposal now supported it. (Some, especially the Quakers, did so unofficially.) For his part, Franklin helped to organize and enlist companies of men and select the officers. In addition he petitioned the Proprietor for cannon and directed the plans to fortify the City. Since the Assembly would not appropriate money for defense, he promoted a lottery. The whole undertaking quickly became a triumph for Franklin's peculiar methods. It was a perfect expression of his ability to arrive at a reasoned solution to a difficult problem.

Behind his glittering success lay certain other problems. Peters and Penn quickly turned their attention to the implications of Franklin's action. Could any government permit the vital military power, which belonged under executive control, to be gathered into the hands of an extralegal, independent body? No matter how obvious the need for action, was it not destructive of the powers of government, and did it not tend further to disturb the balance between the executive and the legislature? Franklin had turned from the established agencies of government and appealed to the people. If he believed this necessary, then he must also believe that there was a fundamental weakness in Pennsylvania's government. Peters declared that the Association was an attack upon constituted authority, and Penn asserted that it created a separate military body within the colony—a situation scarcely permissible in England, and much less so in Pennsylvania.[4]

On the other hand, proprietary leaders were pleased that a way had been found to circumvent the Quaker refusal to let the Assembly pass legislation for a militia. And they found further consolation in the fact that the Association had soon come under the control of the regular leaders of the colony. Although proprietary men were worried about Franklin's unorthodox methods —he might be something of a "tribune of the people"—they also saw that he favored defense. Should the same dispute break out again, he might prove a valuable friend of the government.[5]

Franklin had not considered the theoretical implications of his action or attributed the political impasse that had brought about the crisis to any basic defects in the government. In order to force the leaders to act, he had deliberately avoided the real issues and resorted to compromise, massive application of his personal influence, and an adroit appeal to the people. While some of the politicians might grumble at his solution, he had put enough in his plan to attract both sides. In the process he had nonetheless subverted Quaker pacifism and ignored the proper prerogatives of the executive.

For Franklin the Association was a significant test. His ideas and methods had been put to work in a crisis and had proved sound. Could he not repeat this triumph in other areas? Now retired and provided with a sufficient income to support him in whatever he chose to do, he could afford to consider taking public office. He had a number of worthwhile projects in mind, and a public position might be very useful in winning support for them. He was bound by no factional ties, and he had just demonstrated his freedom to arbitrate between contending parts of the government. Acting as an independent force in politics, he could support the reasonable and the useful on his own terms. If politics should prove a burden, he could always withdraw.

III

PENN'S CHALLENGE

With a long record of success in its conflict with the executive, the Assembly could well afford to relax a bit in 1750, certain that it did not have much to fear from either the Proprietor or his few supporters in Pennsylvania. The end of the War of the Austrian Succession in 1748 let the troublesome problems of the 1740's, especially defense and the management of funds for war, lapse without resolution. Yet the government's failure to meet the needs of the colony and the demands of the Mother Country was an ominous indication for the future. Should such crises arise again, internal and external pressures might seriously threaten a political leadership unable or unwilling to act. For the present, however, the politicians were content to let matters drop.

Penn also contributed something to this moment of political peace. His appointment of James Hamilton as Governor in 1748 was popular in Pennsylvania, and the early messages between the new Governor and the Assembly were fully ornamented with courteous phrases copied from the best English parliamentary usage.[1] Even more productive of temporary harmony was the news that, with Penn's help, Parliament had been persuaded to exclude the colony from a newly passed bill to control paper money. Penn's efforts were warmly appreciated, and even the Assembly found itself able to give unusual expressions of thanks.[2]

But political peace could not last long. Penn was determined to reassert his influence in government and check the growing power of the Assembly. He knew his objectives, but the choice of means was difficult, if not painful. Whatever he did to put a new policy into effect meant a stormy fight in Pennsylvania. It was a high price to pay, and he vacillated, testing first one plan and then another in an effort to find a way through the hazards and conflicting interests involved in various lines of action.

At first proprietary policy was essentially a negative one, designed to block any acts of the Assembly that infringed directly or implicitly upon proprietary prerogatives. Penn warned Hamilton to inspect each measure, however desirable, necessary, or worthy it might appear to be, for any legislative pretensions to his powers, and to obtain explicit acknowledgment of his rights that could be affected by legislative action. This meant that a large number of bills were held up by the Governor while he and the Assembly exchanged messages over the precise meaning and intention of words and clauses. It also resulted in increasingly heated and exasperated conflicts over such seemingly innocuous proposals as a night watch for Philadelphia, regulations for ferries and taverns, and the establishment of new courts.

The night-watch bill alarmed the Proprietor because the wardens were to be elected, and their activities might conflict with the authority of the magistrates.[3] Ferries were a proprietary monopoly, and Penn refused to let the Assembly establish them, although he would allow it to fix the rates in return for "some small certain acknowledgment, so that the rates of ferriage might be moderate if the Assembly wou'd ask it of us in a proper way."[4] As for the right to regulate taverns, which the Assembly demanded because certain taverns and tavern keepers were corrupting the people's morals, Penn was certain that the legislature's real object was to obtain control over the tavern license fees, which went to the Governor.[5] By keeping close scrutiny and raising

numerous objections, Penn and Hamilton attempted to gain recognition of the principle that the Proprietor had specific rights
in government. To the Old Party in the Assembly this was both
quibbling obstructionism and a political challenge that could not
be tolerated.

The first major clash came when Penn renewed his demand for
chancery courts. He failed to recognize the widespread fear that
the courts would enforce land regulations. If they were enforced,
many titles would be in jeopardy, unpaid rents collected, squatters
evicted, and other measures taken. In this dispute, the Assembly's
opposition had the support of nearly all the politicians in the colony, including many of the Proprietor's friends. Reviving an old
argument, the Assembly said that proprietary judges gave the
Proprietor a weight and influence in the courts that no person in
the colony could equal. Penn replied, "All I desire in the establishment of a Court of Chancery is that it may be done in a manner
the most favourable to the People, without giving up the King's
prerogative, with which we are intrusted. Mr Pemberton* and
the People in general should not desire any matters in difference
between us and them to be tryed by themselves only, which is the
Case in common Law Courts, but that we should have some share
of influence [or] the Tryal would not be equal."[6] At issue was not
a free and independent judiciary but a balanced influence in court.

The reaction of Penn's friends revealed the real weakness of the
Proprietors' government. Hamilton declared that "the Gentlemen who are friends to the Government are extreamly averse to
that Court, and upon speaking to Mr Francis† about it, who is
the only man of knowledge in the Law among us, he told me
plainly, He should think himself obliged to oppose its being
held."[7] To which Peters added that he could think of only "three

---

* Israel Pemberton, sometimes called the "King of the Quakers," was Clerk of the Yearly
Meeting of the Society and a member of the Assembly.
† Tench Francis was Attorney General of Pennsylvania from 1741 to 1755.

men in the Province who wou'd bear to hear of a Chancery Court
. . . Mr Allen,* you know, was ever against it."[8] Faced with
this opposition Penn backed down; he lost his courts and divided
his friends, and proved once again to the watchful Assembly that
the Proprietary Party was a fragile, easily cowed opponent. Yet
these preliminary disputes also proclaimed Penn's determination
to re-establish his place in the government.

These issues were still rather minor compared with the crisis
that came from the West. In 1751 and 1752, French activities
among the Indian tribes in the Ohio area threatened to involve
Pennsylvania tribes. A major political question arose: who would
direct Indian relations, Penn or the Assembly? Penn and Hamilton acted upon information received from the West indicating
that the Indians were so alarmed by French intrusions that they
wanted a fort built in the area. The Proprietor responded by
offering money to build and help support a fort if the Assembly
would also act.[9] The Assembly stalled and evaded the problem
because, as Penn told Hamilton, he could not have "the least expectation that any thing will be done by our Assembly, the Majority nay almost all their Members are or pretend to be against
any measure for the defence of the Country in principal, and this
they have a more particular dislike to because it is proposed by
us."[10] Unproductive conferences with the legislators continued
until the Assembly abruptly found a way out of its dilemma.

In response to questioning by the Assembly, Andrew Montour,
a half-breed trader and interpreter, said that far from wanting a
fort in the Ohio, the Indians would surely resist such a plan.
Furthermore, he hinted that the whole idea had been a proprietary
scheme to prod the government into action in the West. Greatly
relieved by this timely exposure, the Assembly rejected Hamilton's urgent appeal for action and rebuked him for what now
appeared to be some sort of plot to involve Pennsylvania in un-

---

* William Allen served as Chief Justice of Pennsylvania from 1750 to 1774.

necessary military measures. It also rejected Penn's offer of £400 for a fort with the suggestion that he would do better to contribute to the Assembly's Indian expenses. Indignant at the apparent duplicity of the Governor, the Assembly tried to get Penn to acknowledge its right to direct Indian relations, claiming that the Proprietor reaped more benefit from its peace funds than any person in Pennsylvania. Peters wrote to Penn, "The Assembly will never be easy till the Proprietaries pay something towards Indian Charges."[11]

Penn was faced with a difficult decision. He was willing to offer money for a fort—a project and an expenditure of his own choosing—but he balked at contributing to the Assembly's particular program. Though he wanted very much to manage Indian affairs, he did not want to spend the money this would entail. And although he was fully aware of the danger to the colony in the events on the Ohio, he feared that any expenditure on his part would be construed as a precedent supporting the Assembly's claim. Thus he informed Hamilton that

We have the opinion of the [English] Board of Trade, who are entirely disinterested in this matter, and who when the Dispute about defence was before them, and some People were foolish enough to say we should provide for it, gave it as their opinion, that we were under no greater obligation to do it than any other Chief Governor of the other Colonys; besides, as to Indian Affairs, we purchase the Lands, and pay that expense which is all any Person of common Sence can expect from us, and we desire the Assembly will not make any application to us of this nature.[12]

Pennsylvanians could hardly regard these as generous sentiments.

Penn's adherence to this narrow legal position in the matter of Indian affairs was undoubtedly a support of principle: if he could not direct policy, he would not pay. Yet it was a costly decision and left him open to a dangerous legislative claim upon his lands in 1756. At the time, however, the Quakers were not displeased with his declaration. It left them in charge of Indian affairs and gave them useful material for anti-proprietary propaganda.

The Indian problem was soon overshadowed by a renewed conflict over finance. The Assembly demanded more paper money
and, as it had in the past, claimed the right to specify how much
would be issued, how long the term of issue would be, and who
would manage it. Paper money was popular in Pennsylvania.
Previous issues had been well managed and had incurred little
loss by depreciation. Most Pennsylvanians accepted it as a necessary ingredient in economic growth: aided by successive issues of
money, commerce expanded, farms flourished with readily available loans, and prosperity spread throughout the colony. The
Proprietor approved the economic benefits of paper money but
strongly opposed the political implication in the Assembly's proposal. If paper money was profitable to Pennsylvania as a whole,
it was especially profitable to the Assembly. Past issues, together
with subsidiary measures, had created sources of revenue that ensured the Assembly's financial independence. Most paper-money
acts specified in general terms the uses to which the money would
be applied—some to replace worn-out bills, some for the King's
use, some to be reissued, and usually some to meet increased economic needs. However, the exact amounts to be thus applied were
often left indefinite or in the hands of Assembly commissioners.
As a result, paper-money issues invariably provided the House
with surplus or unallocated funds, and Penn suspected, in particular, that the amounts requested for replacing worn currency
were actually put to other uses.[13]

The Assembly also voted excise acts to help support the government and to redeem paper money as it fell due. In order to
lessen the burden for any one year, it scheduled the acts to run for
long periods, often for ten or twelve years. The sums thus raised
varied from year to year, and sometimes amounted to more than
was needed by the government or for paper-money redemption.
The Assembly also made a profit from the interest on loans extended by the Loan Office. Most of this interest money also

serviced currency redemption but, like the excise surpluses, interest profits could be added to the Assembly purse. Managed with care, these various incomes gave the Assembly about £6,000 per year for its own use, over which neither Governor nor Proprietor could exercise control.[14] The Assembly placed its own men on guard over this financial power. These men—the treasurer, excise collectors, loan-office trustees, and commissioners—ensured the legislature's authority over appropriations, collections, disbursements, and loans.

Here was a well-contrived financial machine in which all parts contributed to the Assembly's financial and political power. Of course, the legislators paid lip service to the theory that the executive had a half share in financial matters, but, in practice, any Assembly-voted money that came the Governor's way was carefully tied up in detailed appropriation and closely supervised. Penn's decision to fight this machine was courageous; it was also an act of desperation and showed his ignorance of the likely results of his plans in Pennsylvania. Proprietary strength was weak, and against an aggressive counterattack from the Assembly it had little prospect of sustaining a prolonged conflict. The extent of the Assembly's intentions was soon revealed in the paper-money messages and bills coming from its committees.

With help from Penn and the Quaker merchants in London, Pennsylvania's paper currency had escaped Parliamentary control in 1751. Before the bill was passed, Penn had bargained with Parliamentary leaders, and had obtained Pennsylvania's omission from the regulation in return for a promise that the Assembly would not take advantage of Parliament's generosity by rushing into a new expansion of the currency. He had forgotten the strong-willed determination of his legislature in previous money disputes. In 1752 he got a reminder when the Assembly did exactly what he had promised it would not do. In a message to Hamilton, the House proposed a bill to reissue £85,000 in old money and to add £40,000 in new paper. Hamilton rejected the proposal on the ground that it would embarrass the friends of Pennsylvania's money in England (including English Quakers) and antagonize the Ministry. He advised the Assembly to wait until the recent debates in England had receded from memory.

Behind Hamilton's rejection lay a strategy of delay designed to give Penn time to select his position for the struggle to direct the finances and, ultimately, the government of the colony. Penn's first decision was to re-assert the legitimate right of the Governor to a real equality in the expenditure of funds voted by the Assembly. To gain this, the Governor needed a voice in the nomination of the commissioners who applied the funds. If the House refused to approve his nominees, he would insist on naming just as many commissioners as the Assembly chose.[15]

Another way to hedge the legislative power was to keep the issue of paper money as small as possible so that little would be left for private purposes. Most important to the proprietary plan was a way to control the excise, without which the Assembly's financial empire would collapse. Penn determined that at all costs the excise acts must be restricted to short terms, four or five years instead of the ten or twelve usually demanded. This would permit him to review the Assembly's conduct before granting a new excise. Besides, a short term meant less money for the House.[16]

If these measures could be accomplished, proprietary government would gain some authority in Pennsylvania. Ideally, Penn hoped that he might get the Assembly to vote a permanent support for the Governor and other officers and, if possible, attain lump-sum appropriations for the Governor's use instead of tight-fisted, detailed grants. However, these ideas were for the future. Sweeping though his plans were, Penn sincerely believed that they did not endanger any liberties or rights of the people or their legislature. Such changes, he declared, were the best means of preserving a "balanced" government and guarding against "republicanism."

In 1751 the Proprietor instructed Hamilton to demand legislative and executive equality in all appropriations of money, and,
where necessary, to amend money bills until the Assembly recognized his rightful half-share in legislation. Joint appropriation and
amendment of money bills were two highly provocative and
dangerous proposals to try in Pennsylvania. Hamilton knew this
better than Penn, and he stated these political realities in a critique
that ably defined the nature of the problem:

As the Cry for Paper Money is once raised, it cannot now be Stilled again.
There is not the least Doubt, but a Bill will be offer'd at least once in every
year till it be obtained; and therefore this appropriating Clause becomes a
Matter of great Moment to You, and well deserves your most serious consideration. In my humble opinion, It should never be proposed unless You are
determined at all Events inviolably to adhere to it. It is certain that at first
the Assembly will bounce violently, and be very angry, and the Province will
be thrown into a Flame on that Account, and probably You will have but little
Money paid into your Receiver's Hands during the Contest. Added to all this,
(and it ought to be well weigh'd) The Assembly, by the great funds they
have in their Hands of at least £6,000 a year, will be able to accumulate a
Vast Sum of Money before the present Acts expire, with which to carry on
any Contest, or to gratify their Adherents; . . . their liberality will be
stopped to all others. On the other hand, when the Remitting and Excise Acts
expire, which will be in about four years . . . and the money begins to
sink, . . . they will be under a necessity of Complying, rather than want a
Medium of Commerce, but that is a long time to carry on a Contest. And
untill they do comply, Every Officer of the Government who relies on the
Publick for any thing is held in Bondage, the whole dependence of the province is drawn upon them; Men of Fortune, from whom One would expect
better things, gradually slide into their dirty ways of thinking; and by those
means The Government, upon any Contention is left without either Weight
or Adherents.[17]

The Proprietor had to consider not only the effect of his actions
in Pennsylvania but the looming threat of the Board of Trade,
lately roused from years of lethargy under the spirited direction
of its President, Lord Halifax. Halifax envisioned a reformed
and redirected administration of both Crown and proprietary
colonies. His reforms planned, wherever and whenever possible,
the steady extension of royal authority and prerogatives in co-

lonial affairs. The recently passed Iron Act and Currency Act were expressions of this stimulated interest in colonial regulation and reform. Having already announced its interest in proprietary governments, the Board questioned its lawyers about the extent of Penn's authority and the circumstances in which the Crown might act in Pennsylvania. This was no emergency wartime investigation but a basic examination of weaknesses in the proprietary rule. Neither was it particularly directed at legislative poaching on Penn's prerogatives, for in English eyes the blame for bad Assembly conduct rested mainly on the Proprietor because he had paramount authority in the colony. Thus Penn had to be certain that what he did in Pennsylvania was acceptable to the home government, and above all he had to faithfully guard the prerogatives entrusted to him by the Crown. At the same time, he could not permit himself to become a mere servant of the Board of Trade; the prerogatives were, after all, his to use. Here was another dilemma for Penn. It was difficult to determine exactly what the Board had in mind—colonial policy was vague at best—yet he knew that proprietary actions in Pennsylvania were subject to critical review in England. He might innocently do something that would provoke a charge of policy violation.

To counter the threat, Penn turned to the time-honored device of cultivating connections with men of influence in government. Hoping to counter anti-proprietary sentiments, he presented his case at every opportunity to Lord Halifax, Henry Pelham, the Duke of Cumberland, the Duke of Newcastle, and various members of Parliament. He had some success, for despite their conflicting interests Penn and Halifax were on friendly terms in 1752, and Penn told Peters that the President of the Board seemed disposed to "do him every service." By adding these connections to his well-preserved friendships with influential London Quakers, Penn hoped to forestall ministerial meddling while he dealt with the Assembly.

On the surface, rejection of the Assembly's paper-money bill would seem to have been an action calculated to win approval in England. But if Hamilton's predictions were correct and the Assembly's reaction in the future was to be violent and protracted, then Penn could expect it to shower appeals and petitions on the Privy Council and the Board of Trade. There was precedent for this expectation, because on several previous occasions the Assembly had threatened to appeal to the Crown against the proprietors. The ensuing uproar might provide Halifax and the Board with an excuse to interfere directly in Pennsylvania's affairs. From Penn's standpoint, therefore, it was wise to confine the contest to Pennsylvania. But this would place the burden of fighting the Assembly upon his friends.

Before confronting the legislature with their real intentions, Penn and his friends exchanged letters about the proper course of action. He quickly discovered that his supporters in Pennsylvania were divided and few in number. Reluctant to confront the Assembly with instructions for joint appropriation, they complained of their weakness and inability to stand against an enraged legislature.

Hamilton, already in trouble over the chancery courts, Indian relations, and other measures, found it almost impossible to obtain men for government positions. Even William Allen, a principal proprietary leader, was reluctant to accept an appointment as Chief Justice of the province in 1750, though he finally agreed out of a sense of duty. Men in lesser positions were unwilling to expose themselves to "popular" abuse. Hamilton wrote, "It is inconceivable what an inveteracy there is in those people against the Magistracy, to which they so much prefer a seat in the Assembly, that tho there are several in the House, whom I put into commission of the peace, yet they will not qualify for fear of losing their popularity."[18] Peters also tried to find friends for the Proprietor, and advised Penn that "It will be for your Interest to fill up all offices with sensible men who have good friends."[19] But, as the vendue master, Dr. Bard, found out, it was not safe to be a "friend of the government." The Assembly Quakers circulated a petition against him, and "he was frightened to such a degree that he resigned in favour of young Mr Thomas Lawrence," who was one of the Old Party.[20]

Unwittingly, Peters added to the disarray of the proprietary forces. Accompanied by several justices of the peace he journeyed into the West in 1750 to lay out a proprietary manor and, on the way, to remove squatters from Penn's lands. The task was a necessary part of the program to make land-holding in the colony orderly and profitable. However, most of the settlers who were evicted or had their cabins burned were Scotch-Irish. Reports of Peters's foray quickly spread to other settlements and "inflamed the Minds" of both the Scotch-Irish and the Germans. Peters had to tell Penn that "You cannot conceive how much people are offended with Proprietary Surveys, not the meaner sort only, but persons of more sense and a better figure."[21]

The reaction to this event in Philadelphia showed something of the solidarity of the City against the "rabble" in the West. When Peters returned, he reported his action to the Assembly. For a moment the legislators forgot their politics, and, as men of position, praised what he had done. They voted a unanimous approval of his report, stating that they too deplored the unruly, disgraceful squatting of the frontier settlers.

Another large segment of Pennsylvania's population received proprietary attention in the early 1750's. The party leaders knew well how the Quakers used the Germans to win county elections. Added to the political menace was the danger that increasing numbers of Germans threatened to overwhelm English civilization in Pennsylvania. Penn received numerous complaints about the hordes of Germans that were spilling into the province from nearly every ship that came up the Delaware, and his correspondents urged him to try to stop this Palatine threat. Peters suggested that Penn try to get the naturalization law repealed if no other move availed. But Dr. Thomas Graeme, a Philadelphia physician and a proprietary supporter, proposed another solution: a redistribution of county representation would, he thought, dilute German strength. The territory for new counties should be carefully carved out of German areas in Philadelphia, Bucks, and Lancaster, "which will take off their Settlements and leave them only two members to Eight."[22]

As if it were not bad enough for the Quakers to have political control in Bucks, Chester, and Philadelphia counties, they seemed to be winning in the West. Germans loyal to the Quakers had helped in recent York county elections by threatening the sheriff and election officers with violence if the polls were closed early—a move that had previously been attempted by the proprietary opposition. Graeme reported that, for the time being, the Scotch-Irish had the potential political advantage of greater numbers in York and Cumberland countries, and he thought they should be encouraged to gain control of local government before the Germans grew too numerous and powerful. Not only did the Palatines increase more rapidly than other groups, but because they were hard-working and thrifty, they were able to buy lands and qualify for the vote sooner than the Scotch-Irish. Therefore, if the Scotch-Irish did not become active in local county politics, they would find the Quakers and Germans in control.[23]

Penn officially favored the creation of new western counties in the hope that he might gain seats in the Assembly from these areas. However, if the Quaker-German alliance should reap the political benefit in these new counties, the Proprietor would be worse off than before. Until something could be done to wean the better sort of Germans away from their Quaker allegiance, Penn could not expect much improvement in the strength of his faction. Attempted gerrymandering was just a temporary and not very successful expedient. Yet neither Penn nor his leaders in Pennsylvania could bring themselves to attempt to build a party among the ordinary people, many of whom could legally vote. Proprietary men wished often enough that sensible people who believed in "good government"—i.e., who opposed the Quakers—would come forward from the German and Scotch-Irish citizenry. But rather than stoop to ungentlemanly solicitation of such people, they bemoaned the lack of public spirit and accepted election defeat.[24]

All together, these problems, disputes, and weaknesses placed proprietary government in a precarious position in Pennsylvania. Peters summed up the situation for the Proprietor with his usual insight:

Your Quit Rents are shamefully in Arrears—Your Ferrys wrested out of your hands—Your Manor Lands and appropriated Tracts are settled . . . promiscuously. The Assembly [is] provoked by Paper Money being demanded and not likely to be granted—The Sheriffs are the Creatures of and subservient to the People—The Juries without virtue in Proprietary Disputes and no Court of Equity. While matters are in this situation it shou'd be well consider'd where to begin and by what methods to proceed and who will undertake to manage—when this is agree'd on Order and Steadiness may effect every thing.[25]

Any friend would be valuable; one with a seat in the Assembly would be priceless.

Franklin's election to the Assembly coincided with the renewal of conflict between the Assembly and the proprietary. His entry into politics had been unopposed; neither party could see any reason to fear him, and each found reasons to believe in his eventual support. The politicians might be puzzled about his real political principles, but they liked him and knew his ability.

Franklin was precisely in the position he wanted—he was friendly with men in both parties and was courted for his support. For his part, he continued to ignore party affiliation to work with men he liked. He had no quarrel with Penn's government or with

his representatives in Pennsylvania. William Allen, the newly appointed Chief Justice, was Franklin's friend and patron. In 1751
Allen opened negotiations to get the deputy postmastership of the
colonies for him. Both men were busily engaged in boldly conceived plans for an academy; Franklin provided ideas and Allen
gave his considerable money and influence to promote the project
among the non-Quaker gentlemen of Philadelphia. Many prominent Philadelphians were interested admirers of Franklin's ingenious electrical experiments. Peters, assisted by Peter Collinson
in England, solicited a gift of electrical apparatus for Franklin
from the Proprietor. Franklin was grateful for the present, and
in a long letter to Collinson explained his experiments and hinted
that he would like to open a correspondence with Penn.

Penn missed an opportunity by not responding immediately
to Franklin's hints, but he did write Peters that he was "greatly
pleased that most worthless Fellow Pemberton was turned out of
the Assembly, and wish he may always be by Franklyn who is a
man of more temper."[26] The Proprietor also approved when
Hamilton offered Franklin a commission as a justice of the peace.
That he accepted such an unpopular office suggested that Franklin was either oblivious to the danger to his political career or willing to risk certain Quaker censure for proprietary favor. Before
long Franklin found the magistracy not to his taste and resigned
his commission, pleading that his ignorance of the law handicapped him. But as Hamilton had discovered, men who wished
to hold their seats in the Assembly could not afford to be proprietary magistrates.

Franklin's association with leading proprietary men went beyond mutual projects. He shared their attitude toward Pennsylvania society, which was reflected notably in their fear of the German influence on the colony. Except for the scheme to gerry-
mander the Germans, both Franklin and the proprietary came to
similar conclusions in their analysis of the problem, which suggests that they had discussed it. As was usual with Franklin, mat-

ters that deeply interested him found expression in his letters and essays. In his *Observations Concerning the Increase of Mankind, Peopling of Countries, etc.*, outlined in 1751, he dealt mainly with broad imperial or general American topics, such as trade and population growth. But it is noteworthy that here, and in his correspondence of the same period, his discussion of the German menace constituted his sole attempt to analyze a major internal problem of Pennsylvania.

Whatever weight he placed on the proprietary side of the political scale, Franklin balanced with Assembly-Quaker interests and associations. He was, of course, in the Assembly, and he and his son received legislative patronage. If he had any plan for his political career during those first years in the Assembly, it was undoubtedly to preserve his independence from absolute alliances and factions. Should some measure appear which on its merits (defined by reasonableness, utility, and goodness) commanded his support, he could assist the part of government or the faction that seemed most in favor of the proposal. Ideally, he hoped to avoid even this shifting back and forth; rather, he saw himself as an agent whose job was to awaken the natural inclination of all men in or out of politics "to act reasonable and virtuous parts." In pursuing this noble intention, Franklin probably experienced his happiest and most productive years in the Assembly from 1751 to 1753. Without making binding commitments to any faction, he used his influence to found a hospital, assisted the Governor in finding a means of defending the colony and preserving peace with the Indians, and supported a number of useful lesser measures including a bridge survey, a night watch, and a revision of the Assembly minutes. He also devoted much of his time to various studies of the history of paper money, Indian expenses, and official fees; and he wrote messages and proposals for bills that embodied the information from his investigations.

Franklin's subsequent historical reputation as a legislator depended considerably upon the literary talents he displayed in drafting the messages and reports from the various committees on which he served. Increasingly critical of the Governor and the Proprietor, these papers have been offered as indisputable evidence that Franklin was an ardent champion of the Assembly against the Proprietor and the executive power in the province. The facts of politics argued otherwise. Not only was Franklin a professed independent—without open alignment with either the Old Party or the Proprietary—but he was clearly not the leader of the House. The Assembly was the instrument of Quaker politics, and Isaac Norris and Pemberton directed its use for the Society. The committees on which Franklin served were safely composed of Old Party majorities, and their views prevailed. He served as committee penman, writing the decision of the majority. Far from proclaiming an undying opposition to Governor and Proprietor, he undertook to tone down the impassioned antiproprietary sentiments that habitually marked legislative messages.[27] Between 1751 and 1755 he openly disavowed what he regarded as Assembly excesses: he found the Assembly's Address to the King—which had been drawn up early in 1755 when he was absent from the House—"ill-judged and ill-tim'd." He added, "I like neither the Governor's Conduct, nor the Assembly's; and having some Share in the Confidence of both, I have endeavour'd to reconcile 'em in vain, and between 'em they make me very uneasy."[28] This attitude was in harmony with Franklin's policy of promoting calm, reasoned discourse between Governor and legislature.

Had Franklin indulged in extreme legislative partisanship or closely identified himself with the Assembly's denunciation of proprietary government, he could not have maintained his association with the proprietary leaders. Because they regarded him as a moderate and usually temperate member of the House, they excused his writings in the Assembly. It was obvious to them that any messages reported out of the Quaker-dominated committees would necessarily contain a strong assertion of Quaker, legislative, anti-proprietary principles. That Franklin participated in and signed his name to these messages was not construed until later to mean that he agreed with them.

The terms of the political conflict were thus established between 1750 and 1753. The proprietary's attempt to restore executive power was met by a legislative counterattack that also represented a defense of a religious denomination's political supremacy. It was essentially a private quarrel between rival gentleman leaders, and scarcely affected the people at all. Yet there were other influences at work—Indians, the French, English politicians, and possibly, in time, an awakened citizenry.

That Franklin was apparently insensitive to these political conditions was indicated by his attempt to obtain charters for an academy and a hospital. Excited by the prospect of accomplishing these projects, he wanted quick action from Penn. But because the Assembly was also involved, Penn carefully checked the proposals for any dangers to his rights before he would grant the charters. Not surprisingly, he found that the Assembly was indeed guilty of attempting to establish the hospital without the proper letters patent and seals. Although he thought that the Assembly had made a calculated attempt to affront him, he did not believe that Franklin was involved. It was undoubtedly Franklin's exuberance for one of his pet projects that had allowed him to forget his sense of principle and good form. In a letter to Peters, Penn declared, "I believe Mr Franklin had no intention to do a thing disagreeable to us, . . . but no doubt many others had."[29]

Franklin regarded Penn's objections and finicky adherence to rights solely as unnecessary obstacles to the completion of the projects. But results counted with Franklin—even if long in coming—and when Penn belatedly decided to help the academy, Franklin was happy to forgive what had gone before. He rejoiced in the Proprietor's "Beneficence," which "would in my Opinion leave the most lasting Impressions of Gratitude and Respect, and be productive of the best Effects, in a due Regard and Veneration for the Family among those who by their Education and Stations will be most capable of serving it." Furthermore, the "Professor himself, being under the greatest Obligation to the Founders, may take all Opportunities of making and fixing those Impressions in the Minds . . . of the Youth."[30] These were not the sentiments of an opponent of the Proprietor or proprietary government. They revealed Franklin's willingness to let Penn reap political benefits from the academy as long as the students got other educational fare along with their sense of obligation and gratitude to the Proprietors. For the time being Franklin and Penn each wanted, and could benefit from, the good will of the other.

HAZARDS OF WARFARE

Proprietary prospects did not improve in 1753 and 1754. Despite Peters's efforts there was no increase in the party's strength in the Assembly. But Penn had committed himself and his friends to the struggle with the Old Party, and they could not retreat now. Penn conceded, however, that it would be prudent to keep secret the instructions on the joint appropriation of money until the other points had been tested. Hamilton and Allen were certain that the Assembly's reaction to the instructions would completely paralyze the government.[1] Faced with the prospect of battle, Hamilton lost courage. Although he was independently wealthy and was not much concerned with legislative threats to cut off his support, he was more a Pennsylvanian than a Governor.[2] The bitter conflict that was sure to arise over Penn's plans in the province strained his loyalty to the Proprietor and disposed him to resign his position.

For more than a year Hamilton tried to find a way to soften Penn's instructions and thereby avoid conflict with the Assembly. He finally decided that the best strategy would be to apply a suspending clause to paper-money bills.[3] Such a clause would forestall legislative action on the bills until they were reviewed by the Privy Council in England. Other proprietary leaders, including Allen and Tench Francis, supported the idea because it would enable them to evade the unpleasantness of opposing the Assembly and appearing to oppose paper money. Knowing the intransigent attitude of the Assembly better than Penn, Hamilton and his friends hoped to remove both the fight and the ultimate decision from Pennsylvania to England.[4]

Penn had indirectly suggested the logic of this maneuver when, in 1751, he had cautioned Pennsylvania against issuing new paper money because the recent Currency Act and the Ministry's evident distaste for colonial paper-money schemes meant almost certain rejection of further currency expansion. With this in mind, the proprietary leaders in Pennsylvania saw the chance to make the legislature submit to Penn's plans by using English opposition instead of their own. They believed that application of a suspending clause would transfer the Assembly's anger from the Governor and the Proprietor to the Crown. And in time, deprived of its paper money and other sources of income, the Assembly would be amenable to a compromise on proprietary terms. It was a simple, quick solution to a problem that Hamilton and his friends had no desire to face.

Hamilton's use of the suspending clause put Penn in an embarrassing position. To justify his action, Hamilton had referred to the royal instructions of 1741 that required suspending clauses in all money bills. He now declared that until it was known whether Pennsylvania was in any way bound by the Currency Act of 1751, he would not hazard passing such bills. To the legislators these arguments appeared inconsistent and devious. In effect, the Governor was arguing against his own and the Proprietor's authority in government. The Assembly found itself in the novel position of defending proprietary power. It declared that the Crown had delegated its power to the Proprietor, and could not resume it either through royal instructions or through the actions of the Privy Council and the Board of Trade.

Goaded by the "transparently dishonest" reasons advanced by Hamilton, the Assembly went on to question the whole nature of proprietary instructions. If the Crown had delegated its authority to William Penn and could not take it back, then, by analogy, the Proprietor had delegated his authority to the Governor and could not subsequently intervene with instructions. Hence Hamilton alone should accept or reject legislative measures, without proprietary instruction or interference. If a bill was defective, it could be disallowed by the Privy Council. The intention behind this argument was, of course, to isolate the Governor from the Proprietor so that he would be more susceptible to local pressure and influence. Since relatively few colonial laws were disallowed in England, this limitation upon legislative freedom was much less to be feared than proprietary instruction. Penn knew what was going on in Pennsylvania; English leaders usually did not.

Penn was uncertain in 1753 about what course to follow. To what extent did royal instructions, beyond those exactly touching the prerogative in such obvious matters as defense, bind him? After holding several informal discussions with attorneys and government officials in England, he was still uncertain. This question was one about which there were many opinions but to which there was no definite answer. Some members of the Ministry clearly wanted to place the Proprietors under a blanket of instructions, but the lawyers, after much backing and filling, were unable to find specific legal precedents for such action.

In view of this uncertainty, Penn feared that if he and the Governor ignored instructions for royal colonies, the Privy Council might at some future time find a cause for action against the proprietary charter, claiming violation of the royal prerogative. Although he wanted to believe that the Crown had, as the Assembly asserted, irrevocably delegated its power to him, Penn could not be certain. However, Hamilton's use of the suspending clause forced him to make a decision. He wrote Peters in October 1753:

I observe your account of the Governor's uneasiness at the thoughts of passing the Bill for emitting twenty thousand Pounds Paper Money and the objections, as it is drawn, likely to be made at the Board of Trade, but we must not countenance such objections as you instance, the King having reserved a right of repealing only such Laws as are contrary to Acts of Parliament here, to his own prerogative, and the Allegiance due from us and the Inhabitants of Pennsylvania, so that reference to former Laws are not a sufficient cause of repeal, and I have procured a Report from the Board of Trade to the King in which this is acknowledged.[5]

This opinion was not sufficient to stop Hamilton from using the suspending-clause argument again early in 1754, or to prevent the Assembly from hardening its resistance to what seemed to be proprietary hypocrisy and deceit. The Governor finally withdrew the suspending clause in May 1754, but the damage had already been done.

At this point Penn was more worried about the ambitions of the Board of Trade than what the Assembly might do. He was quite willing to fight his battles in Pennsylvania without any interference or assistance from the Crown except its passive legal support of his rights. Exasperated with the shortsightedness of his friends in Pennsylvania, Penn declared, "Whatever I say to Lord President or Lord Halifax must be with great caution. I shall not think it necessary to say so much as you do of the weakness of a Government least [sic] disagreeable consequences should attend it. We must not desire too much assistance from them, least they shou'd think it necessary to give more than we ask."[6] The use of the suspending clause and the arguments advanced in its favor constituted a humiliating admission that, without outside help, the Proprietor was unable to defend his own and the Crown's prerogatives in Pennsylvania. He was well aware that the episode would be interpreted in this light in England. Hamilton, who had made the mistake of applying it, resigned in the summer of 1754, a much battered man.

In the Assembly the leaders watched in growing anger as their paper-money bills fell under a flurry of executive objections. They countered each objection raised by the Governor with assertions of their rights. When he objected to long-term excise acts, they maintained that the Assembly was the proper judge of how long the acts should run. When he evoked the suspending clause, they claimed that royal or proprietary instructions were invalid and that the Governor had, or ought to have, full power to accept bills on their merits. When he asserted his right to a half share in appropriations, they declared that, as representatives of the people, they had the right and the duty to supervise the collection and expenditure of money.

The suspending clause evoked the most extensive barrage of constitutional argument. But it also momentarily divided the Quaker leadership. Israel Pemberton, who had lost his Assembly seat in 1752 but still acted as Party leader from the outside, wanted to accept Hamilton's challenge so that the quarrel might be referred to England. Counting on help from London Quakers and the known ministerial dislike of proprietary governments, he believed that the Assembly would win. He realized (as Penn likewise came to do) that such an appeal to England would bypass the Governor and reduce the Proprietor to a "mere cypher."

Isaac Norris, on the other hand, took a more provincial and perhaps more realistic view of the conflict.[7] He saw it as an endurance contest in which the Assembly had the superior strength. He was not as optimistic as Pemberton about the English reaction to the Assembly's claims. Norris was a practical politician interested in preserving Quaker political power. He believed it wise to confine the struggle to Pennsylvania, where the Assembly had won in the past, and, with its resources, seemed likely to do so again.[8] To bring the Crown into the dispute might result in unfavorable and unpredictable decisions, for, though unfriendly to proprietors, it had shown no partiality toward colonial legislatures. Norris believed that Penn, by himself, would be forced to compromise, and he favored compromises if they preserved the real strength of the Assembly and its Quaker leadership.[9]

The Assembly got encouragement in 1753 and 1754 from the obvious unhappiness of Hamilton. Norris surmised that the Governor would revolt against whatever secret instructions Penn had given him, and thought he could prompt the revolt by increasing the pressure on the Governor. Writing to his brother Charles, Norris confided that Hamilton "pressed [the Proprietors] upon that head with a resolution to resign the Government unless he can be left at Liberty."[10]

When Robert Hunter Morris became Governor in 1754, his term was expected to be short; he was looked upon as a temporary caretaker. All of Penn's friends, and many Assemblymen who were unfriendly to the government, hoped that Penn would soon come to Pennsylvania. They believed that only a representative of the proprietary family could find a solution to the colony's problems. But as the months passed and Penn did not come, all factions united in blaming Morris for creating new disputes and sharpening old ones.[11]

Isaac Norris and the Assembly had confidently expected that the new Governor would bring a more moderate policy and concessions to the Assembly. But Morris immediately proved that he was unlikely to concede or compromise anything. Indeed, he was a legalistic, argumentative match for the Assembly, able to give back as much abuse as he received. He raised every objection he could find to renewed paper-money measures: he revived the suspending clause, attacked the excise proposals and the disposition of money, and said he had sworn to uphold an imperial statute of 1704 forbidding Governors to sign bills that made paper money legal tender or that were not accompanied by sufficient taxes to redeem the paper. He backed up his objections with an opinion of Sir Dudley Ryder, a former Attorney General of England who was now Chief Justice, King's Bench, who declared that it was "by no means safe, advisable or consistent with [the Governor's] Duty to pass such bills without a suspending clause."[12]

As the hope of wearing down the Governors faded, the Assembly's reaction to Morris became even more heated and abusive than its reaction to Hamilton. Penn was also upset by the Governor's tactics. Again he had to consult lawyers to certify his authority, and, since the Assembly reopened its attack on proprietary instructions, he also sought advice on the legality of these instructions from his own attorney, Ferdinando Paris, and from Crown lawyers. Although the Proprietor spent much of 1754 consulting lawyers, waiting on Ministers, and searching for precedents to support his government, his time was not wasted. Such careful attention to law and to important men in the Government provided him with the legal weapons and high-placed connections that eventually helped determine the decision.

In the last months of 1754 it became apparent that if Morris continued to justify his rejection of money bills by invoking royal instructions and former precedents, the Assembly would have to carry its case to England.[13] Events in 1754 also brought Isaac Norris around to Pemberton's interpretation of the situation. After the French and Indian alliance defeated Washington's army at Fort Necessity in 1754, the situation in the West had grown steadily worse. England expressed its concern by issuing an increasing stream of orders for an active colonial defense. The Quaker leaders now saw an opportunity to catch Penn in a nutcracker and thereby shatter his objections to the Assembly's financial measures.[14] If he continued to demand joint appropriation of money, reduced excise acts, and suspending clauses before approving vitally needed money bills, the Assembly could present its case to the Crown, confident that the need for imperial defense would far outweigh what would appear to be legalistic obstructionism by the Governor and his master.[15]

Late in 1754, the Assembly got what it believed to be a sign that it could expect a victory in England. Several letters written by Sir Thomas Robinson, the Secretary of State for the Southern

Department (England), came into the Assembly's hands. They were sharply critical of the government's failure to mount a defense effort and warned that any delay in complying with royal instructions for defense measures, for whatever reason, would be viewed in England with displeasure.[16] And he implied it was the Governor's duty to carry out these instructions no matter how many obstacles the Assembly might raise.[17]

Norris and Pemberton began to prepare the Assembly's case. Pemberton wrote a long dissertation explaining and defending Pennsylvania's paper money and the manner in which the Assembly managed it, and sent it to Hinton Brown, a Quaker banker in London. Norris asked his brother Charles, who was in London, to arouse the colonial agent and bestir the London Quakers to add their support to the coming appeal. All old and new arguments, precedents, and weighty reasons were carefully scrutinized as the Assembly polished its messages to the Governor and shipped copies to England for use against Penn. Some Assemblymen, carried away with emotion, declared that they would rather be captured by the French than concede a single point to the Proprietor. This remark was also sent to England, but in this case for Penn's use.[18]

If the paper-money policy and its ramifications did not confound government in Pennsylvania, the complexities of Indian relations and defense were certain to do so. The Quakers' peaceful Indian policy, based largely on giving presents to the tribes in the colony, was in for a severe test. Priding themselves upon a uniquely honorable treatment of the Indian, the Quakers were suspicious of "outsiders" who might interfere with the Indians or with the policy. But peace was preserved not so much by the Quaker policy as by the Indian policy of "Pax Iroquoia." The Pennsylvania Indians came within the jurisdiction of the League of Six Nations, whose authority over vassal and allied tribes

exerted a stabilizing influence. As long as the power of the Iroquois was strong and it suited their interests to remain at peace
with the English, the treaties and land purchases concluded by
the Quakers or the Proprietor had this tacit power behind them.[19]

Unfortunately for the Pennsylvanians, the power of the Six
Nations was declining by 1753. French intrusions into the Ohio
area had drawn local tribes under French military and economic
influence and, in so doing, had weakened the Iroquois hegemony.
Furthermore, the Long House at Onondaga, where Iroquois
leaders met to decide League policy, was itself divided; some of
the tribes were infected with French influence, and some saw a
greater danger from the land hunger of the English colonists
than from French incursions.

As the influence of the Six Nations declined the vassal tribes,
encouraged by the French, felt free to assert their independence
and to follow their individual inclinations. Iroquois authority was
dealt a further blow when Washington was defeated at Fort
Necessity. It was now apparent that the English could not support their interests and allies against the French.

It was in this larger scene that both the Proprietor and the
Assembly added to the confusion by ill-considered acts and failure
to act at the right time. The Assembly, still complimenting itself
over the exposure of the fort plot, was in no mood to listen to new
warnings of danger on the frontier. Neither the French nor the
Indians had done much in 1753 to cause anxiety, and the old
policy of peace by presents still seemed good enough. The only
improvement the Assembly could suggest was a better regulation
of the fur trade. Ever suspicious, Pemberton warned the Quakers
to pay close attention to any conferences or negotiations in which
the Governor had a part. Out of habit, the Assembly reiterated
that if the Proprietor were concerned with defense of the colony
(which some members doubted), he would do well to contribute
to the Assembly's expenses.

The Carlisle Conference, called by the Board of Trade in 1753 to discuss methods of improving the rapidly deteriorating Indian relations, demonstrated how unprepared the Pennsylvanians were to meet Indian problems. Representatives from Pennsylvania and Indians from the Ohio area exchanged compliments and vows of eternal friendship, but accomplished little else. The Indians begged for more practical help and warned that they would have to look elsewhere if it did not come soon, but the Pennsylvanians thought that a little patching of the old policy would suffice. Franklin, who represented Pennsylvania along with Peters, Norris, and Conrad Weiser (Pennsylvania's chief interpreter), believed that unscrupulous Indian traders were the cause of the trouble and that better regulation and control of the Indian trade would be the best solution. Peters agreed with the need for trade regulation and counted on Franklin to find a way:

The Speaker and Mr Franklyn are fully convinced of the Necessity of a regulation of the Indian Trade, . . . they talk with great assurance of doing something to the purpose at the next Sitting of Assembly, and I believe Mr Franklyn is sincere, and will do his Endeavours to see the Matter in a just Light, and to find out the quickest and most efficacious Remedies—but as to [Norris], he has so perplexed an head, that he will only puzzle, not mend things.[20]

The Proprietor's contribution to trouble on the frontier was a plan to make a new land purchase. He would not embroil his agents with the many separate tribes in the Ohio area or in Pennsylvania, as had happened at Carlisle, but would buy land directly from the Iroquois. This set the stage for proprietary participation in the Albany Congress of 1754, which was called by the Board of Trade to consider a common Indian policy for the colonies. Through the efforts of the Proprietor's nephew, John Penn, together with Peters and Weiser, the purchase of a portion of western Pennsylvania from the Iroquois was negotiated.[21] Repercussions from this sale placed an increased strain on the already precarious inter-tribal relations. Some of the Iroquois chieftains who had not been consulted about the sale tried to repudiate it. Ohio and Pennsylvania Indians, whose lands had been taken without consultation, saw the sale as further proof that the English were after all only interested in Indian land. The action of the Iroquois indicated that the Six Nations no longer cared for the rights of their allies. Thus these Ohio and Pennsylvania tribes listened more intently to French persuasions. William Johnson, the Commissary of New York for Indian Affairs, valiantly trying to hold the northern Indians in line, did not conceal his annoyance at this untimely proprietary action.

Penn's purchase was not questioned by either the Quakers or the Assembly. Neither had yet discovered the political value of a solicitous concern for the poor Indian and an outrage at "proprietary greed." Rather, they were agreeable to land purchases as long as the Indians were paid and appeared content with the bargain.

After the defeat of the Virginians at Fort Necessity, most Quakers rejected any suggestion that they should contribute money or supplies to help pull the southern colony's chestnuts out of the fire. Fearful of any outside interference in Pennsylvania's Indian affairs, the Quakers were deeply suspicious of Virginia's thrust into the Northwest. Their suspicions extended to any efforts made by William Johnson, New York, the Crown, or the Proprietor to further their influence on inter-tribal relations either in Pennsylvania or in neighboring areas. Isaac Norris, who saw affairs on a larger scale than most of his brethren, realized that Virginia's defeat opened Pennsylvania to attack and was a danger of continental importance, but he could not convince the Society to change its traditional policy.[22]

The Quakers guarded their prerogatives in this sphere with the same jealous zeal that they applied to financial matters. If the Governor obtained money for defense, and control over de-

fense and Indian policy, the effect on the balance of power would
be the same as if he gained control over finance. In short, it was
vital that the Assembly achieve full financial control before the
pressure of war forced it to appropriate funds to the Governor
or King without adequate controls. This was one reason why
Norris and Pemberton rushed to present a case to the Crown in
late 1754. The nutcracker could work both ways: they were determined that the Crown would force the proprietary to surrender, not the Assembly.[23]

Quaker accounts of the Society's decline from power in Pennsylvania have usually held that the stern principles of pacifism
were the shoals on which the Party went aground. Religious principles did indeed complicate Quaker response to the need for
defense, but it is evident that these principles were by no means
primary or insurmountable obstacles. It was the conservative
wing of Quakerism, led by Pemberton, that probably felt the
pinch of principle most sorely when it contemplated the military
demands of non-Quakers in the colony and in England. Yet these
"principled" Quakers were a minority faction.

Preservation of political power was the paramount interest of
most Quakers; religious principles came second. Ideally, they
hoped to save both, but if forced to make a choice, the majority,
led by Isaac Norris, would seek to hold on to the Assembly, the
Old Party, and the county offices. Norris wanted desperately to
find some scheme—like Franklin's Association of 1747—that
would free the Society from having to make such a choice. Although emphasizing different aspects of the Quaker tradition in
Pennsylvania—power and principle—both Norris and Pemberton realized that the hitherto impregnable unity of the Party
was in jeopardy. Norris expressed his thoughts on the problem
in letters to his brother Charles. He declared his willingness to
see Pennsylvania fairly bristle with guns, forts, and troops (non-

Quaker, of course) as long as the Governor and the Proprietor
recognized the rights of the Assembly:

And indeed whatever difficultys our Assemblys may have in appropriating
money to Warlike purposes, when there is a good harmony and Confidence in
their Governor, what they give may be made very effectual by leaving the
disposition of it wholly to himself, and can be pretty easily obtained . . . on
all suitable occasions, but when that confidence is lost the difficultys Attend-
ing the Granting money in that manner are very considerable with those
who have otherwise a good influence in our house.[24]

The Quakers had reconciled their religious principles with military necessity in the past. Norris wanted to be able to do so again,
but not at the cost of surrendering anything to the Governor or
weakening the great Quaker bulwark, the Assembly. Norris and
Pemberton were still able to work together in 1754, but signs
of a political split within Quaker ranks were increasingly apparent. There were reports, for instance, that prior to the election
of 1754, some Quakers tried to rebel against the official Party list
of candidates; it was difficult to put these rebels down again with
the old warning that disunity would only aid the enemy.[25]

Proprietary forces in Pennsylvania remained weak and badly divided. Some men openly sympathized with the Assembly. Others,
with only axes to grind, retired prematurely from battle. And
still others simply wanted such proprietary benefits as land or jobs.
Perhaps the only consistent bond joining these political outs was
their dislike of Quaker domination of local government. The
leaders divided tactically on whether to support the Proprietor's
instructions (a minority) or to force him to bring in the Crown
against the Assembly.[26] Their positions depended heavily on personal relationships. It was almost impossible to hold them together and eliminate personal rivalries. Indeed, only the Quaker-
Assembly menace united them and induced them to look beyond
the gentlemen to the "people" for help. Typically, however, they

did not make a straightforward political appeal—that would
have been too much for the proprietary leaders. Instead, they
attempted to enlist German support through education.

Hence after long maintaining a critical attitude toward the
Germans, both the Proprietor and his friends began a positive
change in policy. Stimulated by the creative ideas and plans of
the Rev. William Smith, an Anglican clergyman who had recently settled in Pennsylvania, Penn joined in a plan to found
charity schools designed to educate and "anglicize" the Germans
in the colony. After obtaining generous contributions in England,
Smith and Penn interested their Pennsylvania friends in the project. Smith, a superb promoter, had soon obtained both money and
support from the colony's non-Quaker leaders. Penn chose the
trustees, who included Weiser and Michael Schlatter, on the basis
of their appeal to the Germans. Franklin was happy to join in
the undertaking. He was naturally interested in any project for
education, and especially in one for the Germans, who, he feared,
would soon overwhelm the government and English culture of
Pennsylvania.

For a short time Smith came to be about as close a friend of
Franklin's as anyone in Pennsylvania. Franklin had first recognized the clergyman's abilities when the two had exchanged ideas
for the Academy. He recommended Smith to Collinson as rector
of the Academy, and Smith returned the compliment by recom-
mending Franklin to Penn as a trustee for the charity schools.[27]
Each admired the wit, intelligence, and special abilities of the
other, and, together with Allen and Peters, they soon formed a
group intimately associated with several public undertakings.

The schools were ostensibly established to educate the Germans, but the Proprietor's friends scarcely hid the fact that they
intended them to serve a political purpose. By educating the Germans, they hoped to instill in them a proper sense of gratitude
and duty to their proprietary benefactors, and, eventually, to

wean them from the old Quaker alliance. This practical, political reason was obvious from the start, but Franklin offered no objection. He accepted it with the same complaisance that he showed in recognizing Penn's political benefit from the Academy—as long as the schools provided a useful education, he was willing to join in furthering both educational and political good works. That the Quakers were conspicuously absent from the organization of the charity schools was hardly surprising. Any proprietary solicitude for the education of the Germans was but a thinly veiled attack upon one of the props of Quaker power.

The Germans who were closest to the Quakers vehemently rejected the schools. Christopher Saur, the spokesman for this body of German opinion, wrote in 1755:

I have been thinking . . . whether it is really true that Gilbert Tennent, Schlatter, Peters, Hamilton, Allen, Turner, Schippin, Schmitt, Franklin, Muhlenberg . . . have the slightest care for a real conversion of the ignorant portion of the Germans in Pennsylvania. . . . Concerning Hamilton, Peters, Allen, Turner, Schippen and Franklin I know that they care very little about religion, nor do they care for the cultivation of the minds of the Germans.[28]

Opposition to the schools was especially strong among the Pietists. These people had been agents of Quaker politics among other Germans and, as such, had wielded an influence greater than their numbers warranted. Hence their dislike of the charity schools reflected political as well as religious motives.

The charity schools were judged a failure because they attracted relatively few pupils and roused a noisy opposition. Yet the eager support offered for the schools by congregations of German Lutherans and Reformed in Philadelphia, Chester, and Lancaster counties is significant. The Lutherans and Calvinists who petitioned for the schools were chiefly from older, settled areas in the colony, and were established in congregations under the discipline of such educated clergymen as Henry Muhlenberg, a Lutheran, and Johannes Leidig, a Reformed. Both Lutheran and Calvinist ministers disapproved of what they considered to be the wild, undisciplined "lower sort" of German, who, as Franklin affirmed, violently resisted ecclesiastical and governmental discipline. It was a common charge in Pennsylvania that Quaker and Pietist leaders encouraged the Germans to resist the proprietary government and the extension of Lutheran and Reformed Church authority in the province.[29]

Prosperous Germans in the older areas often had more in common with their English neighbors than with the ignorant, poor, recently arrived immigrants. This was especially true if the prosperous Palatines were also members of a Reformed or Lutheran congregation in the eastern part of Pennsylvania. Within Philadelphia, Lutherans and Anglicans had a good history of cordial relations, and even the Calvinists, both Reformed and Presbyterian, could find much in common. If they accomplished nothing else, the charity schools provided the leaders of the "better sort" of Lutherans, Calvinists, and Anglicans with an opportunity to discuss mutual problems and interests. In time, they might lean away from the Old Party and toward the Proprietor.

Cooperation in the school plan was not the only activity that placed Franklin in close and cordial contact with the Proprietor and his friends. When Franklin was appointed deputy postmaster for North America in 1753, he was deeply grateful and considered it a valuable honor. He was chosen after two years of negotiations with the English dispensers of patronage, carried on largely by Allen and Collinson.[30] One of those who approved of Franklin's application (and whose opposition would have blocked it) was Penn. Penn reported to Peters that he had told Sir Everard Falconer, the secretary to the Duke of Cumberland, "I thought Mr Franklyn as capable as any man in America to serve the Crown, and find he desires some Plan for the extention of correspondence, without any view to present advantage, which I desire you will consult Franklyn upon."[31]

The appointment was frankly a bribe to ensure Franklin's "proper" behavior in the Assembly. Peters reported to Penn, "Mr Franklyn is made Post Master General [deputy postmaster] with one Mr Hunter of North America owing to Mr Allen's Interest, and Mr Allen told me that I might depend upon it, he would act a fair and good Part in the Assembly tho he would have a difficult time of it, and was not unsuspected, and this last Office would encrease the Jealousies of [the Quakers]—but set him aside, and there is not a man who can write in the Assembly."[32]

Franklin responded warmly to Penn's help. Accepting with particular pleasure the chance to correspond with Falconer, Franklin stressed his personal disinterestedness.[33] In Pennsylvania the appointment, and the means by which it was obtained, carried strong political implications. Such major patronage, especially with the blessing of Penn, marked Franklin as a friend, if not an outright ally, of the Proprietor. Peters noted that the appointment would *increase* Quaker suspicion of Franklin—a suspicion that already bothered Pemberton.

Good personal relationships with the proprietary men in Pennsylvania continued to bring Franklin both pleasure and profit. He shared many interests with Smith, and worked with Peters at the Carlisle and Albany conferences. He and many of his proprietary friends were members of the Masonic lodge in Philadelphia, and they worked together on various civic projects. In 1754 it was to Peters that Franklin wrote the friendly, amusing sort of letter reserved for his friends. In one, he declared that, while he did not wish for a moment to change the secretary of the province, he did wish that the Secretary would change his handwriting.

There were, however, some indications that these pleasant relationships were coming to an end. When the Assembly got around in 1753 to answering Penn's assertion of 1751 that he was no more bound than the royal Governors to contribute to the defense of the province, its reply was sharp and angry. Franklin was a member of the committee that drew up the reply, and Peters and Penn, in an exchange of letters, expressed shock that Franklin would sign his name to a message "Full of indecent and abusive Invectives against a Gentleman whom he esteems."[34] The Proprietor's need for friends, and especially for Franklin's support, forced Peters to offer him the excuse that Franklin had softened the Assembly's message, reduced the passion of the Quakers, and thus had actually served the government. Peters's apology was true only in part; Franklin clearly considered it Penn's moral and legal duty to contribute a full share to the defense of the colony, no matter what legal opinion might hold to the contrary.[35]

Some of Franklin's other actions in the Assembly also drew proprietary criticism. In a letter to Peters, Penn flatly rejected Franklin's suggestions for the regulation of the Indian trade: "I do not at all approve of Mr Franklin's Boston method, or of any thing that comes from thence."[36] The Proprietor was also cool to the Albany Plan, although he acknowledged that Franklin's motives were probably good.

Strong though Franklin's connections with the proprietary men were, he frequently found himself in disagreement with the means they used to carry out policy. What seemed to be unnecessary delay, obscure argument, and doubtful honesty in their tactics irritated his direct, pragmatic mind. In Philadelphia, he could rely on the force of his arguments, his personality, and his cleverness to influence these men and achieve the results he desired. But no matter how hard he worked to influence these proprietary adherents in Philadelphia, he could not bring the same techniques to bear on the final authority, Penn. Penn was far away, and Franklin did not work well at long range. This difficulty was also

apparent in his relations with colonists in the more remote parts
of his own province.

Lacking in sympathy for the German third of the population,
Franklin also cared little for the other settlers or their problems. Even the defense of the West, which Franklin advocated
strongly, was to him more of an international or imperial question than a local one. Uneducated, boorish, poor, lazy, shiftless,
lacking in respect for property, government, or church discipline,
emotional, intemperate, and savage—these were some of the
judgments he applied at various times to the people living beyond
the old, settled areas near Philadelphia. At other times he praised
virtues in these people, but his benevolence toward them was
general rather than particular. Until 1754, Franklin had exhibited nothing in politics to distinguish him from any of the city
oligarchs.

If Franklin failed to appreciate the complexities of the problems of his own colony, he was hardly better informed about the
realities of proprietary or English government. In letters to Jackson and Collinson in the 1750's, he showed his developing mys-
tical attitude toward England. In the *Observations* he championed the greater glory of England and the empire in America.
Toward men in the Mother Country who would carry this empire
forward in culture, government, and wealth, Franklin adopted
an almost reverent attitude. He chided Jackson for believing that
English politics was decaying and that the politicians were corrupted. Franklin regarded English leaders as men of intelligence,
education, understanding, and virtue, who composed the true
aristocracy of enlightenment.

Franklin was willing, even anxious, to see Penn in this light, as
long as the Proprietor did not act irrationally or factionally. Unfortunately for Penn, many of his actions and those of his friends
appeared to Franklin in 1754 to be inspired by just such party
motives. The delays in chartering the Academy and the hospital,

the Governor's objections to money bills, the denial of personal responsibility in provincial defense, and other actions shook Franklin's confidence in the Proprietor, though not yet in proprietary government. To cap it all, Penn had sent that quarrelsome legal bickerer Robert Morris to govern the colony in 1754.

To Franklin, politics was a highly personal affair between individual men, not a matter of forms of government, institutions, or theories. He worked with people; his patience with men was great, and his essential optimism about their action even greater. Only when they exhausted his patience and directly threatened his personal interests did he react against them and what they represented. This was true in Pennsylvania in 1755; it would be true in England in 1774. Whatever his particular objections to politicians and policies in Pennsylvania, it required a personal quarrel with Penn before he rejected proprietary government. Until that quarrel took place in 1755, he continued to profess friendship for Penn and acceptance of proprietary rule.

However slight Franklin's interest in political theory, he undertook to devise a political structure for his plan of colonial union. Although the final Plan of Union that emerged from the Albany Congress in 1754 included contributions and amendments from other conferees, the basic form and ideas were his, and he accepted it as a proper and workable expression of his views.[37]

Franklin's ideas of an inter-colonial government could not but have been affected by what he knew of Pennsylvania government. He had lived in Pennsylvania a long time; he had heard discussed all of the issues, constitutional problems, and arguments over powers in government that had been the business of politics for years. If these had not stirred him before 1750, he could not have failed to be aware of them after he entered the Assembly in 1751. Thus, although the Albany Plan had to blend both colonial and Crown interests to produce a workable union, it nonetheless reflected a measure of Franklin's understanding of his own political world and that of England. He had the chance at Albany to grapple with some of the problems of government that tormented Pennsylvania politics.

The astonishing result was a form of government that denied many of the claimed powers of the colonial legislatures. Franklin apparently favored a stronger, more independent executive than existed anywhere in the colonies. His Plan provided that the chief executive, the President-General, would be appointed by the Crown and would be supported by a salary from the Crown so that "such disputes which have been frequently of mischievous consequence in particular colonies" might be prevented. The salary would be paid out of quit rents. This amounted to a civil list—a salary free from legislative control. (In Pennsylvania the legislature voted the Governor's salary only after all business had been completed.) In addition, the President-General was to have a veto over all acts passed by the representative Grand Council. With the advice of the Council he could make treaties and direct the military forces, and with its approbation nominate military officers. Civil officers, "chiefly treasurers and collectors of taxes," would be nominated by the Council and approved by the President. In Pennsylvania, Morris was endeavoring to get the Assembly to recognize precisely this right of executive approval of treasurers and collectors of taxes.

Franklin explained that in order to establish the financial power of the proposed union on a sound basis and "To prevent misapplication of the money, or even application that might be dissatisfactory to the Crown or the people, it was thought necessary to join the President-General and Grand Council in all issues of money."[38] This was, of course, a plan for joint appropriation. Finally, to underline the power of the executive, Franklin added, "The President-General, besides one half of the legislative power, hath in his hands the whole executive power."[39] Penn wished for little more than this acknowledgment from the Assembly in Pennsylvania.

Franklin also dealt with other matters of Pennsylvania government in the Plan. He stressed the need for adequate regulation of Indian trade and the acquisition of Indian lands for new settlements by the Crown (except in proprietary colonies). "It is much cheaper to purchase of them, than to take and maintain the possession by force; for they are generally very reasonable in their demands for land."[40] This opinion agreed with Peters's advice to Penn that land purchases could be made easily because the Indians demanded very little in return.

Franklin believed that a representative council was necessary to protect Englishmen from taxation without representation. But he had no notions of democratic government: "Popular elections have their inconveniences in some cases; but in establishing new forms of government, *we cannot always obtain what we may think the best*; for the prejudices of those concerned, if they cannot be removed, must be in some degree complied with."[41] Agreeing fully with the eighteenth-century, pejorative meaning of "popular" and "democratic," Franklin wanted no such leveling principles expressed in the Plan of Union. He saw no virtue in the mass participation of people in politics. The representatives to the Grand Council, or to the Pennsylvania Assembly, must be men of the "better sort." To ensure that they were, Franklin desired that they be chosen by the respective colonial assemblies. He declared, "As the choice was not immediately popular, they would in general be men of good abilities for business, and men of reputation for integrity."[42]

This conservative, aristocratic, strong-executive Plan, together with his letters to Governor William Shirley of Massachusetts in 1754, also reflected Franklin's ideas of imperial relations. He proposed that the Albany Plan be imposed by Parliamentary act if it did not pass in the colonial legislatures or was not accepted by the Ministry.[43] He was not concerned that such an act would reshape colonial charters, redistribute powers, and undermine local privileges. A Quaker Assembly, at that moment fighting to maintain its powers, could hardly be any more receptive to Parliamentary dictation than it was to Penn's. Little wonder, then, that the Plan of Union was almost insultingly brushed aside when it was presented to the Pennsylvania Assembly. Only Franklin could have been, and was, surprised.

Franklin was above all convinced that Reason would solve any problem, whether it be in Parliament, in a Plan of Union, or in the government of Pennsylvania. The interests of a petty corporation, Quaker politicians, or the Proprietor could be all managed or overcome by its enlightened application. In a letter to his friend James Parker, written in 1751, he stated his political creed:

Now, if you were to pick out half a Dozen Men of good Understanding and Address, and furnish them with a reasonable Scheme and proper Instructions, and send them in the Nature of Ambassadors to the other Colonies, where they might apply particularly to all the leading Men, and by proper Management get them to engage in promoting the Scheme; where, by being present, they would have the Opportunity of pressing the Affair both in publick and private, obviating Difficulties as they arise, answering Objections as soon as they are made, before they spread and gather Strength in the Minds of the People . . . such an Union might thereby be made . . . For reasonable sensible Men, can always make a reasonable Scheme appear such to other reasonable Men, if they take Pains.[44]

Franklin's ideas were singularly out of touch with the reality of politics and government in Pennsylvania, which were now approaching a crisis of major proportions. Still holding on to a concept of society and his role in it that had changed little since the 1730's, he expressed an idealism inappropriate to the situation.

FRANKLIN'S QUARREL WITH PENN

Neither the Proprietor nor the Assembly had been able to win a clear decision over the other before 1755. Still determined to force the Assembly to acknowledge his rights, Penn had found in Governor Morris a blunt, unyielding instrument capable of upholding his instructions. The Assembly, now fully aware of Penn's intentions, was likewise determined not to yield. The result was close to a stalemate.

The outbreak of the French and Indian War in 1754 put great pressure on both parties. At first Penn and Morris felt the pressure most—they were under instructions to implement defense in the province and aid the army when it arrived in America. But without cooperation from the Assembly, Penn was nearly helpless to obey. On the other side, Norris and Pemberton saw in this situation a glittering opportunity, and worked out a strategy to make the most of it. The Assembly would profess its patriotism and desire to help the war effort, but plead that while it was harassed by Penn and Morris it could do nothing. If General Braddock and the army won a speedy victory over the Indians and the French, the war might end and the Assembly would not have to act. It would lose nothing to Penn, and he and Morris would still be blamed for not assisting the army or, at least, would get no credit for the victory in England.

To show itself capable of full cooperation when not menaced

by Penn, Morris, and loathsome proprietary instructions, the
Assembly responded to a request for aid from Massachusetts,
transmitted by Josiah Quincy on behalf of Governor Shirley.
Franklin worked out a plan in the winter of 1755 to provide the
assistance quickly and directly. Quincy and Shirley were grateful
for the timely help; Morris was not so pleased, however. He had
been virtually ignored in the proceedings and denounced the
Assembly's action, stating that "If the House claimed the privilege of sitting when and as long as it pleased, and of keeping its
proceedings secret from the Governor, and could borrow and cir-
culate money as it chose, it would probably use the power against
the government under whose authority it acted."[1]

At the beginning of 1755, the Assembly had not yet formu-
lated its full constitutional claims. It declared that if the Proprietor were limited in his capacity to instruct the Governors, and if
suspending clauses, limitations on the excise, and similar obstacles
were removed, it would be able to respond to whatever was required for the safety of the colony. When Norris and the Quaker
leaders in the House petitioned against Penn's right to instruct
his deputies, they had good reason to expect a favorable reception
in England. They presumed that ministerial antipathy to the
Proprietor plus the realization that the Assembly, not the Proprietor, had the means to raise money and supplies, would weigh
heavily in English considerations and win the support of non-
Quakers as well as Quakers.

Ministerial criticism of Penn and his difficulties with the Assembly was widespread in the first months of 1755. Because the
Ministry desired practical results instead of disputes over powers,
it was disposed to accept the Assembly's terms.[2] So strong was
the belief in England that the proprietary government was inadequate to meet the urgent problems created by the war, that
Penn was offered the chance to sell his government to the Crown.

Despite this lack of favor in England, Penn succeeded in getting the Board of Trade to reject the Assembly's petition early

in 1755. The Quaker Richard Wells wrote to John Smith of the Pemberton faction in Philadelphia: "The Assembly Remonstrance was referr'd from the Lords Committee of Council to the Board of Trade for their opinion, which they gave that it should be rejected, and subjoined a State of the Proceedings of the Assembly taken from the last Votes which they have set in so bad a Light that tis thought twill greatly prejudice the Lords in Council against the House."[3]

Whatever their opinions about proprietary government, the ministers and lawyers in England were obliged to agree that Penn legally had the right to instruct his Governor and to insist on an equal or predominant share in the appropriation of money. Nevertheless, the ministers warned that he must seek some compromise with the Assembly on the question of contributing to colonial defense even if this meant a temporary lapse in his rights.[4]

This might also have warned the Assembly that it was pursuing actions which were legally objectionable in England. But the Assembly was interested only in the news of the Crown's offer to buy the government and its criticisms of proprietary policy, which indicated that Penn might yet be forced to give way. At this time—early in 1755—Isaac Norris suggested that an appeal to the Crown to vacate the proprietary Charter and establish royal government in the colony would be the ultimate weapon against Penn.[5] The Quaker leaders in the Assembly believed they could safely resist proposals from the Governor that in any way conflicted with their concepts of legislative rights. Their refusal to seek Morris's approval of the loan to Quincy was one example of this unyielding attitude in the first months of 1755. Closely calculating its strategy, the leadership counted on a quick military victory by Braddock to end the need for distasteful military preparations. They knew that a long war would again raise the question of Quaker pacifism and its effect on the Society's fitness to govern in wartime. This was a vulnerable point, certain to be exploited in England by Penn.[6] However, much as the Old Party wished for Braddock's quick success, it was unable to do much to help him. A real contribution would mean some surrender to Morris and a recognition of the normal military function of the executive—and this the leaders refused to do.

In the meantime, there was the problem of Braddock's persistent criticism of the Assembly. He and many other officers were exasperated with the quarreling politicians and their failure to help. His Commissary General, St. Clair, was almost as willing to use the troops against Pennsylvania and the Assembly as against the French, or so St. Clair wrote to England.[7] To counter these complaints and win army favor, Franklin suggested that the legislature demonstrate its good will by making gifts to the army officers. This was done, and William Smith reported that the Assembly gave "sweetmeats, Horses and Presents to conciliate themselves to the King's officers, who threatened us with Fire and Sword if we sat idle."[8]

The Assembly thought highly of Franklin's clever idea and cooperated heartily in its execution. Soon afterward it approved his scheme to procure wagons and animals for the army. Both schemes aided the cause of British arms and enhanced Franklin's and the Assembly's reputation in England. Neither the Proprietor nor the Governor had been able to match the presents dramatically bestowed on the officers and the wagon trains assembled for the army; Norris confidently expected that the Assembly would be rewarded when credit was apportioned in England for the General's anticipated victory.

Braddock's defeat in the summer of 1755 was a political catastrophe for the Assembly and the Quakers. Norris realized that the colony would be subjected to even greater pressure to help revive the military effort. The Quakers were now vulnerable, and reports from England soon told of a perceptible change in English sentiment toward the Friends in Pennsylvania.

The intensity of the conflict had forced most of the influential Pennsylvanians into an open political alignment with one side or the other. Tench Francis, for example, wavering between his desire for proprietary position and income and his dislike for the policy and leadership of Penn's government, finally threw his support to the Assembly in the election of 1755.[9]

Almost alone among the major political figures in Pennsylvania, Franklin remained uncommitted. Before July 1755, he bestowed his interests and friendships equally among the competing factions with no apparent regard for the irreconcilable differences that embittered not only politics but personal relationships. To the most "principled" and zealous party leaders, Franklin's behavior seemed inscrutable, vacillating, and suggestive of some hidden, possibly sinister, motives. It was impossible, they concluded, for a man to maintain common ties with the friends of the Proprietor while at the same time "scribbling those vile messages from the Assembly" that were designed to destroy Penn's power and government.

Attempting to find some explanation for Franklin's actions, William Smith, soon to be one of Franklin's most despised enemies, described his perplexities to Penn:

Mr Franklin frequently observed with seeming Surprise that you had taken no notice of the Letter he wrote to you, and I made the best excuses in my power. He might then have been so reconciled that he never would have prostituted his Pen to help the Assembly out in their present Embarassment, tho' I believe he never would have warmly been your Friend, for he generally blamed both Sides and seemed to have a Scheme of his own. Tho' I flatter myself with having as much of his confidence as he gives any Body, I can neither learn nor conjecture what he means, unless it be to overset the *Quakers.* I would still think he could not have deceived us and all the world so long as to carry about any wickedness in his Intentions.[10]

To elicit some commitment from Franklin, Smith plied him with strong arguments supporting the proprietary position. He emphasized the dangers from popular unrest and Indian warfare in Pennsylvania. Their discussion always returned to Franklin's writings for the Assembly. Smith wrote to Penn:

The Substance of these late inflammatory messages I have often had from him as his real sentiments, but never thought they would be so unseasonably brought on the carpet. When by ourselves he seldom failed to introduce public affairs and freely spoke his sentiments, and seemed pleased to hear mine. I told him how heartily you was endeavoring to serve him all this while by representing the Service he did in procuring Waggons, to the Ministry, Sir Everard Falconer, etc. He said he was obliged to You and was heartily your Friend, but never could think you did wisely in sending the present Governor. All of these arguments I have occasionally used with Mr Franklin, who admits the Force of many of them, and declares he would be *the last man to hurt your Estates and would readily give his whole Interest to procure a Law for the more effectual Recovery of your Quit Rents*, whenever it should be wanted, and that it was wrong to attribute the Conduct of a public Body to a single member. In short, I must suspend my Judgement of my Friend for a little, for I cannot yet believe so ill of him as many do, and perhaps it would be wrong to drive him entirely from us by a hasty Judgement. A little Time will discover all.[11]

While still professing the highest regard for Penn, Franklin thought his actions in the Assembly neither harmful nor derogatory to proprietary interests. He declared that if his support for the Assembly's money bills, his doubts about some of the Governor's instructions, the suspending clause, and limitations on the excise, or his demands for proprietary contributions to colonial defense suggested that he was a partisan of the Quaker legislature, there were equally important considerations that inclined him to the proprietary side.

Pemberton, who carefully appraised any man or measure affecting either Quaker or Assembly strength, was unable to find any certainty or consistency in Franklin's politics. In a rare moment of enthusiasm for a possible Franklin-Quaker alliance, Pemberton declared in July 1755, "The Governor Just upon sending them [the Assembly] a message full of falsehoods and most malicious misrepresentations . . . animated Franklin so effectually that I am in hopes it will engage him to Act steadily and zealously in our Defense."[12] Despite Franklin's work in the Assembly since 1750, Pemberton was unable to consider him a real friend of the Quakers or a steady defender of the legislature against the Governor.

Franklin's earnest efforts to work with Penn and the Proprietary Party came to an abrupt end in the summer of 1755. The suddenness of the quarrel and the subsequent furious and revengeful spirit displayed on both sides indicate that personal grievances and misunderstandings contributed fully as much as conflicting political principles.[13] Certain points of the dispute did increase the sensitivity of both sides and prevented them from reaching a compromise on who should receive credit for aid to Braddock, but in essence it was a personal quarrel between two men who did not understand each other.

Always proud-spirited and sensitive to any slights—real or imagined—to his honor, Franklin had undoubtedly been uncomfortable under the patronage and patronizing attitude of William Allen. In 1753, Allen had declared that in return for the deputy postmastership, Franklin would act well in the Assembly. The mighty and haughty Allen certainly did not let Franklin forget the source of the favor, and, as Franklin became more important in the Assembly, Allen tried to influence what he did there. There were hints that proprietary leaders demanded Franklin's support in the campaign against the Quakers. At some time between Franklin's return from Albany in 1754 and the spring of 1755, Allen evidently tried to force him to declare himself. Although he refused to make an open commitment of this sort and declined to submit to the direction of Allen or any other proprietary leader, Franklin nevertheless showed some willingness to see a number of the "stiff rump" or uncompromising Quakers deprived of their seats in the Assembly. Even though he rejected Allen's demands, he did not entirely dash proprietary hopes for an eventual alliance. Such possibilities were the subject of continuing speculation—by both parties—until well after Franklin's quarrel with Penn.[14]

The Proprietary Party did not possess so many political advantages in Pennsylvania that it could allow influential organizations or persons to enjoy the luxury of independence, if by any means they could convert them to political usefulness. Both the Academy and the charity schools offered just such opportunities. Prior to 1755 they were ostensibly non-political, though in fact proprietary influence in them was already strong and only partly concealed by the philanthropic motives originally claimed for their establishment. In 1755 and 1756 both organizations were turned into avowed instruments of anti-Quaker politics. Although he was not averse to a modest amount of proprietary influence in and benefit from the charity schools and the Academy, Franklin now resisted the blatant intentions of the proprietary leaders, and they offered him the choice of acquiescing or getting out. Peters was determined to use the charity schools and the Academy for political purposes, but he expressed dismay at the tactless behavior of his colleagues:

Mr Franklin is alone in the German Schools but in the Academy he has among the Trustees several minions who are already disobliged at a slip taken by the Trustees . . . they made a change in their President putting me in the room of Mr Franklin. I objected very heartily and told them that they were doing a wrong thing and it would be construed that Party was introduced by them first into the Academy, and so it really was so far as that Mr Franklin was deem'd Head of one Party and Mr Allen of the other and just at this time a change was made.[15]

In the charity schools, the Academy, and the Philadelphia Common Council, Franklin found proprietary politicians assuming control and demanding submission to their direction.

Franklin fully appreciated the value of the work he had done to aid Braddock and the army. While he accepted the praise and gratitude from ministers in England, colonial governors, and ordinary citizens in Pennsylvania, he waited for acknowledgment and thanks from Penn.[16] The Proprietor was pleased with Franklin's efforts, but he was annoyed by Franklin's recent behavior in the Assembly—especially by his part in the loan to Quincy and in the several messages from the Assembly to Morris objecting to proprietary instructions and policies. However, he asked Peters to convey his appreciation to Franklin for supplying the wagons. He made an excuse for not writing directly, declaring that he would wait to consult Falconer about Franklin's plans to extend the postal service in the colonies.

At first, proprietary leaders in Pennsylvania joined in the general applause for Franklin's work. But before long, Peters and Morris showed their jealousy of the honor paid him and the implication that his efforts alone had saved the reputation of the colonies. They claimed that their assistance had been just as important, and in order to diminish his standing in England, they presented Penn with fresh evidence of his questionable actions in the Assembly.[17] Penn responded with a stiffer, more critical attitude. He declared to Peters:

The Report of the Committee of Assembly comes up to the account you gave it. It is so strained, and they have made use of such low and malicious observations, as must convince every Candid Impartial Reader, of the baseness of it, but can I be brought to court any man that has signed such a Paper, before he has expressed any concern for it? I cannot yet resolve to do it. I will do Mr Franklin all possible Justice, and am so much disposed to live in peace with all men, that I can heartily forgive on the least acknowledgement . . . I think it is no small Act of Friendship that I have recommended him to Sir Everard Falconer.[18]

With this attitude it was not difficult for Penn to decide to reclaim part of the credit that had gone to Franklin for the wagons. He wrote to Peters, "I wish I had known with more exactness, before, as I gave all the merit of supplying both waggons and forage to Mr Franklin When he did it, I apprehend, by direction of the Governor and in concert with you."[19] This was typical of the letters Penn sent to Peters, Hamilton, and Morris.

Their contents also reached Franklin. There were no political secrets in Pennsylvania; the letters and opinions of one party soon became the property of the opposition.

Meanwhile, Franklin waited with increasing impatience for a letter from Penn. There was, of course, no thought of his writing to Penn to explain his work in the Assembly—he would not humble himself before Penn—and Penn would not write until Franklin did.[20] Nor did Franklin think he had done wrong: he had told Smith that "it was wrong to attribute the conduct of a public Body to a single member." Each waited, and each grew angrier.

Peters and others had increased Penn's stubborn attitude, and certain men had acted upon Franklin in the same way. The Quakers and other enemies of the Proprietor (including Tench Francis, whom Richard Hockley, Pennsylvania's Receiver General, called Franklin's "crony") worked to widen the breach. Informed of the proprietary greed for credit in the assistance to Braddock, Franklin confronted William Smith with a letter from Collinson. Smith reported to Penn, "I much fear from a Letter Mr Franklin shewed me that our Friend Collinson is part of the innocent cause of Franklin's Conduct. He told Franklin that you could not be persuaded to think him your Friend. I only mention this to put you on your Guard and beg Mr Collinson may not know of it; for it would destroy all my Confidence with Franklin, with whom I yet hope to do some Good."[21]

By the autumn of 1755, Franklin and Penn were avowed enemies. Each accused the other of insincerity and of engaging in unprincipled schemes. When Peters discovered that Franklin was moving into complete opposition, he frantically tried to undo the damage. He implored Penn to write Franklin and to be generous in expressions of personal regard and good will. But it was too late. When the disputes arose over the militia law and the proposals to tax the proprietary estates (which Franklin had denied any intention to harm earlier in the year), Penn, like Franklin, sought revenge.[22] He applied to Falconer for Franklin's removal from the post office, and asked him to discover Franklin's real intentions: "Which Letters were wrote at my desire to see whether he would act a better part before I would apply to his removal." By asking Falconer how Franklin could expect to hold an important place and at the same time "so much oppose the lawful prerogatives of the Crown," Penn threatened Franklin, "and he was told what was expected of him."[23]

Convinced that the Proprietary Party had acted falsely, attempted to damage his reputation in England, threatened his postmastership, and interfered with some of his favorite measures and projects, Franklin thought he had reason enough to take the strongest action against Penn and his followers in Pennsylvania. One of his immediate reactions was to associate himself openly with the Assembly's attack upon the Governor and the Proprietor. Franklin got encouragement and justification for his new course of action from men outside the province. Shirley, Collinson, Richard Jackson, a London barrister, and Thomas Pownall, secretary to the Governor of New York, found him receptive to anti-proprietary ideas and provided him with reasons for attacking Penn that transcended particular issues in the colony.

At the Albany Congress, Franklin had established associations with men who thought of colonial problems in imperial terms. Already receptive to grand concepts of the glorious future of the British Empire, he delighted in finding men such as Pownall and Shirley who seemed to share his sentiments. For the first time he had the opportunity to discuss politics, government, and imperial relations with important leaders outside of Pennsylvania. He discovered in the middle of 1755 that anti-proprietary and imperial ideas harmonized. Both could be applied to the politics of Pennsylvania and to his new opposition to Penn. Neither Shirley nor Pownall had any reason to favor proprietary government;

they generally advocated expansion of royal authority in the colonies and ardently championed increased colonial efforts against the French and the Indians. Despite his friendship with Penn, Collinson was opposed to proprietary government and favored the interests of the Quaker Assembly. Likewise, Jackson informed Franklin of anti-proprietary opinion in England. Pownall, who was corresponding regularly with Norris and Franklin, was even more critical (he was influenced in great measure by private reasons), and predicted an early assumption of the government by the Crown. Governor Morris, alarmed by letters from Pownall, Sir George Littleton, and others to people in the province, wrote Penn about the injury these reports were doing to proprietary interests. One letter from Littleton, circulated widely in Philadelphia, informed Penn's enemies that all proprietary governments would "in a short time fall into the Hands of the Crown, but above all [Littleton] wonders that you [Penn] should attempt to keep yours at this juncture."[24]

After his quarrel with the Proprietor, Franklin accepted these opinions as justification for taking measures against Penn and the proprietary government. Interested above all in victory over the French and the prosperity and glory of the Empire, Franklin concluded that Penn was the greatest obstacle to the colony's proper participation in the war. If he helped to diminish proprietary power, he would contribute to his own interests and to those of England and Pennsylvania. The removal of bad governors such as Morris and the termination of proprietary instructions and opposition to measures that Franklin approved, seemed consistent with colonial and imperial unity and, in a sense, a local application of the Albany Plan. If he needed an added incentive, Penn's enmity demanded a counterinfluence with important men in England. Pownall's interest and friendship provided one such connection, and through it Franklin later sought to gain access to Lord Loudoun and the Duke of Cumberland.[25]

In the meantime, Franklin threw himself into the Assembly's attack on Penn. Although he joined this old controversy quite late, he more than made up for his earlier independence by the fury of his hatred for Penn and everything associated with the proprietary. The Quakers, a little startled by this abrupt change of policy, welcomed him to the fray—at least most of them did.

ENGLISH INFLUENCE

After his bitter quarrel with Penn, Franklin turned to direct the Assembly's most masterful assault upon proprietary power. He was not yet the leader of the House, but his ideas for attacking Penn won the enthusiastic backing of the Norrisite Quakers and helped to carry the conflict into new areas. In an able presentation of the case for taxing proprietary estates in Pennsylvania, he declared that the Proprietor, the largest landowner in the colony, would actually reap the greatest benefit by "sacrificing a portion to save the whole."

Aware that the power to tax was indeed the power to destroy, the Assembly sought to deny the Proprietor any voice in the selection of the tax assessors and any share in the expenditure of the money raised. In addition, it proposed that quit rents and all lands, occupied or not, improved or unimproved, be taxed as it saw fit. Writing to "my Friend Mr Oswald, one of the Lords of Trade, with whom I correspond," William Smith assessed the Assembly's plans.

The Quarrel now is Taxing the Proprietary-Estate and Quit Rent; a new Branch of Power assumed contrary to a positive Law of their own. This they think will serve at your Lordships Board as a better Pretence and Plea for their doing nothing in defence of the Province, than their former Quarrels about Instructions, which they find will no longer do. That the Proprietor should bear his Part of the general Burden is but reasonable. But that the Assembly should fix both the *Mode* and *Quantum* of his Tax is unjust in itself. They have already wrested too much of the Powers of Government from their chief Governor; now they want to complete their Scheme by wresting his Estate also. . . . All other Subjects are taxed by those who may be called their *Peers*; Persons interested to deal equitably; but here the Proprietor would be taxed by Persons who are taught to think it *Justice* to do him *Injustice*, and who the more they can make him pay will have less to pay themselves.[1]

The Assembly reiterated its contention that Penn did not have the right to amend money bills or to instruct his Governor, and declared that if he or the Governor continued to deny its rights, it would appeal directly to the Crown. Apparently determined to establish that the real executive power lay in the English government, the Assembly argued that whenever Penn's pretended power conflicted with its interests, it could ignore him and appeal to higher English authority. The Proprietor's reaction was a mixture of surprise and bravado: "I am sure I have no desire to have any authority inconsistent with the well established Liberty of the People, and am so far from dreading it that I am impatient to see the Dispute if there must be one began [sic]."[2]

In reply Governor Morris stated the proprietary case, which was essentially the one presented to the Crown between 1757 and 1760. He declared that the Assembly could not exercise power over those from whom it derived its authority. The Proprietor held the grant and the title to both the government and the soil, and therefore had authority over both. Morris insisted that such authority could not be separated or divided without destroying it. Although the Proprietor did not personally govern, he had the legal right to do so. Denying the Assembly's contention that its powers were similar to Parliament's, Morris argued that the constitution of Pennsylvania was established upon royal and proprietary charters,

being subordinate and in no way similar to that of England nor composed of the like constituent parts. Here the whole power is lodged in the governor and assembly, who have all along exercised equal legislative powers, each of them having the right to propose laws and to amend what is proposed by the other. Till, therefore, you can show that the constitution of this province is similar to that of England, composed of the like parts, and that each of them have the like or similar powers and privileges, you can found no claim upon the usage of Parliament for having your money bills passed without the governor's amendments.[3]

In response to the Assembly's threat to appeal to England if the Governor should reject money bills containing provisions for the taxation of proprietary lands, Morris declared that the King could not consent to parts of an act and that the Assembly's intention, in effect, gave immediate legislative power to the Crown. The Charter made no provision for direct royal interference. Neither could the Assembly tax proprietary quit rents, which, like those belonging to the Crown in other colonies, were not liable to taxation.[4] When the House also claimed that the Governor could not prorogue the legislature, Penn replied, "The power claimed by the Assembly was not conferred upon them by Charter, for the most they can claim is the same Powers that other Assemblys in the English Plantations have a right to, so that their pretence not to be prorogued is without any foundation."[5]

Penn's difficulties increased as English anti-proprietary sentiment grew during 1755. Reports from Pennsylvania told of constant political fighting and local outrage at his instructions to prevent the Assembly from touching any proprietary estates or revenues to aid local defense. Although he had long attempted to forestall ministerial direction of his policy, Penn was now forced to turn to members of the government for help. Earlier he told Peters of his efforts to remain independent: "While I can have anything I want done by the direction of the head of the Board [Halifax] . . . this is a rule I observe where I have any concerns, and I think it has a good effect, I never go to the Board on any common occasions, but on a hearing, or when my Lord Halifax desires I wou'd meet him there."[6] Now, however, the intensity of the Assembly's attack pressed him into a closer dependence upon ministerial favor and advice. He needed legal support for his policies and friends in high places to block any attempt in England or Pennsylvania to take over the government. Penn worked hard to cultivate connections; he succeeded, but at a very high cost.

The Duke of Cumberland, Falconer, Halifax, Sir Thomas Robinson, the Duke of Newcastle, Henry Fox, and William Pitt (in 1757) were all objects of Penn's attentions, and their influence upon provincial politics rose as the threat to his government and estate increased.

Dependence upon the help of "great men" cost Penn his freedom of action. He became obliged to heed their advice, which often differed from man to man and from week to week.[7] His policy in Pennsylvania reflected the vacillations and contradictions (and to a considerable extent the ignorance) of the numerous English politicians who dabbled in colonial and Pennsylvania affairs. In the morning, for instance, Halifax might tell Penn that the Ministry was "perfectly assured" that he was justified, even required, to reject the terms of the Assembly's money bills; in the afternoon, the Duke of Newcastle might say that it was not expedient to press the Assembly, or that "it would better serve the Crown to compromise." In 1755 and 1756 the anxious Proprietor, faced with such conflicting views, relinquished his claims to make joint appropriations, select commissioners, impose excise limitations, and exercise several other powers he later discovered he was not obliged to give up.[8]

One of the most damaging results of Penn's reliance upon the favor of English politicians was his surrender of control over patronage. Very proud of his association with the Duke of Cumberland, he allowed him to choose a successor to Morris, who resigned in 1756. Cumberland and his secretary, Falconer, selected Pownall.[9] The choice, which Penn meekly accepted, was scarcely believable in Pennsylvania. Pownall was a champion of royal government for the colonies; he disliked Penn personally and was known to be a frequent correspondent of Isaac Norris and Franklin. Proprietary supporters in Pennsylvania were horrified at the prospect of his accepting any position in the colony, and their report that the Quakers were delighted with the selection was condemnation enough.[10] Pownall saved Penn by rejecting the position in a manner that disguised his real motives. By demanding from Penn an almost independent authority and discretion as Governor and specific concessions in financial matters and by indicating his sympathy for the Assembly's claims, Pownall finally convinced Cumberland that he was not exactly the right choice. Evidence suggests that, much as Pownall disliked proprietary government, he made his conditions and objections so excessive that he knew they would be rejected. Penn reported that "He would not indeed submit to any Instructions, but Mr Fox, my Lord Loudoun and Halifax thought he was wrong to refuse them, but he refused, believing if he took Pennsylvania he should lose Massachusetts which was both more honorable and profitable, so that his behaviour was to extricate him out of that difficulty without refusing what the Duke recommended him to."[11]

News of Pownall's conditions and opinions about Pennsylvania's government was gleefully received in the Assembly. Penn was too deeply committed to his royal and ministerial patrons to profit from the lesson of the Pownall debacle, and when Cumberland recommended William Denny as a replacement, Penn accepted. Denny proved to be, if possible, an even worse choice. A man with no evident principles or abilities, he was easily managed by the Assembly, betraying his instructions and obligations and eventually succumbing to bribes. But although it cost Penn a great deal in 1756 and 1757 to preserve access to influential men in the English government, his investment soon reaped a profitable return.

Toward the end of 1755, Penn found that the Assembly's proposal to tax his estates had once more tipped changeable English opinion against him. Some drastic countermeasure was necessary. The ingenious Dr. Graeme, who had devised the gerrymandering plan to dilute German strength, suggested that Penn restore his prestige by giving the colony £5,000 for defense. Penn offered to donate this money from proprietary revenues provided that the Assembly would specifically exempt his lands from taxation. The Assembly was caught off guard. It could make no valid objections, and sourly accepted the terms. Penn thus scored enough points in the contest over taxation to carry him through most of 1756.[12]

While he worked to protect himself in England, Penn found the opportunity to strike back at his enemies in Pennsylvania. Those responsible for the prosecution of the war looked for someone to blame for Braddock's defeat. Penn did not escape censure, but the more obvious scapegoat was the pacifist-professing Quaker membership in the Assembly. With full assistance from his friends in Pennsylvania, Penn turned English attention from proprietary failures to the notoriously poor record of the Quakers in past wars. He found members of the government more willing to listen to proprietary charges that Quaker power was the great obstacle to imperial interests—at least in Pennsylvania. And in 1756 antagonism to the Quakers had developed to the point where leading members of the government, led by Halifax, agreed to present to Parliament a bill to exclude Quakers from the Assembly.

Pacifism was not the real reason, of course, for removing the Quakers from the Assembly. Whatever the religious scruples of the Society, the real issue was political power—a fact not clearly understood in England. The Quakers in Pennsylvania were caught in a trap. They could not suddenly deny pacifism to save their power, nor could they hold power without seriously compromising their traditions. Isaac Norris and his followers in the

House were only too anxious to find a way out, and Norris wrote in 1755, "That money can and ought to be given to the Crown is I think acknowledged on all hands."[13] But money could not be given on proprietary terms or in a manner advantageous to the Governor.

Proprietary men also saw the dilemma and stepped up their efforts to get both the Quakers and their German allies excluded from colonial politics. Most of them sent anti-Quaker letters, pamphlets, and petitions to England. Perhaps the most influential piece of propaganda was William Smith's pamphlet *Brief State of the Province of Pennsylvania*, which blamed the Quakers and the Germans for most of the colony's past and present troubles. It charged the Quakers with pacifism and the Germans with allying openly with the Quakers and secretly with the French enemy! If the Germans were capable of such duplicity they were indeed a menace, but lack of logic in these matters did not much concern the proprietary propagandists.[14]

In their zeal to bring down the Quaker political system, the proprietary leaders in Pennsylvania pushed Penn further than he wished to go. Much as he wanted to hurt his old enemies, he could not really swallow the argument that pacifism was a valid or just reason to exclude them from the Assembly. He could not promise that this would solve the problems of provincial government, and was obliged to report, "I have been asked whether if the Quakers are disabled I will engage the other Party will pass such a Law as the Ministers or I myself can approve of. I could not positively engage for it, but told them I believe they would, as they have so long blamed the Quakers for wanting to weaken Government and not giving what they could for the King's Service; some are of the opinion they will not do it."[15] After years of experience with the contrary and fickle attitudes of his own supporters in Pennsylvania, Penn was well aware that he could not "engage for" their actions. Although he went along with Quaker exclusion, he refused to support similar action against the Germans, who might be his political enemies but were certainly not traitors in the employ of the French.

The English government's attempts to establish qualifications for voting and for election to the Assembly, and to set up standards of proper conduct and thinking for legislators on the Quaker-German problem, raised an unprecedented constitutional issue. If Parliament or executive agencies of the English government could manipulate the membership of a colonial legislature and regulate its actions, then nothing remained of the idea of legislative liberties and the sanctity of charters, which had been fundamental to English constitutional theory since 1688.

Despite the implications of the exclusion bill, no Pennsylvania "Sons of Liberty" rose to protest and no constitutional arguments were advanced to show that Parliament had no such authority over colonial legislatures. Even the members of the Assembly, whose messages were so full of claims of powers and rights, did not deny Parliament's competence to deprive Pennsylvanians of their political rights. Perhaps this was only another example of political naïveté in Pennsylvania. In its conflicts with Penn, the Assembly repeatedly demonstrated an ignorance of law, of constitutional precedents, and of its own and English history. It failed to perceive that the destruction of proprietary or royal executive authority could not be tolerated indefinitely by England, ignored specific precedents in the colony's legislative history that refuted many of their claims, and flagrantly misread and misinterpreted the colony's original charter. It appeared to base its actions on methods that would win it immediate advantage in a given contest with the Proprietor rather than on any comprehensive knowledge or theory of government.

Pennsylvanians, and possibly other colonials, were saved from this blow at their liberties by the reluctance of the English government to undertake so radical a reformation of the Pennsylvania Assembly and by the often deprecated intricacies of the factions that governed English politics in the middle of the eighteenth century. Lord Granville in the Privy Council and Lord Hyde helped the English Quakers block Parliamentary attempts to exclude Pennsylvania Quakers from the Assembly.[16] Dr. John Fothergill, John Hunt, Peter Andrews, Collinson, and Edmund Peckover, all English Quakers, worked with Granville and Hyde to devise a scheme whereby the overseas Society could guarantee that a certain number of Pennsylvania Quakers would voluntarily resign their seats and decline to stand for re-election, which would —they hoped—enable the Assembly to speedily engage in passing war measures.

Only with great difficulty did the English Quakers succeed in forcing the compromise on their Pennsylvania brethren. Fothergill implored them to accept it so that no further damage would be done to the Society, but it took threats that no further help would be forthcoming from England to bring compliance. Suspecting only partly that the real interest of most Quakers in the province was to preserve their political power in the Assembly, the English Quakers were bewildered by the seeming lack of good faith (and good sense) shown in Pennsylvania.[17]

Cooperation between the English Friends and their ministerial allies ended the matter in England. The political leaders were sensitive to the power of the Quaker lobby, which skillfully played one faction against another and maintained a steady influence in politics. Penn advised his friends that "As the Quakers are a Body of People much respected here, [and] were the chief Settlers of the Province, and as a considerable Body there, they [politicians in England] are not willing to make them Enemys by a permanent disqualification."[18] Halifax, who had been greatly influenced by proprietary reports of Quaker iniquities, advised Penn to accept the compromise. Penn was not satisfied, but all he could get from Halifax was the empty assurance that some further measure might be considered if the Quakers failed to keep their part of the bargain.[19] That the compromise was largely a face-saving measure to satisfy English and American opposition to the Quakers was demonstrated at the end of 1756, when the Quakers quietly resumed their political activities and the English took no further action against them.

The exclusion crisis had a revolutionary effect on Pennsylvania politics. However, it did not greatly affect the long-established basis of Quaker political power—although weakened, the Quakers were and would continue to be the most important political group in the colony, because most of the social and political factors that had sustained minority rule still operated. Rather, it produced an irrevocable division in the Old Party and its leadership. Two factions emerged, one under Isaac Norris and the other under Pemberton, and both were unhappy with the compromise worked out in England—for opposite reasons. The Norrisite Quakers wanted to remain in the Assembly and in other positions of power even at the cost of substantial concessions to the demands of war. Pemberton and his smaller following believed that principles could not be sacrificed; they lay at the heart of the Society, and neither its religious nor its political powers could survive for long without them. He therefore wanted total rather than partial or token exclusion, believing that the Quakers would remain united even if they temporarily lost their hold on the Assembly.

Penn and his allies had thus contributed to a political change beyond their most optimistic expectations: the shattering of Quaker unity and the weakening of the power of the Quaker oligarchy in politics. But it was a pyrrhic victory. Although they accomplished an ancient objective, they also helped their most dangerous enemy, Franklin, to take over leadership of the Assembly. In alliance with Norris and the "war" Quakers, Franklin became the principal leader. He supplied defense schemes that were acceptable to both the Norris faction and to English critics of Quaker pacifism, and furthered Norris's anti-proprietary plans. In return, he got the votes and the still great political backing of the Quaker majority in the Old Party and in the Assembly.

It is significant that this opening for Franklin and the frightful prospects now facing the proprietary (and many Quakers as well) were not really the result of efforts made by politicians in Pennsylvania. They were effected, directly or indirectly, through English influence, which had become an increasingly important (if often confusing) factor in Pennsylvania politics. It was this influence that had saved the Quakers from more severe punishment and forced Penn to make concessions to the Assembly, and the Assembly to respond to the military needs of the province and the Empire. In 1756 the era of "salutary neglect" for Pennsylvania came to an end.

A PHILADELPHIA BOSS

Franklin was virtually the only person involved to benefit politically from Braddock's ignominious defeat. The fact that he could not be charged with a lack of zeal for the Crown's military interests despite his place in the Assembly was especially advantageous to him and significant to the Quakers. Isaac Norris was no longer able to command the undivided support of the Old Party, and relinquished much of his leadership to Franklin. And Franklin demanded a great deal from his allies: never before had the Assembly passed an act for a militia or attempted to interfere directly with the property of the proprietary family. Under his leadership it did both, and much more.

For decades, Pennsylvania politics had been controlled by the Quakers. The shift of power affected the delicate political balance and the relations between factions. Norris's description of the structure of Pennsylvania factions revealed that intergroup rivalries and religious animosities were so intense that many men allied with the Quakers in order to prevent the rise of some more dangerous group to power:

The Church of England makes but a Small part of the Inhabitants. The Quakers are much more numerous. And by Great Importations from Ireland and their Encrease and Such as have come among us from other Parts, The Presbyterians exceed the Quakers. And the Germans are without Doubt, more than either of the others. The Anabaptists and Moravians etc. are but few. The Church of England are well apprized that Their Interest is not sufficient alone, and upon search they have found it Difficult to find men among themselves with whom they Could Confide their Liberties. They dread the Presbyterians and the Germans more, so that in the nature of things—upon a Political System only—the Church of England know they must keep in with the Quakers to keep the others out. The Presbyterians are divided into Several Sects mostly Disliking, if not hating one another as is the Case between the new and old Lights as they Call themselves and the People know themselves so well That they will not Trust one another. Under these Circumstances, the Church of England and Quakers Continue in very strong Terms of Union without any formal Cabals for that Purpose—and the Dutch Joyn them in dread of an arbitrary Government—so that it Seems Absolutely Necessary to keep the Quakers as a Ballance here.[1]

In October 1755, Norris reported that "The Frontier County of Lancaster, composed of all Sorts of Presbyterians and Independents, of all sorts of Germans and some Church of England Electors, have chosen all their Representatives out of the Quakers, tho there are scarcly [sic] One Hundred of that Profession in the whole Country."[2] The Quakers were therefore looked upon as an essential stabilizing force in politics. They could not really withdraw from power unless they were willing to risk social and political anarchy. To many, anarchy or tyranny seemed synonymous with Scotch-Irish Presbyterians, and Peters declared that the Quakers often told him they were "afraid of the Presbyterian interest." Thus to the Quakers and those who looked to them for political safety and stability, it was worth nearly any sacrifice to preserve the power of the Old Party. Many Quakers believed that no matter what dangers there might be in Franklin's politics, he offered them the best chance to preserve their position and block the rise of the Presbyterians. Moreover, he had never demonstrated any desire to encourage the political strength of the "unruly" Scotch-Irish Presbyterians outside of Philadelphia. This situation produced an alliance of mutual benefit—the Quakers needed Franklin's help, and he needed their backing in the counties. They had no intention of surrendering the Party leadership to him permanently; he was a useful interim leader who filled a void left by the withdrawal of the "principled" members.

The key to control of the Party and the Assembly remained in the hands of the county Quakers. Threatened expulsions and the split between Norris and Pemberton had wrecked the Party's unified oligarchic control, but the strength of the county Quakers was still great. In fact, in Bucks, Chester, Philadelphia, and even Lancaster counties, they now had more power than before, and more freedom to determine their own political actions. Because they controlled local politics, the election machinery, and the bulk of the German political allies, they could win elections and keep a majority of seats in the Assembly. They were vitally interested in protecting their local political advantages. Fearing the Presbyterians and being more inclined to favor some form of defense than the safer City conservatives, many county Quakers, who were as much exposed to Indian or French attacks as the neighboring Germans and Scotch-Irish, ignored the advice of the Yearly Meeting not to participate in elections. Although some of them did quit the House, most were re-elected in 1756. Even when a Quaker Assemblyman did resign, the county Quakers ensured the Party's continuing influence by selecting candidates from other faiths who would do their bidding. Peters called these new Assemblymen "Quakerized Presbyterians and Quakerized Churchmen."[3] Thus the withdrawal of professing Quaker members from the Assembly did not really impair Quaker political influence. Yet the shattering of long-established leadership, unity, and discipline left them confused and divided, without a clear policy to follow. In 1756 Franklin came forth with a policy and energetic, forceful leadership, and attracted enough support from the Norrisite group to direct the business of the Assembly.

In Philadelphia, Franklin acquired a personal following that formed a typical political faction, loyal to him and to his interest and responsible for his election to the Assembly. He could proudly claim that he never campaigned for his seat, but it was customary for any gentleman leader to depend upon his faction for his election. He also attracted a number of the young, ambitious City Quakers who refused to bow to the dictation of the old leadership. His most important follower and political protégé was young Joseph Galloway, who would soon become his chief assistant in the Assembly and watchman of Isaac Norris's political activities.

Rebellion among the young was not confined to the City. Peters informed Penn that in the election of 1756 the county Quakers "were never more assiduous, nor more of their young People avowedly busy" to win seats for their candidates—despite the Quaker bargain in England to remain outside of the Assembly.[4]

In addition to the Quakers in Philadelphia, Franklin won over many of the anti-proprietary men of the Church of England. He capitalized on an old dispute among the Churchmen of the City to gain

a Considerable Interest in the Church. The Poyson has never reached the Plumsteds, the Ingless's, the McCalls nor those who live in the South part of the Town and applied for a New Church—these ever were and always will be friends of good Government, and of the Proprietaries and their Governors and they have a considerable Interest—but the Old Churchmen—Evan Morgan, Jacob Duché—Thomas Leech and others and their Friends and Relations—are infected, they are meer Franklinists . . . some of these are promoted in the Military way and can thence encrease their Interest, and are very high in favour of Franklin, the Captains, Officers and Granadiers waiting on him . . . as if he had been a Member of the Royal Family.[5]

Peters had contributed to the quarrel within the Church when, in the 1730's, he tried to seize a rectorship and special preferments from the dominant faction. Remembering his opportunism and political ambitions, the old Churchmen were happy to throw their support to Franklin.[6]

Pemberton led the conservative Quaker faction in Pennsylvania. He did not deny that retention of political power was essential to the well-being of the Society, but he and his adherents were convinced that maintenance of unity under the old leadership and through the Yearly Meeting was the paramount requirement. He rejected the compromises that Norris and the majority of Quakers in the Assembly were willing to make with Franklin on the militia act and on raising and paying taxes for war purposes. It was apparent to him that such concessions would permanently destroy the Society's leadership, principles, and discipline, and would permit new men to assume political control in the colony.[7] A divided and weakened Quaker Party would only help Allen, Peters, and the other proprietary supporters to seize power. Those who were not Quakers would take advantage of any split in the ranks to draw rebellious Friends into compromises and acceptance of political favors, which would eventually undermine both the Old Party and the religious society.

Consequently, Pemberton was scarcely grateful for the compromise devised by Granville and the London Quakers. He resisted the enforcement of partial exclusion, and his attitude brought forth Fothergill's angry warnings. Although he realized that total exclusion would deprive the Society of political power for a time, he thought the exiles would remain united and would be prepared to resume control of the Assembly when the war was over.[8]

Pemberton's actions during 1755 and 1756 were devious, but they marked a consistent effort to hold the religious and political interests of the Quakers together by rigid adherence to the heritage that had made them supreme in Pennsylvania. He sought to curb their tendency to deny their principles while pursuing temporary political advantage under Isaac Norris and Franklin. Although he and the conservative Quakers bowed to the compromise and, in 1756, effected the withdrawal of all but twelve of the Quaker members from the House, he attempted several maneuvers to preserve his and the Friends' strength. These added further confusion to provincial politics.

Pemberton was alarmed at Franklin's growing prestige and influence in the Assembly, and jealous and suspicious of his alliance with Norris. He therefore decided to seek an understanding with Penn. Uncertain whether Franklin was deliberately plotting to destroy the Quakers or innocently following a course of action that would bring about the same result, Pemberton, encouraged by Fothergill, tried to build Quaker resistance to the legislative measures Franklin proposed. He criticized Franklin's attacks upon the Governor and opposed the militia act and the taxation of land for war purposes (as a large landowner, Pemberton would have been taxed heavily). The old enemy of the Proprietor found himself supporting Penn and the Governor against some of the Assembly's most important legislation.[9]

After Braddock's defeat, Pemberton knew that the English government might attempt to coerce the Quakers or to limit their power, and he saw that a reconciliation with Penn might be the most effective way to protect the Society from this danger. The English Friends were warmly in favor of such a policy, and they acted as mediators between the Proprietor and the Pemberton faction.[10] Penn, however, suspected this new cordiality; he wanted practical signs of good faith in the form of changed policies and favorable votes in the Assembly: "The friends here do not approve of the behaviour of their brethren in the Assembly, and both those of Pennsylvania and this Country profess a regard for us, and aver that their People never desired any change of Government . . . and much desire to settle matters amicably; however . . . I shall never agree to an accommodation but on proper conditions."[11] Actually, the obstacles to any workable political alignment between these rivals for provincial power were insurmountable. One of the most important obstacles was William

Allen, who so despised Pemberton that he refused to consider any attempts to mediate differences between the factions, even if the results might hurt Franklin—who became Allen's enemy in 1756.[12]

While he was seeking better relations with Penn during the autumn of 1755 and the winter of 1756, Pemberton turned to a problem that had long been of special interest to the Quakers. Indian relations had deteriorated after Braddock's defeat, and for the first time in Pennsylvania's history a brutal Indian war swept across the province. At first Pemberton blamed the alienation of the Indians on bad colonial policies, partly proprietary, which did not coincide with the traditional Quaker methods of preserving peace with the tribes. He frantically tried to prevent a declaration of war by the Governor and reprisals against the Indians by the enraged settlers.

By the middle of 1756, Pemberton discovered the immense political possibilities in a separate Quaker-Indian policy. Governor Morris did not cooperate sufficiently to satisfy him, and even attempted to exclude the Quakers from the first Easton Conference in July, which was called in an effort to preserve peace between the colony and the Pennsylvania tribes. However, when the Quakers offered to give Morris money for Indian presents, the Governor changed his mind. It was a mistake, for he soon discovered that the Quakers intended to take over the Conference. Pemberton also made some discoveries at Easton: the value of the newly formed "Friendly Association for Regaining and Preserving Peace with the Indians by Pacific Measures," and the possibility that he had an excellent tool to serve Quaker interests in the drunken, self-proclaimed leader of the Delaware Indians, Teedyuscung. After convincing the gullible Delaware that the Quakers were his true friends and that Morris, Peters, and the other proprietary officers were the enemies of peace and justice, Pemberton launched a private attack that put the blame for the

colony's Indian troubles on fraudulent proprietary land purchases. He suddenly found himself equipped with an organization that was united under his leadership and free from outside
contamination and had a program acceptable to all Quakers. It
was possible that the Friendly Association might serve as a temporary focus of Quaker power in place of the Assembly, which
had been corrupted by Franklin and the war. With money, an
organization, and general approval from the Friends in Pennsylvania and in England, Pemberton was prepared to make Indian
relations the means to revive the Quakers' exclusive political
leadership.

Pemberton's tactics were shrewd; the blame for the Indian war
could now be charged to the proprietary and to the betrayal of the
honorable Quaker policy. Thus the Quakers were absolved from
any responsibility for the war and for its prosecution. And a
divided Society could now rally around the Friendly Association
in defense of honesty, honor, and the old ways of dealing with
the Indians. Perhaps equally important in Pemberton's mind was
the possibility that the English Quakers might accept his charges
against Penn and thus restore English faith in the "true" leadership of Pemberton and his faction.

The Quakers completely dominated the Easton conferences,
and, to the dismay of Penn and his friends in Pennsylvania, the
proceedings became an exposé of proprietary mistreatment of the
Indians. Yet by impugning proprietary Indian policy and land
purchases, the Quakers also succeeded in further upsetting relations between Pennsylvania tribes and the Iroquois. They thus
endangered the work of William Johnson, the Crown superin-
tendent of Indian affairs, and involved Governors and military
leaders throughout the colonies in a series of investigations of
Indian complaints—all in the middle of the war.

For the moment Pemberton reunited the Quakers on a single
issue, resumed power in Indian affairs, embarrassed the Proprie-

tor, and, altogether, did much to stir up trouble. Left alone to develop this opportunity, Pemberton might have found a way to regroup the Society under his personal leadership. But Franklin and Norris and their followers in the Assembly took steps to turn Pemberton's work at Easton in another direction. If properly exploited, the charges against the proprietary could be used in England as grounds for revoking Penn's Charter. The chance to place the blame for the war on Penn was too good to pass up, and, added to other charges against the Proprietor, it seemed certain to bring about the overthrow of his government.

Franklin and Norris failed to consider a more likely English response to the Easton conferences. The case against Penn was hard to prove or disprove and investigation would be prolonged, but it would not be difficult to prove that Pemberton and the Quakers had arrogantly violated all proprieties in their zeal to manage Indian affairs. English leaders who thought there might be some truth in the accusations against Penn were astounded by the reports from Peters, Weiser, and, most significantly, William Johnson describing how the Quakers had disobeyed explicit instructions not to interfere with the Indians, and how they had privately carried on their own scheme without any regard for English interests. Johnson, who had hitherto been unfriendly to Penn, now supported him, declaring that as far as he and the Iroquois were concerned, Teedyuscung's complaints were unfounded. Moreover, the Quakers had caused trouble for the Iroquois by inciting the Delawares, who were vassals of the Six Nations, to make charges, conduct treaties, and make peace—all matters that should have been managed at Onondaga.[18]

Whatever the truth or untruth of the accusations made by the Quakers and the Delawares, the Ministry could not allow a private organization to brazenly assume diplomatic authority, no matter how laudable its intentions. Responsibility for this untimely meddling might have fallen solely on Pemberton and the

Friendly Association, had not Franklin and Norris rushed in to join the attack. In English eyes, the Assembly was thus co-defendant to the charge of usurping the diplomatic prerogatives of the Crown.

As soon as Franklin and Norris appropriated the Indian complaints for their own political purpose, Pemberton began to retreat. He had never really wanted to bring about the total destruction of proprietary government, but desired only a weakened executive and a secure, strong Quaker rule. Above all, he did not want to give any advantage to Franklin.

Franklin undoubtedly supported this Quaker policy in order to strike at Penn; he also needed Quaker backing and accepted their Indian policy as the price. However, his cooperation with a unilateral Quaker policy that demanded peace with the Indians was as inconsistent with his usual opinions about the Indians as it was contrary to the interests of England and the war effort. In August 1756 Franklin told Pownall, "I do not believe we shall ever have a firm peace with the Indians till we have well drubbed them."[14] He had also proposed a *Plan for Settling Two Western Colonies in North America,* which envisioned a vast expansion of English settlements beyond the mountains—a plan that required extensive acquisitions of Indian land. Penn therefore had reason to be surprised at his sudden solicitude for the Indians. It was especially annoying that Franklin now agreed with the criticism of the land purchase of 1754, for both he and Norris had participated in the negotiations without any complaint.

In the long run, the political expediency of joining with Pemberton in the Easton conferences did not serve Franklin well in England. It was but one of his actions in 1756 that Penn later used against him and the Assembly.

Despite Franklin's well-intentioned efforts, his scheme for a Pennsylvania militia proved unacceptable to both Penn and the

Ministry, and, contrary to his expectations, aroused intense opposition among important groups in Pennsylvania and in England.
Believing that almost any measure could be put into effect by
well-disposed men, he again expressed in his militia law a confidence that governments, institutions, and laws, whatever their
faults, could be made to work effectively if men acted together
upon a given problem, under the direction and stimulus of a talented leader.[15]

To apply these ideas in Pennsylvania affairs, Franklin sought
to draw out what he thought were the inherent good intentions
of his fellow citizens. He again employed the methods he had
used so successfully in the past: organization, massive applications
of personal influence, propaganda in the *Pennsylvania Gazette*
and in pamphlets, and specific appeals to the interests of several
groups. At the expense of clarity and workability, Franklin drew
up a measure that provided something for everyone. He hoped
to achieve the results he had obtained with his Association in 1747.
England and the Proprietor got a militia, and the Governor could
choose one or more officers from a slate of three elected by the
troops. The election of officers appealed to the Quakers and to
other gentlemen who were not of the Proprietary Party, as well
as to the enlisted militiamen. Limitations upon the extent of
service and the lack of coercive military law attracted both the
troops and those suspicious of the Governor's power. Voluntary
enlistment was a sop to the Quakers, winning support in the Assembly and undermining objections from such Friends as might
claim "tender consciences."[16]

In a diligent campaign for the militia act, Franklin used all of
his personal influence and the authority of his pen. In *A Dialogue
Between X, Y, & Z,* as in *Plain Truth* (1747), he presented objections to the measure and then demolished them in his typically
humorous, easy manner. In 1756, however, the objections he
presented and so easily knocked down were superficial—they did

not reflect the real reasons why important men in Pennsylvania
and England opposed the militia act. As Penn reported from
England, "Some are for passing a proper Militia Law here . . .
by the Law lately passed in [the] Pennsylvania [Assembly], the
Militia is taken out of the hands of the Crown, and the appointment of Officers given to the People which can never be allowed,
this they say has nothing to do with the Principles of Quakers."[17]

Angry at the Governor's rejection of the act, for which he
blamed Penn, Franklin failed to realize that Pennsylvania was
not amenable to ingenious schemes that compromised too much.
The Pennsylvania of 1756, in real danger of invasion by the
French and Indians, was not like the unharmed colony of 1747
at the end of a war. Conditions had changed in the province, but
Franklin, remembering the success and acclaim accorded to *Plain
Truth* and the Association of a decade earlier, again employed the
strategy that had worked then.[18]

The militia act, the Assembly's abusive treatment of the Governors (especially shocking to English officials), and a number
of other measures contributing to the attack on the proprietary
gave Penn useful weapons to apply in England. In a number of
specific contests with Penn and his governors, the Assembly did
win some important victories and concessions. Many of the bills
it offered to the Governors were obviously needed, and on several
occasions, notably when the question of taxing proprietary estates
arose, Penn was hard pressed to find ways to defend himself without appearing, as the Assembly claimed, arbitrary and unjust.
Despite these victories, Penn was able to find in nearly every
measure some proposal or device that undermined his power or
usurped royal prerogatives. The Assembly provided Penn with
a series of claims which, when presented to the Board of Trade
and Privy Council, could not be ignored for long. By 1756 Penn
was almost pleased at the extravagance of legislative pretensions,
and he instructed the Governor to keep pressing the Assembly,

"for if they will not do what is right the more indecent their behaviour is the better, as it may be attended with good consequences
here."[19] Much of what the Assembly did was Franklin's design
and responsibility. He was to spend ten years trying vainly to win
English approval of this record.

As Franklin rose to power during 1756, the Proprietary Party
sank deeper into confusion and despair. Unable to achieve an
agreement with the conservative Quakers who feared Franklin,
Peters sadly told Penn, "It is a Pity that Mr Allen is in so bad an
humor, for I think with Prudence and a decent and honorable
Coalition of his and the Quakers Interest all Mr Franklin's iniq-
uitous Schemes may be frustrated."[20]

Proprietary Party strength in Pennsylvania was still ineffectual
despite the efforts of the leaders to exploit the charge that the
Assembly was to blame for the lack of defense in the colony. The
rise of Franklin to leadership of the Assembly lessened the effect
of this accusation, for he was recognized as a champion of military
preparedness. His influence was, however, only partly responsible
for the failure of the war issue to affect legislative representation.
More members elected in 1756 were willing to permit increased
Assembly support for the war, but they were influenced less by
popular demand in Pennsylvania than by fear of further English
action against the Quakers and the Assembly. Governor Morris
declared that even after they were threatened with expulsion the
Quakers "used every Means in their Power to put in Men that
would oppose a general Militia Law, and maintain the perpetual
War which they say they have waged with the Proprietors."[21]
By a general militia law, Morris meant one that placed military
authority in the hands of the Governor, not a measure such as
Franklin offered. For those who managed elections in the counties, the old fears and jealousies of rival factions, Presbyterians,
and "mobbish sorts" ensured that there would be no rebellion at
the polls. The majority of the Germans remained loyal to the

Quaker alliance and, forgetting Franklin's criticism of them, gave him their votes in the counties, because "Mr Franklin is very popular among the Dutch, by his Waggon-Project."[22]

The selection of representatives for the Assembly continued to be controlled by political bosses. The changes of 1755 and 1756 simply added Franklin to the list of Philadelphia leaders. He directed the Old Party, which was now composed of "war Quakers" and his faction, and, following the practice of the other Philadelphia leaders, exercised his new power by dictating the choice of the ticket for the election of 1756. To salvage something from almost certain defeat, the proprietary leaders were forced into a humiliating meeting with their enemy. "Mr. Hamilton, Mr. Allen and Mr. Chew have had two Meetings with Mr. Franklin, in the last Meeting a Ticket was agreed on."[23] The Old Party let its opponents put up only two men in Philadelphia County, and Peters complained that although "the ticket is extreamly disagreeable to the Town in general and the Gentlemen are bound in honor to support the Ticket yet I do not know that it will be carried. It will depend on the determination of Friends at their Publick Meeting at Burlington."[24] Just before the elections, Franklin repudiated the agreement, apparently deciding that it was not necessary to give the Proprietary Party even two seats. Peters reported the sad results to Penn: "Mr. Allen and his Friends have taken a great deal of Pains but after all their Industry and the Exertion of their whole Interest they have lost the Election entirely."[25]

Dictation from Philadelphia was not confined to the Franklin-Quaker party. In fact, the leaders of the Proprietary Party attempted to gain an even tighter control over their supporters. Edward Shippen of Lancaster, rich and powerful in his own right, nonetheless submitted his political decisions to Philadelphia approval. In a letter to his son Joseph, he described a meeting of the

leaders of Lancaster County, where the election ticket was determined: he had proposed "Alex Stodman and Neddy" [his son,
Edward Shippen, Jr.] for the Assembly, and "they were agreeable to Cousin Allen and the other Gentlemen in Philadelphia."[26]

For political purposes Franklin was, in 1756, a Philadelphia
boss, and he practiced politics in the traditional manner, albeit
more adroitly and with certain advantages. As a boss who approved the exclusion of "stiff" Quakers from the Assembly, criticized the Germans (although he ceased to demand their exclusion from politics), and shared the general Philadelphia dislike
and distrust of the turbulent Scotch-Irish, he led no "Party of the
People." The persons to whom he appealed outside of his faction
had diverse political interests that often bore little relation to his
own plans and principles.

One of the favorite subjects in the correspondence of Franklin's
opponents was the nature of his ambition. Some accused him of
interest in "the fashionable Arguments of Pension and Places."
Others were certain that he wanted to govern Pennsylvania under
the Crown. As William Peters, Richard's brother, informed Penn,
"Many People think their mighty Favorite Mr Franklin has a
Design to Dupe them as well as you, by working his Scheme so
as that the King shall be oblig'd for saving the Province to take it
into his own hands."[27] As early as October 1755, Penn was preparing to resist any such scheme: "I think if he could overthrow
the Government with regard to us they [the Ministry] would
not advise the King to appoint him."[28]

With the Assembly apparently behind him, Franklin worked
to remove the proprietary obstacles to harmonious government
in Pennsylvania. He believed that if the executive were reformed,
there would be no limit to the beneficial measures that men of
reason and good will might effect in the colony. Expecting that
the leaders in England would assent to such a worthy undertaking, he prepared to go to England to battle the Proprietor in

person. Morris was as yet unaware of Franklin's decision to cross the Atlantic. He wrote:

The Quakers, under the Direction of Franklin, are doing their utmost to accomplish a Change in the Government of Pennsylvania, without knowing what they are about, or without considering that they will be almost the only Sufferers by it, the Change I mean is the making this a King's Government, which I believe is a Matter settled between Pownall and Franklin; the former is to use his Interest with the Ministry, and the latter to furnish Materials, and obstruct the public Measures here in order to make the Measure necessary.[29]

Certain that his arguments and reasoning would defeat Penn in England, Franklin was confident as he left Pennsylvania in February 1757 that he would soon return with the blessings of royal government for the province. It did not occur to him to inquire into the nature of royal government. He saw no similarity between proprietary instructions and those given to royal governors; he did not perceive that the Crown was no closer to Pennsylvania interests and problems than was the Proprietor. Believing in the "goodness" of England and English leaders and judging royal governors from his associations with men like Shirley and Pownall, Franklin thought he had found a quick and easy solution to the old political problems of Pennsylvania. He likewise underestimated his opponent—a man with considerable experience in English politics. Franklin was not long in discovering the extent of the obstacles facing him, but it took him longer to realize that the methods and personal resources that had been so useful in Pennsylvania would not automatically be effective in England.

MISSION IN ENGLAND

When Franklin sailed for England in 1757 with the Assembly's commission to prosecute its case against the Proprietor, he appeared to be the most powerful and influential member of the legislature. His apparent strength contributed to the confidence he expressed in asserting that his visit to the Mother Country would be a wholly enjoyable personal experience as well as a successful political venture. He assumed that the Assembly's business would take little time away from the more pleasant association with old friends and newly made acquaintances among the most interesting men in England. In fact, it was the prospect of participating in the exciting cultural life at the center of the Empire, not his political mission, that made him eager to cross the Atlantic.

In a private capacity, Franklin's experiences from 1757 to 1761 indeed gave him great personal satisfaction. His *Autobiography* describes them as the triumphant pilgrimage of a colonial scientist, writer, student of imperial affairs, and observer of mankind to an England and Scotland that soon rivaled Pennsylvania for his affections. It was this happy memory that he fully recounted for history. The frustrations and defeats he met with in his assigned task were omitted. In a peculiarly Franklinian way he got even with men and events that displeased him, especially those he could not retaliate against more tangibly, by largely ignoring them in his records. Certainly Penn and the political events of the period merited greater attention in the *Autobiography* than they got, if only because they cost Franklin so much time and trouble after 1757.[1]

Most of the politicians in the colony agreed in 1757 that the affairs of government were in such a deplorable state that only direct negotiations with the Proprietor or an appeal to the Crown could "re-establish those principles of justice and harmony which should subsist between the several parts of the government." They also agreed that with Franklin as its representative the Assembly was likely to emerge the winner if the dispute with Penn came to a showdown. Even Franklin's enemies in Pennsylvania conceded this. Fearful of what might happen when he reached England, Peters, Allen, Smith, and Hamilton all warned the Proprietor of the danger to his government and of the very real possibility of his defeat by Franklin and the Ministry.

The Assembly based its hopes for ministerial favor in 1757 on the same circumstances that had encouraged it to press its attack upon the Proprietor in 1755 and 1756. The British Army still depended upon the Assembly to obtain supplies in large quantities, and general ministerial opposition to proprietary governments was strong. Moreover, the Indians' charges against proprietary land policy and the Ministry's skeptical reaction to Penn's refusal to let the Assembly tax his lands made the Proprietor's prospects look poor indeed.

Gratifying as these advantages were to the anti-proprietary faction, its hopes were immeasurably raised by the belief that Franklin possessed great personal stature and prestige in England. There was little doubt in Pennsylvania that the abilities and assets which had so recently made Franklin the most powerful member of the Assembly would serve him equally well overseas. While paying due regard to his affable personality, wit, intelligence, and knowledge of political affairs, as well as to his spectacular ability as a writer, the colony's political observers believed that Franklin's scientific reputation would tip the balance in the Assembly's favor.[2]

Peters advised Penn, "But certain it is that B. Franklin's view is to effect a change of Government, and considering the popularity of his character and the reputation gained by his Electrical Discoveries which will introduce him into all sorts of Company he may prove a Dangerous Enemy. Dr. Fothergill and Mr. Collinson can introduce him to the Men of most influence at Court and he may underhand give impressions to your prejudice."[3] Another opponent, former Governor Robert Morris, added his realistic appreciation of Franklin's assets: "Mr Franklin has sense and knowledge enough to make himself considerable, especially as Ld Loudoun's Letters, and his Electrical Reputation, will Introduce him to the first men of the Kingdom, who wanting information as to America will be glad to have it from a man of his parts. I wish Mr Hamilton had gone home . . . and having the Ear of the Ministry he might have kept F and his Schemes at a distance from them."[4]

As Peters reported, Franklin believed that the solution to Pennsylvania's political problems lay in a change of government. He felt that negotiations with Penn would serve little purpose, and therefore planned to appeal to the Crown for royal government. For his part, the Proprietor likewise saw nothing to be gained by any discussions with Franklin; the antipathy between them had grown too strong. Penn was scarcely willing even to receive Franklin when he came to England. Nevertheless, despite their inclinations, both Franklin and Penn were forced to profess a willingness to negotiate. The farce had to be played out before the critical audience of English political leaders, who, wanting an end to provincial squabbles so that the colony might play its proper part in the war, would probably decide for the side that seemed most disposed to compromise. Consequently, it was incumbent upon both Franklin and Penn to place the blame for any failure to restore harmony between the legislature and the executive upon the evil intentions and schemes of the opposition.

On the surface, the Assembly seemed solidly behind Franklin, and placed few restrictions upon the measures and means he might use to gain his ends. Actually, there were significant divisions among the anti-proprietary factions. Because he had risen to power in the Assembly only recently, Franklin had not had time to establish a large personal following in the House. The small cadre that comprised his faction had its main strength in Philadelphia. It was loyal to Franklin, and, although a minority, it did dominate the Assembly. This domination was possible, however, only with the support of the Quaker and Quaker-nominated members from the counties. These allies were by no means political captives of Franklin in 1757, and they followed his leadership only as long as it was to their advantage.

Many Quakers still looked forward to the resurrection of the Society's political power after the war. Israel Pemberton's brother John testified to their impatience when he wrote to Samuel Fothergill, a London Quaker, "Our Country People seem already to repent Friends being out of the House of Assembly. And if we do not use much precaution it will be next to impossible to prevent a majority of them being chosen next year."[5] While they might dispute about the party's methods and leadership, their basic allegiance to the powerful Quaker position in religion and in politics had not been destroyed by the events of 1755 and 1756. Franklin was a useful interim leader who might obtain benefits for the colony and the Assembly from the Proprietor, but whatever their political persuasion, the Quakers were unlikely to follow meekly behind a leader who was neither a Quaker nor fully trusted by all members of the Society.

Among the leaders of the Quaker oligarchy in Philadelphia there were already indications—strong from Pemberton and tentative from Norris—of uneasiness over Franklin's avowed intention to appeal for a change of government. Weakened though their power in politics was, their opinions were still influential in the councils of the faithful. Whatever the faults of the Proprietor, an increasing number of Quakers suspected that there was a greater measure of security and certainty in politics under a weak proprietary government than under the greater power of the Crown. To add to the anxiety of Quakers, there was the possibility that Franklin might succeed too well in England and then return to Pennsylvania strong enough to do without Quaker support. This possibility did not accord with their plans to restore the political supremacy of the Society after the danger of further English censure had passed.

Hence Quaker support for Franklin's mission was cautious. As Franklin's implacable hatred for Penn grew, he tried to prod Norris and a majority in the Assembly into taking a firm stand for royal government. In his reports from England to Norris, Franklin urged the Assembly to this course, but even a supporting opinion from Richard Jackson could not move the Quaker majority to commit itself to the outright overthrow of the Proprietor.[6]

There was no rebellion in the Assembly against Franklin, but an open quarrel between Franklin and Norris was only narrowly averted. In 1759, Norris learned of the contents of a letter, written by Franklin's son, William, to Joseph Galloway, which very frankly discussed the political senility of the Speaker. Young Franklin wrote, "It is not to be wonder'd at, if, as the Speaker grows more and more in Years he should become more and more capricious. The Speaker having been long a Member, and accustom'd to have considerable Weight and Influence in the House, it is not unnatural to suppose he would readily take Umbrage at any one whom he thought likely to interfere with his Power. I have myself seen several Instances where he [has] given such an Opposition to some Measures propos'd by my Father, as could not be accounted for but from Motives of Jealousy."[7] Norris knew that an open break with the Franklins would only help the Proprietary Party. He therefore concealed his anger, but took care to let the senior Franklin know that he had learned of William's opinions. Needless to say, relations between Norris and Franklin grew more strained, and the Speaker could not be counted upon to rally Quaker support behind the more radical of Franklin's plans.

Much of what Franklin hoped to achieve in England depended upon how many important connections he could establish with influential men in the government. He especially had to arouse a favorable interest among the members of the Board of Trade and the Privy Council. These two bodies heard petitions concerning, and made decisions on, colonial policy, and sometimes suggested that Parliament take certain measures under consideration. However, Parliament usually took little interest in colonial affairs, and, with few exceptions, the decisions and recommendations of the Board and the Council determined colonial policy.

In view of Penn's constant and perceptibly successful cultivation of good relations with members of the government, Franklin had to find a compensating influence. Before he left Pennsylvania it appeared as though his hitherto friendly association with Lord Loudoun and Thomas Pownall might serve this purpose. Both men possessed considerable power in the Board, and Pownall's brother was its secretary. Moreover, as clients of the Duke of Cumberland, they were in a position to challenge Penn's hard-won interest with the Duke. Although the Duke was not officially concerned with colonial policy, he nonetheless exercised, personally and through his secretary, Falconer, a very real influence on ministerial deliberations upon colonial affairs and on the dispensation of patronage. Just a few months before, it had been his favor that had nearly put Pownall into the Governorship of Pennsylvania. Hence, if the Pownalls and Loudoun exerted themselves in Franklin's behalf they could ensure, at the very least, a friendly and interested reception for him when he brought his case before the Board and the Committee for Plantations of the Privy Council. Armed with such a favorable introduction, Franklin could then effectively apply his other weapons to good advantage against Penn.

These plans and prospects dissolved in the three-way dispute that broke out between Pownall, Loudoun, and Governor Shirley of Massachusetts. The exact details of Franklin's part in the quarrel are not clear, but one of the results was an apparent coolness of Pownall and Loudoun toward Franklin. Vexed with the Assembly's intransigent attitude toward the proprietary government, disturbed by the interference of the Quakers and the Assembly in Indian relations, and possibly a little jealous of the lofty position Franklin held in the military planning of Pennsylvania, Loudoun replaced his formerly favorable reports of Franklin with accusations that he was not to be trusted, was overly ambitious, and was known to have been drunk on the crossing to England. This last charge Loudoun had on the authority of the ship captain.[8]

There were numerous rumors in Pennsylvania during 1757 that Franklin and Pownall had also quarreled. Pownall was the center of the larger dispute, in which Shirley accused him of being a scheming and ambitious opportunist who was plotting his ruin. The basis of the allegation was found in Pownall's efforts to obtain Shirley's removal from the Governorship of Massachusetts. Pownall had also schemed, proprietary forces believed, to overthrow proprietary government in Pennsylvania, partly because he opposed such government in principle, and partly because he desired to make another position available in the event that he was unable to secure the more profitable Massachusetts place.[9]

The proprietary leaders, who were very attentive to such de-

velopments, repeatedly denounced Pownall for meddling in
Pennsylvania for his own advantage. These designs, moreover,
"produced a jealousy between Mr. Pownall and Mr. Franklin,"
as Peters happily informed Penn.[10] After obtaining the Governorship of Massachusetts, Pownall was no longer active in Pennsylvania politics. Because he was busy defending himself against the
charges sent home to England by his enemies and was less intimate with Franklin than in the past, he did not give him the help
that might have smoothed his way in English official circles. In
fact, Franklin soon found that Penn's work had made Halifax,
Cumberland, and Falconer unfriendly and prejudiced toward his
agency. Penn took pleasure in reporting that "The Duke of Cumberland told me he had spoke to Sir Everard Falconer, by no
means to support Franklin unless he acted another part."[11] The
Duke went on to advise Penn that "The Resolution of a Committee of the House of Commons, in the Affairs of Jamaica, would
be of use, in letting the Assemblys of the Plantations know they
will not abet them in their extravagant Claims."[12] This resolution
had declared that the Assembly of Jamaica had no right to raise
and apply money without the Governor's consent. If this were
applied to Pennsylvania, it would dispose of one of the Assembly's
major demands and one of Franklin's chief arguments against
proprietary instructions.

The chances for a favorable outcome to Franklin's mission
would have been immeasurably greater if he had received the
wholehearted assistance of the English Quakers. With their
strength in English politics the Quakers, especially those in London, were in a position to provide Franklin with connections, information, and influence in the most important places in the
government. Their power had been amply demonstrated in the
exclusion crisis when, with the help of Lord Hyde and Lord
Granville, they had blocked Parliamentary action against the
Quakers in Pennsylvania.

Franklin did have the promise of help from individual members of the Society such as Fothergill and Collinson, but the Society as a whole refused to join in the all-out struggle with the Proprietor that Franklin thought necessary. It was particularly reluctant to assist in any attempt to get royal government for Pennsylvania. As in Pennsylvania, many of the Quaker leaders in England were not convinced that Quaker interests and prospects would best be served by continued warfare with Penn or by Franklin. When these interests did coincide with Franklin's plans—as they did in the investigation of the Indians' charges of mistreatment—the Quakers were willing to help.[13] However, during 1757 and 1758 the English Friends repeatedly urged their Pennsylvania brethren to avoid controversies that might rearouse English criticism and possibly result in penalties. The anxiety of the English Quakers over what they considered dangerous and ill-considered politics in Pennsylvania was reflected in Fothergill's pointed plea to Pemberton: "If you think it beneath you to clear Yourselves; at least endeavor to clear us of the imputation we lie under on your account—you expect we should serve you when occasion[s] arise, and justly we are disposed to do it, many of us cordially, but our ability to Serve you depends upon our credit here; in proportion as this sinks, our ability ceases . . . restore us to a degree of credit which we have fallen from by your inattention, or neglect."[14]

By 1758, the English Quakers had further cause for concern. Instead of seriously damaging the Proprietor, the charges made by Teedyuscung and the Delawares were now turned against the Quakers. Fothergill, once again the voice of alarm, described a growing sentiment in England that held the Quakers responsible for the Indian War in Pennsylvania. It was reasoned, he declared, that "When the Delawares demanded the Hatchet and a beginning of war against the French, the Assembly influenced by the Quakers refused and the Indians went over to the French to get revenge. In turn the Quakers tried to cover this up and keep the Delawares quiet" by inciting them to blame Penn for fraudulent land purchases.[15] Regardless of whether this opinion was accurate, the Quakers in England were certain that a very cautious policy was desirable in Pennsylvania.

The Quakers in England did not "hate" Penn; their relations with him had remained generally amicable through the years.[16] They held to the belief that with good will on both sides the disputes between Penn and the Assembly could be settled by negotiations and compromise. Therefore, when Franklin professed his hatred and contempt for Penn and proprietary government, the Quakers drew back. The uneasiness many in England felt about Franklin's plans and opinions was demonstrated after his famous interview with Penn in 1759. Franklin's furious denunciation of Penn resulted from the Proprietor's insistence that the Assembly, and Pennsylvanians in general, could not regard the rights or privileges they had received or seized from William Penn as absolute and indisputable if they conflicted with English law, custom, or prerogatives. The Crown, or the Proprietor acting for the Crown, could at any time change the "constitution" of the colony to make it conform to English practice.

Franklin exploded with rage. He later declared, "The contempt I felt for Thomas when he so readily gave up his Father's character as an honest man, and allow'd that he had pretended to grant privileges which were not in his Power to grant, in Deceit of the People who had come over and settled on the Faith of those Grants."[17] When he informed his friends in Pennsylvania of this new example of the Proprietor's treachery, he spared few words in describing his feelings for Penn.

Fothergill and Penn soon acquired copies of Franklin's remarks, and the doctor was shocked at what he considered their abusive and intemperate nature. By Franklin's own account,

Dr Fothergill blam'd me for writing such harsh Things; but I still see nothing in the Letter but what was proper for me to write . . . and it is of no small Importance to know what Sort of Man we have to deal with, and how base his Principles. — I might indeed have spar'd the Comparison of Thomas to a *Low Jockey* who triumph'd with Insolence when a Purchaser complain'd of being cheated in a Horse; an Expression the Dr particularly remark'd as harsh and unguarded. I might have left his Conduct and Sentiments to your Reflections, and contented myself with a bare Recital of what pass'd; but Indignation extorted it from me, and I cannot yet say that I much repent of it.[18]

Penn found it difficult to understand Franklin's reaction, and in reports to Pennsylvania he stated that he had only "represented to him that it was as unsafe for the people, as it was for us, to claim Privileges by my Father's Charter, that could not be warranted by the King's Charter to him."[19] The Proprietor's observation was logical and soundly based in English constitutional theory, and it was one that his long and troublesome experience with officials in the English government had confirmed. One of the strongest objections in England to proprietary governments was that they failed to maintain the powers entrusted to them. It was the duty of the King's representatives to restore these powers no matter when or under what conditions the colonials had usurped them.

Legislative opinion in Pennsylvania strongly opposed such a strict theory of colonial rights. The belief was firmly maintained that rights or powers once obtained and exercised, by whatever means, became part of an inviolable constitution. Franklin also shared this view. Nevertheless, his personal remarks about Penn's character were excessive. And Fothergill, like many Englishmen, was alarmed by the abusive language the Americans often used in discussing their executives—be they royal or proprietary. Penn, for his part, used Franklin's remarks to advantage: "I have shewn it to my Lord Hallifax and some other People to shew how well disposed this Man is to settle Differences."[20]

During his years in Philadelphia, Franklin had demonstrated how valuable the skillful use of his pen could be in obtaining support for his ideas and causes. Although he had used his newspaper sparingly in the political disputes of the colony, such tracts as *Plain Truth* and the *Dialogue Between X, Y, & Z* testified to his ability to overcome opposition and achieve success for his plans. When he reached England, he therefore wasted little time before commencing an extensive campaign against the Proprietor in the London press. Through messages from the Assembly, pieces of his own composition, and useful works by others devoted to the Assembly's case, he took full advantage of the help and facilities that were provided by his old friend and fellow printer, William Strahan. One of the most successful fruits of their cooperation was the publication of Charles Thomson's *An Enquiry into the Causes of the Alienation of the Delaware and Shawanese Indians*—a forceful condemnation of proprietary injustices to the Indians culled from the Quaker discoveries at the Easton conferences. Thomson's work was widely circulated in England and for a short time had some success. However, many Englishmen saw a greater evil in the untimely interference of a private group in the delicate and intricate relations with the Indians, in the middle of war, than in Penn's supposed lack of principles or honesty in Indian affairs.

All of this was but small fire compared with the chief instrument of Franklin's press campaign, *An Historical Review of the Constitution and Government of Pennsylvania.* Work on this devastating and definitive book designed to eliminate Penn and proprietary government from Pennsylvania, was begun soon after he arrived in England.

Although Richard Jackson wrote the *Historical Review* in its final form, there can be no doubt that its content, direction, and purpose were inspired by Franklin. His help, and contributions from Robert Charles, who was an Assembly agent in England, and William Franklin, provided Jackson with the information about Pennsylvania history he needed to attack the Proprietor. It was expedient that the authorship be not clearly that of the Assembly's agent, but for political reasons Jackson did not wish to take sole credit or responsibility for the work. The mystery that later surrounded the real authorship appears to have been calculated and deliberate. Those who admired Franklin were allowed to give him credit; those in England who were suspicious of Franklin and the Assembly were informed that the *Historical Review* had been written by an eminent English student of Pennsylvania history.[21]

In part planned as an answer to William Smith's *Brief State of the Province of Pennsylvania*, which had been quite successful in turning English opinion against the Quaker government in the colony, the *Historical Review* was an equally partisan piece of political propaganda. With little regard for the facts of history or a just presentation of the causes of the political disputes, the work's chief aim was to glorify the Assembly and defame the Proprietor. In letters to his friends, Franklin clearly stated his purpose: "The Publication of the Defense of the Province, mention'd in mine of Sept. 2 [1757] will probably be one of the first Acts of Hostility on our Side, as being necessary to prepare the Minds of the Publick in which the Proprietary will be gibbeted up as they deserve, to rot and stink in the Nostrils of Posterity."[22] In April 1759 he announced that publication was near, "tho' perhaps not Time enough to send any Copies by these Ships. I hope this Work will put a finishing Stroke to the Prejudices that have prevailed against us and set the Proprietary Character and Conduct in their proper Lights, and without expresly taking Notice of the infamous Libellers [William Smith, for one] they have employ'd or encourag'd, fully expose and confute their Falshoods and Calumnies."[23]

If Franklin's purpose was to arouse English opinion and persuade Parliament and the Ministry to support and confirm the Assembly's pre-eminent place in provincial government, he did not succeed.[24] The Ministry was neither convinced nor much influenced by the book; Parliament did not overturn ministerial policy; and private citizens in England did not petition the government to help Franklin. Those few in England who were disposed to favor Franklin and his cause applauded the book; those who opposed the legislative pretensions of the colonies or backed Penn largely ignored it. In these years Englishmen did not respond to the power of Franklin's pen when it was devoted to a cause of little interest or political value to any important group in politics.

Hence one of the political devices that had worked so well in Philadelphia was not successful in England. The Assembly gained little, and Penn was not overthrown. Indeed, Franklin's special talents proved something of a disadvantage. Fothergill, who was often critical of Franklin's tactics but was nonetheless a loyal friend, noted in 1758:

B. Franklin has not yet been able to make much progress in his affairs. Reason is hard with fear: the representations are considered as the effects of Superior Art; and his reputation as a man, a philosopher, and a Statesman, only serve to render his Station more difficult and perplexing: Such is the unhappy turn of mind of most of those, who constitute the world of influence in this country. You must allow him time, and without repining. He is equally able and Sollicitous to serve the province, but his obstructions are next to insurmountable; Great pains had been taken and very successfully to render him odious and his integrity suspected to those to whom he must first apply.[25]

Penn had shrewdly predicted Franklin's failure in England. When Peters and other proprietary men in Pennsylvania had expressed their fear that Franklin's reputation and accomplishments in science would open the doors and minds of English leaders, Penn calmly replied, "I think that I wrote you that Mr Franklin's popularity is nothing here and that he will be looked very cooly upon by great Peeople, there are very few of any consequence that have heard of his Electrical Experiments, those matters being attended to by a particular Sett of People, many of whom of the greatest consequence I know well, but it is quite another sort of People who are to determine the Dispute between us. I do not care how soon he comes, and am no ways uneasy at the determination."²⁶ The Proprietor knew English politicians; neither the reputation of a scientist nor the skill of a philosopher counted for much in their deliberations.

Some of the obstacles Franklin faced in England were unavoidable; he could not change the mentality of the politicians nor convince them against their will. What he failed to show was the skillful politician's adroit ability to avoid actions and situations that increased his difficulties and strengthened his opponents. Obsessed with a hatred for Penn that was far greater than the Assembly's grievances warranted, he could not endure the leisurely pace of negotiations with the Proprietor. English politicians and Quakers warned him not to press too hard, but as early as February 1758 he wrote, "My patience with the Proprietors is almost tho' not quite spent. They continue to profess a sincere Desire of settling everything with the Assembly amicably on reasonable Terms . . . so I am oblig'd to wait from time to time, or take upon myself the Blame of Rashness, if I should come to open War with People suppos'd to be so well disposed, who, it will be said, might have been brought to very reasonable Terms by an Agent of more Temper."²⁷ There was some justice in Franklin's charge that the Proprietor was acting slowly, but there were large issues at stake. Time served Penn; for while he delayed, Franklin and the Assembly might take hasty and ill-considered actions that would strengthen his case against them.²⁸

As the negotiations dragged on into 1758, Franklin repeatedly sought to make the Assembly take a positive stand in favor of royal government for the colony. At his request Jackson drew up a legal study that examined point by point the soundness of the Assembly's claims, the probable reactions of the Crown, and the course the Assembly might take to obtain its wishes. Although profusely expressing his personal sympathy for the legislature's cause, Jackson offered some serious doubts and obstacles for the Assembly to consider. These reflections should have served as a warning and a brake upon further aggressive measures against the Proprietor. After examining some of the most important rights demanded by the Assembly, Jackson declared:

The Models of Bills, especially those for raising Money sent over by Mr Penn are certainly improper in general, yet I doubt if they would be generally disapproved by the Council, as our Administration goes further in framing Laws for Ireland. . . . The Disposition of Publick Money, and a Militia, are Points on which tho' I entirely agree in my private opinion with the Assembly of Pennsylvania, yet which I am convinced would be determined against them, both by the Privy Council and the Parliament, were they formally to be brought before either. But I should not think it at all advisable to drive any of these Points, much less all at once to a formal Decision at present, if at all; the Safest is the Dispute on the Tax Mr Penn is to pay . . . to keep up the Ball of Contention 'till a proper Opportunity offers either to dispute, or amicably to determine [the matter]. . . . If Mr Penn continues to thwart the Province in necessary Measures of Government . . . they should return him the same Treatment, and Harrass him from time to time, with Applications on every small Point.[29]

Admittedly, Jackson seemed to encourage the Assembly to sustain the conflict, but at the same time he offered them little hope of winning ministerial or Parliamentary support. He bluntly stated that the Ministry could carry its policy and wishes in Parliament "with as little Struggle and Opposition as possible. A formidable Opposition to them, either within Doors or without they provide against."[30] Jackson could argue on both sides of a point, but in 1758 he was clearly of the opinion that Parliament would not overturn ministerial policy, especially upon a colonial question. He thus was offering little hope that Franklin's *Historical Review* would win support for the Assembly. Yet Franklin continued to expect that the publication of the *Historical Review* would achieve important results in Parliament. Though the work had been completed, Franklin delayed the printing because "It is thought best not to publish it till a little before the next Session of Parliament."[31]

Both Franklin and the Assembly disregarded Jackson's advice

against pressing for a formal decision. In view of the subsequent actions of the Assembly in 1759, the admonition "to keep up the ball of contention" was the most popular advice in Jackson's message. Generously interpreting the phrase, the Assembly went far beyond the "safe" question of land taxation and initiated a general assault upon all powers of the executive part of the government.

It has been customary to praise the rise of legislative power in the colonial period as a sign of the maturing ability of the American colonies to manage their own affairs. The record of the Pennsylvania legislature in the 1750's, however, is dominated by a single theme: the legislature's unbridled determination to have its way. A small group of men exploited every executive weakness, extracted from the war crisis every possible concession and advantage, and—at the expense of the safety of the province—sustained their private policy of securing absolute legislative supremacy. By American or English constitutional standards of the eighteenth century or later, many of the Assembly's actions were petty, unprincipled, and tyrannical. Included in its measures was a systematic invasion of the legitimate powers of the executive by engrossing its authority over taxation, expenditure, appointment of fiscal officers, military establishments, Indian relations, and land management. It attempted to gain control over the judiciary and threatened the opposition with libel suits. When Governor Denny expressed some reluctance to bow to the Assembly's will, he was bribed. William Franklin's only regret was that the Assembly had not done a better job with opportunity: "I wonder when there was so good an Understanding between the Assembly and Governor they did not make an Attack on the Licenses for Taverns, Marriages, etc. It would have been worth while for the Province to have given him a considerable Sum of Money to have the Matter put on a Different Footing."[32]

Part of the blame for this destructive performance must fall on Franklin, who advised the Assembly that either Penn would surrender or the English government would assume control over the colony if there were "Tumults and Insurrections, that might prove the Proprietary Government insufficient to preserve Order, or show the People to be ungovernable." To this he piously added, "But such I hope will never happen." Then he continued, "I know not but a Refusal of the Assembly to lay Taxes, or of the People to pay them, unless the Proprietary Estate be taxed would be Sufficient."[33]

Just as Penn took advantage of Franklin's open hostility to discredit him before the Ministry, he found that the case of the Assembly vs. William Smith and William Moore helped him in England. The affair developed in Pennsylvania after Franklin left, but he was soon called upon to defend the Assembly's action when the case was reviewed in England. Sensing an opportunity to strike at both Smith and Penn, Franklin enthusiastically accepted the responsibility.[34]

To the anti-proprietary men in Pennsylvania, William Smith came to be the most detested representative of the proprietary faction. Happily received by Franklin when he first arrived in the colony, he had betrayed his friend by remaining loyal to Penn after the quarrel of 1755. Smith, the penman for the government party, was a skilled propagandist, and his writings, particularly the *Brief State*, rivaled Franklin's in their facile exposition and influence. His enemies were determined to punish him for this treason and opportunism and for the damage he had done to the reputation of the Quakers and the Assembly.

The opportunity for revenge came when it was discovered that Smith had assisted William Moore, a proprietary magistrate and later Smith's father-in-law, in the publication of an attack upon the legislature. The Assembly seized the two men and charged them with libeling the House. They were then brought to trial, wherein the justice was as speedy as it was political. Given little

chance to present a defense, they were condemned and hurried off
to jail, and those who attempted to assist them were threatened
with similar treatment. Hugh Roberts, a friend of Franklin's,
was pleased with this petty legislative tyranny and wrote him,
"The proceedings of the Assembly . . . had had this happy
effect to make the Scots clan who were very public in their
Clamours against the Conduct of the House, now communicate
their thoughts to each other in whispers under the thistle."[35]

To ensure its complete triumph, the Assembly refused to release the men on writs of habeas corpus. The only course open to
Smith—who, unlike Moore, refused to make the slightest submission to the Assembly to secure a release from jail—was an
appeal to the Crown for a review of the proceedings. Although
the Assembly tried to block this attempt for justice, Smith was
released and left for England to gather support for his case.

After considerable delay and legal maneuvering, the opinions
of Attorney General Charles Pratt and Solicitor General Charles
Yorke, acting for Smith and Penn, won out over the case presented by Franklin and his Solicitor, Joshua Sharpe, and Counsels
Parrot and De Grey.[36] The retention of Yorke and Pratt for the
plaintiff was a significant advantage for Penn. Under English law
Yorke and Pratt had to admit that a libel had in fact been committed against the Assembly. But on the technicality that the libel
had been done against an expired Assembly and the charge and
trial carried by a newly elected Assembly, which could not take
cognizance of a libel upon its predecessor, the case against Smith
was dismissed.[37]

This was a gratifying victory, but the real significance of the
case lay in the condemnation of the Assembly that Yorke and
Pratt presented to the Privy Council. In response to the Assembly's claim that its action against Smith and Moore was based
upon the precedents and like powers of the House of Commons,
the report declared that colonial legislatures were inferior bodies

and that there were no grounds for such claims or comparisons with the House of Commons. The specific charges were more serious: the Assembly was accused of denying the power of the King's writs, interfering with the powers of magistrates and judges, and attempting to hinder the application of a subject to the justice of the Crown. These were, the Privy Council agreed, high invasions of the Crown's prerogatives; the Assembly received formal notice of "His Majesty's displeasure."

Not stated in the formal presentation of the case but included in the general rebuke of the Assembly's methods was evidence of the legislature's vindictive tyranny over its political enemies in Pennsylvania. However involved in politics Moore and Smith truly were, they were regarded in England as a magistrate and a clergyman of the Church of England who were suffering legislative persecution. Penn took full advantage of this English sympathy to show that his case against the Assembly was also a defense of Crown, Church, and Justice. Acting with Smith and Jacob Duché, an Anglican clergyman in Philadelphia, Penn enlisted the interest and support of prominent clergymen in England. Duché wrote in May 1758, "I laid an Abstract of Mr. Smith's Case before the Bishop of Oxford, now his Grace of Canterbury, before Dr. Bearcroft, Dr. Nicolls, Dr. Chandler and others, who are all convinced that Mr. Smith is extremely injured and oppressed, and will use all their interest to serve him."[38] Penn thus gained friends among the leading clergy, whose political connections were sometimes just as valuable as their spiritual ones.[39]

Even Franklin had to admit that Smith had become something of a martyr. "He represents himself as a Clergyman persecuted by the Quakers, for the Services done the Church in opposing and exposing those Sectaries, and in that Light a Bishop recommended him to Oxford for a Degree of Doctor of Divinity, which it seems he has obtain'd; and if he can get a Benefice here, as possibly he may, it is not unlikely he will desert poor Philadelphia and by removing his Candle stick leave the Academy in the Dark."[40] Later, Smith had the pleasure of knowing that his degree from Oxford came before Franklin's.

Toward the end of 1759, Penn gathered together eleven bills passed by the Assembly and prepared objections to them for the consideration of the Privy Council.[41] Retaining the Attorney General and Solicitor General once again, Penn achieved, from the outset, counsel whose influence and prestige Franklin could not match in the presentation of his case.

The acts under review pertained to the granting and remitting of paper money; surveys and warrants; the appointment of judges, relief officers, and flour and stave officers; and the appointment of Franklin to receive money from Parliament for Pennsylvania's share of the reimbursement for war expenses. Judges, paper money, and the methods of taxing lands were the most important issues, and the ones over which the two opponents labored most diligently. But early in 1760 it became evident that there could be no real doubt about the outcome. Penn cheerfully declared, "Our objections to the several Acts are said by the Council and some proper People who have seen them to be very strong and very full and I believe we shall generally prevail—Sir Matthew Lambe,* I wrote you, had reported against several of the Bills."[42]

In June 1760, the Board of Trade made its report to the Privy Council and recommended repeal of "The Act for granting £100,000, The Act for remitting the £30,000 Paper Money, The Supplement to the Same, The Act for Warrants and Surveys, The Act for appointment of Judges, The Act for the Relief of Heirs and Devisees, and The Act against Lotterys and Plays." The Assembly was upheld only in the acts for the flour and stave officers,

---

* Lambe was adviser to Lord Mansfield in the Privy Council.

and the provision appointing Franklin receiver of Parliament's grant.[43]

On all the major issues Franklin and the Assembly suffered an overwhelming defeat. When the Privy Council took final action, based on the advice of the Board, it sustained the principles and opinions contained in the report, although it modified their application in some particulars. Penn obtained confirmation of his power to instruct his Governors and to require bonds from them for the performance of their duty. His right to an equal share in the selection of commissioners to spend appropriated funds was upheld, as were his claims to a fair determination of the amount and mode of land taxes. The Assembly was completely blocked in its attempt to secure control over the appointment of judges. Most of the other acts had been likewise rejected because they embodied some plan repugnant to the powers of the Proprietor, the laws of England, or the prerogatives of the Crown. As Penn had declared earlier, much to Franklin's anger, local laws or provincial constitutions and charters were subordinate to English interests and interpretations. When colonial usage differed, it must give way.[44]

This study of the legislative concepts and practices in Pennsylvania awakened the Ministry to the realization that a serious erosion of proprietary power, and by analogy of royal power, had taken place in the colony. To Penn's dismay, the Ministers now strongly rebuked him for not exerting his authority long before. Previously accused of taking too great an interest in his lands and rents, Penn found himself criticized for failing to uphold the powers entrusted to him by the Crown and to restrict the Assembly to a proper place in the government. In England Penn was blamed for leniency to the Assembly; in Pennsylvania he was accused of a monstrous tyranny.

In plain and unmistakable terms, the Ministry in 1760 presented to Pennsylvania a theory of English supremacy in colonial government which, if and when it were applied, would leave little substance in the Assembly's claims to competence in the larger areas of provincial government. There could be no doubt that the Crown intended to have strong and instructed executives, no legislative interference with judges, limited power to tax and to apply money, and an Imperial Indian policy instead of one managed by a local faction. In criticizing Penn, the Ministry told Pennsylvania that proprietary government had been easy, lax, and overly generous. Direct government by the Crown would be firmer and stronger.

Franklin chose not to interpret these opinions in this fashion. He saw in ministerial criticism of Penn the probable assumption of the government by the Crown. And if Penn were removed, Franklin had faith that no matter what theories of English supremacy might be advanced by the Ministry, a wise, informed, and reasonable government would not apply them. This faith that enlightened Ministers would eventually accede to power can be the only explanation of Franklin's incongruous pursuit of royal government for the colony after the debacle of 1760. His attempt to create a favorable interest in Parliament for the Assembly suggests that this may have been his long-range hope.

However strongly the Ministry declared its policy, there was no direct way of enforcing it in Pennsylvania except through the repeal of objectionable measures or through the cooperation of the Proprietor and the Assembly. It was still Penn's responsibility to apply and maintain the prerogatives and powers delegated to him. In view of his weakness and inability to manage the colony in the past, an increasing number of thoughtful politicians in Pennsylvania were certain that a weak Proprietor was more desirable than the greater power and influence of the Crown. The Charter of 1701 might be safer under Penn's government.

A LULL BETWEEN BATTLES

By all standards, Penn had achieved a resounding victory, and at the same time he had seen all of Franklin's efforts fail. Indeed, so great was his success that he was somewhat frightened. Too great a dependence upon the Crown put him in danger of being "swallowed up" by ambitious royal officials. Not wishing to become a "mere cypher" in the management of the colony, Penn was amenable to compromise in 1760. If the Assembly did not press him too hard, he was willing to relax the strict application of his rights so that the necessary functions of government might continue.

It would have been almost un-ministerial in 1760 to have allowed such a firm declaration of policy as was handed down by the Board of Trade to stand without some temporizing qualification. Hence, after accepting the report, Lord Mansfield in the Privy Council found it expedient to soften the Board's stand by compromise.

In 1759, at the height of its drive to stamp out the remains of proprietary power in financial matters, the Assembly had passed a measure proposing an issue of £100,000 in paper money, with taxation of proprietary estates and distress sale of lands to redeem it, if necessary. Governor Denny, succumbing to a bribe from the Assembly and pressure from Generals John Stanwix and Jeffrey Amherst, waived his instructions and passed the bill. When Penn protested the measure before the Board of Trade, the Solicitor

General and the Attorney General convinced the Board that the Assembly had seriously threatened the prerogatives of the Crown. Citing the Assembly's refusal to allow Penn a share in the nomination of tax officials and the inequality in the method of taxation —especially in the taxation of waste, unallocated, and unimproved lands—the Board agreed that the bill was discriminatory, inconsistent with natural equity and the laws of England, and in effect a confiscation of property for political reasons. It was further noted that the Assembly had passed the measure independent of the Governor, though management of revenues was properly shared with the executive, and he alone was competent to handle it.[1]

These serious charges would have doomed the measure in the Privy Council had not Lord Mansfield proposed a solution that would allow it to pass while still preserving the Proprietor's rights. Without denying the objections to the bill, Mansfield suggested that if Franklin would agree to a number of concessions, it might be saved. These concessions, embodying Penn's major objections to the measure, were designed to ensure that the Assembly would, in the future, carefully respect the Proprietor's rights concerning all tax and paper-money bills. Behind Mansfield's action lay the British Army's obvious need for Pennsylvania's help in the coming military campaigns. Stanwix and Amherst had begged Governor Denny to accept whatever the Assembly offered on any terms. If the money bill, presented in 1759, were repealed, Pennsylvania would contribute nothing to colonial defense in 1760 and 1761. The Privy Council could not afford to uphold principles at the price of endangering the war effort.

Surprisingly enough, Penn quickly consented to Mansfield's scheme, and advised his friends in Pennsylvania to accept it: "I hope you will approve of the Agreement entered into with the Agents, rather than the Tax Bill should be repealed, as it now obliges them to induce the Assembly to pass Laws, to remove all the reasonable objections . . . this was my Lord Mansfield's Scheme and I must confess I prefer it to the other method, tho' the Attorney General was of opinion it ought to be repealed, that is it would have been more for the Dignity of the Crown to have done it."[2] Part of Penn's relief over the Council's decision stemmed from his appreciation of what would have happened to the economy of the province if the Assembly had been forbidden to issue additional paper money. He also believed that he was protecting the colony from both the aggression of the Assembly and the ambition of the Crown. He was striving, he declared, for "a just ballance in the Government, as the most permanent security of the Liberty of the People."[3]

Franklin also promptly accepted Mansfield's proposal, and in so doing showed an abrupt change of attitude about his power to speak for the future action of the legislature. When Penn had previously offered terms for a settlement, based upon certain concessions on his part in return for the Assembly's promise to refrain from introducing wholly objectionable measures, Franklin had flatly refused.[4] He reported to the Assembly, "The Truth is, I did refuse to take upon me to settle a Money Bill with the Proprietors, as having no Power to do an Act of that kind that should be obligatory on the Assembly, for that they neither had given nor could give me such a Power, it being no less than giving me a Power of making Laws for the Province; a Power which, tho' the Assembly are trusted with by the People, they cannot delegate to another."[5] But Franklin now had no such scruples. His acceptance was necessary if the bill was to survive, and he willingly gave it.

Whether he never intended to honor the agreement or knew that the Assembly would ignore his advice in any case, Franklin made no real effort to convince the House that it should respect the bargain made with the Ministry. His later remarks suggest he believed that the conditions imposed to protect Penn's rights were unjust and not binding. The Assembly did not censure him for the part he took in the affair, but it was unhappy with the result. Peters declared, "The Assembly, enraged at the Repeal of their Laws and the Force put upon their Agents to stipulate for them Amendment of the exceptionable parts of their Supply Acts by a new one, have refused to pay the poor Soldiers for their over time. . . . They still think they are in the Right and that the Privy Council and Proprietaries are in a Confederacy against them."[6] At any rate, the Assemblymen found ways to avoid compliance with the agreement, though they never formally denied it.

At first Penn placed great hope in the compromise.[7] He believed that not only would the Assembly be bound to follow a more cautious policy in the future, but Franklin could not very well repudiate an agreement that he had accepted in England. This limitation upon Franklin's political power was uppermost in Penn's mind when he wrote, "Mr Franklin hears so much said by both the Attorney and Sollicitor General of the Assembly's intention to establish a Democracy, if not an oligarchy in the place of his Majesty's Government, and of the Duty we were under to oppose it . . . that I think he must use his endeavours to bring his Friends into a compliance with that Agreement."[8] But the old problem remained; there was no effective way to coerce a rebellious legislature. Rejection of bills by appeal to the Privy Council was a clumsy and time-consuming procedure that confused and paralyzed the government of the colony. But aside from this, there was little that Penn or the Crown could do to limit legislative pretensions. In the end Penn would have to depend upon the Assembly's willingness to work with the proprietary government. It was not a hopeful prospect—especially as the Ministry had shown an easy inclination to compromise principles in order to satisfy the need for money.

Despite the fact that from 1761 to 1763 the Assembly failed to follow the agreement and continued to harass both Governor Hamilton and Governor John Penn with objectionable bills, the disputes over paper money and taxation did recede from the center of political contention. With the end of the war the colony needed less money and less taxation, and Thomas Penn was more willing to accede to money bills because his revenues from Pennsylvania were rising rapidly.[9] The colony was finally beginning to pay large dividends to the Family—so much so that in 1765 Penn would contemplate using these revenues to support the proprietary Governor. Moreover, Penn found that, in practice, taxation of his lands did not prove to be an intolerable burden. He also discovered that, with a few exceptions, the local assessments were justly and reasonably made.

Disputes between the Governors and the legislature continued through 1763, but much of the fury and bitterness went out of them. Governor Hamilton, who had resumed office in 1759, was a much abler executive than Denny had been; he was also a Pennsylvanian and had the respect of most politicians in the colony— even the Quakers. When John Penn, the Proprietor's nephew, succeeded Hamilton in 1763, the Pennsylvanians had to adjust to the novel experience of having a resident member of the Family in the executive position. Young Penn was given a chance to prove himself a friend or an enemy to the legislature. Even Franklin expressed his willingness to allow him a period of grace:

The new Governor arriv'd before my Return; I waited on him to pay my Respects, and have since met him often in various Places at Dinners, and among the Commissioners for carrying on the War of which I am one. He is civil, and I endeavour to fail in no Point of Respect; so I think we shall have no personal Difference, at least I will give no occasion. For tho' I cordially dislike and despise the Uncle [Thomas Penn] for demeaning himself so far as to back bite and abuse me to Friends and to Strangers, as you well know he does, I shall keep that Acct open with him only, and some time or other we may have a Settlement.[10]

The Assembly also knew that there were limits beyond which it could not go without inciting Penn to attempt repeal, with the certain support of the Ministry. To this extent, the wild aggressiveness of 1757 to 1759 had been curbed. Direct attacks on Penn had not worked; the Assembly found more subtle ways to gain its wishes. Caution was advisable from another standpoint; as early as 1759, there were rumors about the sweeping reformation of colonial policy and administration that would take place when the war ended. One of the most certain reforms was a uniform regulation of colonial paper money. Penn warned his friends in Pennsylvania, "Our disputes with the Assembly about Paper Money will soon be at an end, as a Bill is to be brought into Parliament, to put all the Colonys in that respect on the same footing with New England."[11]

Representing the affairs of the province in England had been a tedious and unrewarding task for Franklin. It had not, however, taken all of his time. Travel, visits, entertainment, and illness occupied him during much of his stay. After the decision of the Privy Council in 1760, Franklin devoted more and more time to these non-political pursuits. All of his activities were of interest in Pennsylvania, and Thomas Penn reported, "He has spent most of his time in Philosophical, and especially in Electrical Matters, having generally Company in a Morning to see those Experiments, and Musical performances on Glasses, where any one that knows him, carrys his Friends."[12]

Although Franklin's popularity remained great in Philadelphia, there were signs that many of the old Quaker leaders were working for his political downfall. The mixture of jealousy, ambition, and Quaker exclusiveness that William Logan displayed in letters to John Smith in 1761 presaged political danger for Franklin when he returned to Pennsylvania:

As to Benjamin Franklin, I cannot on all the Enquiry I could make in London find out where nor how He spends his Time, excepting it be in travell about and seeing the Curiosities of the Countrey. I find Doctor Fothergill, John Hunt and most other Friends here in London have no Extraordinary Opinion of him nor any Good he has done or Intends to do our Countrey, and Greatly admire at his Continuance here. I know he is looked upon on our side of the Water as a Second Sir William Pitt, perhaps their Eyes may be opened in time and they may see clearer. Pray let these Hints of him be to thyself.[13]

The English Quakers were indeed moving toward open opposition to Franklin's plans and his domination of the Assembly. Their opposition would contribute to his defeat in 1764.

Although political warfare between Penn and the Assembly diminished, the battle between Penn and Franklin continued. Penn did his best to prevent Franklin from receiving the Parliamentary grant to Pennsylvania. His delaying tactics, which found ready support in the Treasury, were largely responsible for Franklin's continued stay in England. In time, Franklin succeeded in obtaining the funds, but his temper was not improved by Penn's actions.[14] The Proprietor and his friends in England maintained their untiring efforts to undermine Franklin's reputation and standing. To a considerable extent their work was successful. As Fothergill had reported, many powerful leaders in the government had a natural suspicion of Franklin, not only because he represented the distasteful Assembly cause, but also because of his scientific and intellectual attainments. Although Franklin used his charm and talents to remove some of this prejudice, much of it remained and was increased by Penn's efforts. That these attitudes in England injured his political career in Pennsylvania was clear. It is also likely that they affected his later work in behalf of compromise to preserve the Empire. Part of the ministerial fury that fell on Franklin in 1774 may be traced to Penn's campaign against him in the 1750's and 1760's.

Of course, Franklin was anxious to repay the proprietary leaders in kind. He had an opportunity in 1760, when William Smith toured England seeking contributions for the Academy in Philadelphia. Franklin was willing to sacrifice the welfare of the Academy, whatever the cost, in order to strike at Smith. Charging him with perverting the Academy for political and sectarian purposes (a charge that contained considerable truth), he warned his friends not to give aid to the enemy. Politics had engendered such passion and spite on both sides that worthy institutions suffered.

Before leaving for Pennsylvania, Franklin undertook a highly secret project against Penn which he hoped would topple him if nothing else did. After establishing an acquaintance with Springett Penn, who was a direct descendant of William Penn and a nephew of Thomas Penn, but who had no direct rights of succession to the government or lands of Pennsylvania, Franklin wrote to Old Party supporter Edward Pennington in Philadelphia requesting him to investigate some disputed property holdings that were believed to belong to Springett. Hoping to prove that Thomas Penn had defrauded his nephew out of his property, Franklin declared that evidence of such fraud would be sufficient to have Thomas removed from the government by English courts. Franklin had found lawyers in England who doubted that the government of Pennsylvania had ever been legally conveyed to its present holders. In May 1761, he urged Pennington to the "utmost secrecy" and declared that Springett was a "sensible, discrete young Man, which makes me the more regret that the Government as well as the Property of our Province should pass out of that Line."[15] But lack of evidence forced Franklin to drop the issue. These opinions and plans suggest that Franklin's real antipathy to proprietary government was directed at the person of Thomas Penn rather than at the type of government.

A chatter of speculation broke out in Pennsylvania in 1762 when the news arrived that William Franklin had secured the royal governorship of New Jersey. All parties in the colony wondered what the appointment meant for Pennsylvania politics: was this a sign that Franklin was favored by the new Ministry under Lord Bute? If so, then the recent decisions against the Assembly might be revised or reversed. The anxiety of the proprietary faction in Pennsylvania was intense. Hamilton wrote to Penn, "Every body concludes that this must have been brought about by some strong Interest his Father must have obtained in England, but with whom no Body here pretends to know. If you do, I beg You will be pleased to inform me."[16]

Penn's answer provided the probable explanation: "The New Jersey Government was refused by Pownall, and less Interest was sufficient than to any place of two hundred Pounds a year here, it was done by the direction of Lord Bute, and Dr. Pringle came from that Lord to the Secretary of State about it, whether he recommended him himself I cannot tell, he is Lord Bute's Physician and a friend of Franklin's—young Franklin sollicited less than a Month before to be Deputy Secretary of Carolina."[17]

There was no evidence that Lord Bute regarded the appointment as a sign of favor for Franklin's political views or for the Assembly's case. Later it was believed in Pennsylvania that Bute and the Ministry were trying to influence the actions of the father by making the son a royal official. Both of these opinions largely represented wishful thinking on the part of Franklin's friends and enemies. Penn's guess that William obtained the position because Pringle used the requisite interest at the proper time appears to be the most likely reason for the appointment.

When Franklin returned to Philadelphia in 1763, receiving an almost royal reception from his friends, he found the City and the Assembly thoroughly tired of war and of all the expenses, troubles, requisitions, and discomforts that had accompanied it. Philadelphians were preparing to enjoy the peace that had been so long in coming. For a time, this general weariness had a soothing effect upon political warfare. But hope for peace was quickly ended in the summer of 1763 by the news of the Indian rebellion in the West. With the frontier areas of the colony once again under attack, the politicians responded almost exactly as they had in 1754 and 1755. Political issues were quickly reheated when Governor Hamilton requested the Assembly to provide funds and men for defense. Led by the strengthened Quaker and Quaker-nominated faction, the Assembly showed that it had learned little in ten years. Rejecting the Governor's proposals together with similar requests from General Amherst, it would do no more than give a trifling number of men for guard duty.[18] In time the rebellion was put down, but the government of the colony could not claim any credit for Colonel Bouquet's victory at Bushy Run. The people and settlements on the frontier had once again received nothing more than political arguments from their government in Philadelphia.

Without political organization, direction, or much political consciousness, the settlers in the West, who were predominantly Scotch-Irish and German, had needed time to focus their grievances upon some object. The disaster that had struck them had been sudden; there had been little time for organization, petitions, and remonstrances. After the danger had passed, a reaction set in. Hatred for all Indians, fear of Indian treachery, fury at what seemed to be Quaker and Moravian coddling of the Indians, and bitter resentment toward the eastern politicians—especially the Quakers—contributed to their spontaneous and brutal attacks upon the "peaceful" Indians at the Conestoga Moravian settlement. The massacre of these Indians and the destruction of their settlements was an act of violent protest that had been long in coming, and it reflected the settlers' inability to make their discontent felt in lawful political action through their legislature.[19]

The fact that the Quaker candidates continued to hold seats in the Assembly for York and Lancaster counties testified to the Old Party's still firm grip on the election machinery. However, there is little evidence that the westerners, especially the Scotch-Irish, had the capacity to play a more forceful role in politics before 1763. Discontent existed, but it had not been sufficiently organized to be effective in politics. Therefore, undemocratic as the political domination of Assembly by the three eastern counties was, it had gone unchallenged.

In Philadelphia the reaction to the brutality of the massacre was revealing, if not surprising. Horrified and badly frightened by the affront to law and order, the politicians dropped their private quarrels to form a united front to the western menace. The solidarity of the politicians was spontaneous, and Governor John Penn, Quaker and proprietary leaders, and Benjamin Franklin responded as one.[20] From December 1763 to February 1764, the Assembly and the Governor worked together in unprecedented harmony. Both issued orders demanding the prompt apprehension of the murderers. In addition, the government, under Quaker direction, sought to provide protection and refuge for other threatened Indians in the colony.[21]

The first signs that the political harmony in Philadelphia would not last came in December 1763, when it became evident that the leaders of the massacre were not being apprehended. Suspicious that proprietary magistrates were not being diligent in searching for the criminals and that such proprietary leaders as Edward Shippen in Lancaster County and Colonel John Armstrong in Cumberland were sympathetic to the westerners, the Assembly demanded that the sheriff, the coroner, and the magistrates from Lancaster County be called to Philadelphia to testify. In addition, it prepared to pass a bill to require that the men charged with the murder of the Indians be brought to the eastern part of the colony for trial.[22]

Neither the Governor nor the proprietary leaders could accept the political motives implicit in this criticism of the magistrates and the leaders in Lancaster. Moreover, the proposal to remove men to the East for trial was regarded as an infringement upon proper methods of justice. This bill aroused heated opposition in Philadelphia, and the Assembly prudently withdrew it. But it continued to charge that John Penn was dilatory and indecisive in upholding law and order and in seeking the guilty.[23]

A renewed danger from the West in January 1764 again brought a temporary end to these arguments in Philadelphia. Weary of attacks by the westerners, many Indians had sought refuge in the City. When neither the Governor nor the Quakers could find a new home for the refugees and returned them to Philadelphia, the western settlers, who thought the Philadelphians were coddling the Indians, rose up in a new fury and threatened to march to the capitol. Faced with this danger, the politicians joined together to provide a defense for the City against the threatened invasion. Franklin spoke for the Philadelphia gentry when he later denounced the settlers from the western counties of Pennsylvania as "white savages."

Between the massacre of the Indians in December 1763 and the March of the Paxton Boys in February 1764, the Assembly passed some remarkable measures. It belatedly gave General Amherst the 1,000 men he had earlier requested to defend the province against the Indians. Governor Penn received a bill of credit, without the usual squabbles about constitutional issues, and the Assembly passed an "Act for Preventing Tumults and Riotous Assemblies."[24] At Franklin's suggestion, an association for defense was hurriedly formed, and it got full support from the gentlemen of the City. As a final measure of military preparedness, some 200 Quakers abandoned pacifism and took up arms to defend Philadelphia.

The vigorous defense efforts against an invasion of white settlers offered a startling contrast with the niggardly help that these same settlers had received from their government when Indian attacks had occurred. Likewise, the spectacle of Quakers eagerly assisting in military measures and even arming themselves made a mockery of the professed principles of the Society. The contrast between the past professions and the present actions of the Assembly, the Quakers, and the Governor increased the bitterness of the western settlers.[25]

Franklin threw his whole support behind the preparations under way in Philadelphia. In the Assembly, and with Governor Penn, he took a leading part in the legislative actions and in rallying Philadelphians to join the association. Like the rest of the leaders in the City, he urged swift punishment of the murderers and a firm defense against any invasion from the West.

When the Paxton Boys approached fortified Philadelphia the ending was an anticlimax. In orderly fashion, the marchers listened to the mediation of Franklin and Galloway, who represented the Assembly, and Benjamin Chew and Thomas Willing, who represented the Governor. It was agreed that the marchers' representatives would present their grievances to the government and then retire peacefully. After it had done so, the delegation received assurances of prompt consideration by the Governor and the Assembly. In a few days the Paxton Boys broke up and returned to their homes.[26]

As soon as the danger to Philadelphia was removed, the massacre, the march, and the grievances became violent political issues. The temporary unit of Governor and Assembly dissolved into an acrimonious exchange of charges and countercharges. Attempting to place the blame for the recent events upon the Governor, the Assembly declared that the failure to preserve peace and law in the colony arose from the weakness and cupidity of John Penn and the proprietary government. As was to be expected, the intimate association of Franklin and the Governor had been too artificial to last. As soon as John Penn no longer needed Franklin's help, the alliance ceased. Piqued by this abrupt change, Franklin led the Assembly party in denouncing the whole proprietary government including both John and Thomas Penn. Lost in the melee of political recriminations, the grievances of the West went unanswered.

During the preparations for defending the City, the leaders found that many people were openly sympathetic with the western counties and almost as strongly hostile to the Indians. This hatred for the Indians had been demonstrated against the refugees lodged in Philadelphia, and it had been necessary to assign troops to protect them.[27] It was an ominous sign that when the danger to the City from the Paxton Boys was at its height, many Presbyterians and a sizable number of Germans refused to join the association or bear arms. By appealing to the clergy and telling frightening stories of what would happen to lives and property if the marchers entered the City, the leaders did succeed in rallying the population, but the response had not been enthusiastic.[28] The gentlemen, including Franklin, could sneer at these uncouth people, but many Philadelphians must have been impressed by the orderly and peaceful effort of the westerners to secure justice and redress of their grievances. A sympathetic link between the "meaner sort" in Philadelphia and the settlers in the western part of Pennsylvania was established in 1764.

About the only persons to prosper from the tumults of 1763 and 1764 were the printers. From February 1764 until the election in the fall, every group and most prominent leaders in politics rushed to publish their views, accusations, and defenses. This was a rare event in Pennsylvania's political history: an election for the Assembly was now to be fought over real issues and with a wider popular participation than before. The pamphlet war opened a campaign that asked for more support than the politicians of Pennsylvania had needed or wanted in past elections.

THE ELECTION OF 1764

Proprietary government had not been popular in Pennsylvania for many decades. What thin support it could muster came chiefly from the non-Quaker gentry of Philadelphia and from office-holders and a few county magnates. The proprietary leaders rarely sought a broad support for the government from the ordinary citizens of the province; on the few occasions when they did seek it, their attempts were so halfhearted and showed such obvious distaste and disdain for "democratical" politics that they usually failed. As gentlemen, they were willing to receive support but not to solicit it.

Over the years, the opposing factions had won elections and control of the Assembly almost by default. Posing as the champions of local rights and powers against the tyranny of a distant, greedy landowner who cared so little for the welfare of the colony that he would not come to govern it in person, the partisans of the Assembly used skillful propaganda and a firm hold on the election process to dominate provincial politics. As if this advantage weren't enough, the proprietary forces often contributed enough inept tactics, ill-considered policies, and private rivalries among themselves to ensure their opponents' success.

That the proprietary government in 1764 could suddenly win substantial support from people hitherto outside the political order, defeat the two leaders of the opposition, and gain an increase in Assembly seats suggests that Pennsylvania almost achieved a long-overdue political reformation. At a time when the executive part of government throughout the colonies was being battered by legislative and popular pressures, Penn's government emerged for a brief moment as the leader of a rebellion against the domination of the so-called popular, legislative party. To Franklin and his Quaker allies must go a large share of the responsibility for so misunderstanding and misjudging the interests and aspirations of their fellow Pennsylvanians that the proprietary was able to gain a following that it had never before achieved through its own efforts.

When the Paxton Boys withdrew from Philadelphia, without settling their grievances, the Assembly immediately attacked the Governor for allowing the tumults of the past months to happen. The Quakers, on their own, added a shrill denunciation of proprietary Indian policy including a restatement of the old charges of land fraud and general mistreatment of the Indians. In their pamphlets asserting that peaceful treatment of the Indians would have prevented the uprising of 1763, they included explanations and justifications for the martial actions of the armed brethren of Philadelphia.

Franklin and John Penn had faced the danger of the march of the westerners as brother Philadelphians. This camaraderie might have meant better days for Pennsylvania politics if John Penn had not dispensed with Franklin's help and advice as soon as the danger had passed. Once again a member of the Proprietary Family had hurt Franklin's pride. His jocular tone in a letter to Fothergill scarcely hid his resentment: "This Proprietary Governor did me the Honour on an Alarm, to run to my House at Midnight, with his Counsellors at his Heels, for Advice, and made it his Head Quarters for some time: And within four and twenty Hours, your old Friend was a common Soldier, a Counsellor, a kind of Dictator, an Ambassador to the Country Mob, and on their Returning home, *Nobody* again."[1]

Franklin's retaliation was prompt in coming: he drove through a series of resolves that virtually declared the Assembly in rebellion against the Proprietor.[2] Pleased with his work, Franklin wrote to Strahan in March 1764, "Such a Necklace of Resolves! and all *nemine contradicente* . . . If you can find room for them and our Messages in the Chronicle . . . I should be glad to have them there, as it may prepare the minds of those in Power for an application that I believe will shortly be made from the Province to the Crown, to take the Government into its own Hands.—They talk of Sending me over with it."[3] This letter and others like it announced to those in England who might help that Franklin had taken the offensive against the Proprietor.

As leader of the Assembly, Franklin, with Galloway's help, chose and defined the issues. He declared that the proprietary government must bear the full blame for the massacre, for letting the "white savages" of the West go unpunished, and for endangering Philadelphia by failing to preserve order and prevent the marchers from entering the City.[4] To these charges, he added the whole list of past grievances against the Proprietor. Denunciation of Penn's government was normal practice and would probably have gained Franklin the traditional backing of the groups and factions who opposed the power of the executive, but his solution, royal government for Pennsylvania, was not easily accepted. The Quakers, moreover, had something else to add: unless the Old Party continued in power, proprietary-Presbyterian anarchy would result. By defining the enemy as the proprietary government plus the Presbyterians, the Quakers naturally drove these two together for common defense.[5]

John Penn and the other leaders in Philadelphia had joined the Quakers in denouncing the shocking massacre of the peaceful Indians and the disorderly behavior of the western settlers. The proprietary gentlemen had not, at first, thought of these events in terms of factional or political advantage. But as the attacks by

Franklin, the Assembly, and the Quakers increased, they were forced to change their position and seek support from the West.[6]

Before 1764, most settlers in the West had made little distinction between the Governor and the Assembly in placing the blame for the lack of provincial defense. The whole government in Philadelphia seemed equally at fault. Now the proprietary leaders tried to make the distinction clear, and with the help of friendly clergymen, they told of repeated efforts by the Governor to build forts, to supply men and money for frontier defense, and to prosecute war against the Delawares in 1757. The pamphleteers hammered away at the notorious record of Quaker pacificism, the Friendly Association, and the recent example of Quaker arming against the westerners. Another western grievance was the lack of equitable representation in the Assembly. Penn had made some effort in behalf of obtaining a greater number of seats for the new counties so that Quaker domination in Bucks, Chester, and Philadelphia might be counterbalanced. The proprietary claimed that if the Old Party won the election, there would be little chance for a redistribution of seats.

To the Quakers, the lawlessness, savagery, and leveling spirit that had recently terrified Philadelphians, was not only "lower sort" and western; it was Scotch-Irish and, especially, Presbyterian.[7] Quaker fears were transmitted to England, where Peter Collinson used anti-Presbyterian information to warn Lord Hyde in 1764:

I presume my Dear Lord is no Stranger to the comotions in Pensilvania, in which the Riotous Presbyterians by Illicit Arts and contrivances Jockeyed out of the Assembly my Ingenious Friend Mr Franklin. The legislature here in England may do well to think of some Checks to the Torrent of Presbyterian Power which prevails in the Governments to the Eastward of Pennsylvania—they still have Oliverian spirit in them, and if ever a Revolution is attempted to sett up themselves independent of their Mother Country, it will arise from this prevailing Presbyterian Faction. Mr Allen mention'd in the Letter sent lately over, he is their Chief Justice, a strong Presbyterian a crafty man, is secretly the Head, Spring, and Support of that Interest.[8]

While Franklin did not publicly rant at the Presbyterians, he did nothing to distinguish between groups or people in the West. He had called them "white savages" and "those mad People on the Frontier." And he added, "But they and their Abbettors are filling up fast the measure of their Iniquity, and Justice will ere long overtake them all."[9]

The Presbyterians responded in the obvious manner; they joined the proprietary side. Penn found that the Presbyterian clergy, no longer as seriously divided by old controversies, became very useful allies in the West, and William Allen was for the first time able to command their strong support in Philadelphia. Sympathetic with their co-religionists and countrymen of the West, and daily abused by the Quakers, the congregations in Philadelphia and nearby responded to the call of their clergy and Allen. Haughty and aristocratic as ever, Allen instructed his people on the proper behavior at the election. He informed Penn, "I told all the people, particularly the Presbyterians, that I would not serve in Assembly if they were guilty of the least breaches of the peace, and these my sentiments I conveyed to all parts of the Province."[10] Pennsylvania did have a peaceful though hotly contested election: Allen's imperious orders were obeyed.

Franklin made his most serious blunder when he made the petition for royal government the essential part of his re-election campaign, for he thereby divided his friends and drove his opponents into a closer alliance. The Presbyterians, for example, were less interested in the question of a change of executive than they were in defeating the Quakers. But by tying the Quakers, the Assembly, and royal government into one package, Franklin forced the Presbyterians and others into strong opposition to the whole in order to defeat or protest against a part.

This dilemma bore equally hard on the Quakers. Whatever hopes they had of restoring their old unity and power were demolished in 1764. Many of the leading Quakers in Philadelphia could not accept the idea of royal government, and Pemberton, Logan, and Norris rebelled on the issue, refusing to support Franklin.[11] Norris resigned his long-held place as Speaker of the Assembly rather than agree to the petition, although he gave ill health as his official reason. Pemberton spoke for these Quakers when he declared that "the Quakers will suffer under the Proprietor rather than risk losing all."[12] The "all" was the Charter of 1701, which secured the liberties and rights not only of the Quakers but of all Pennsylvanians.

In England the Friends remained strongly opposed to any change of government, and they cooperated with the Quakers in Philadelphia who held similar views.[13] Logan wrote from London, "It is generally thought here that our Assembly have been much too precipitate in petitioning a Change and that it proceeds more from a Malevolent Heart than a right way of thinking. I am afraid there is too much truth in their Surmises." He later reported that the English Friends were pressing Jackson to act against the petition. "Our agent Jackson would not proceed in the Affair without further orders and the advice of Friends of our Society there to encourage it, which He is assured that they will Not, as they are in General against the change."[14]

However, opposition from the "best" Quakers in Philadelphia and London did not carry the weight that it once had. Neither the decision of the Yearly Meeting "to stand against the Petition and Petition signers" nor the commands of the old leaders brought obedience from the Friends in the country or even in Philadelphia.[15] Faced with the frightening specter of Presbyterian ascendancy and a powerful new rival to their political power, allied with the Proprietor, most of the county Quakers and many in the City remained loyal to Franklin. They had no real choice. With Franklin they had a guarantee of continued power in the Old Party and the Assembly; without him or in opposition to his policies, they invited proprietary-Presbyterian domination. Allen chided these political Quakers, stating, "I have taken a good deal of pains with the contending partys and find that many of the serious Quakers say they disapprove of the change of Government and of Franklin's measures; But still they appear to be afraid of disoblidging him, and as I tell them they worship him as the Indians do the Devil, for fear."[16]

On the other hand, Franklin still could not do without the Quakers, for only with their support could he command a majority in the House. Whatever differences of opinion Franklin had about defense or the Indians, he was obliged to accept and defend Quaker policies and interests in the election campaign. Thus, he associated himself, and was associated with, the faults and weaknesses of the Quakers as well as their advantages. In the eyes of many, he was the leader of the eastern, Quaker-dominated, pacifist, Indian-coddling, undemocratic Assembly party. During 1764, moreover, Franklin did nothing to show any sympathy or understanding for the large number of people who lived beyond Philadelphia. He and his party did not apply in Pennsylvania the rights he had frequently mentioned in England.[17]

Like other groups in Pennsylvania, the members of the Church of England were divided in politics. They were not, as has been said, all on the proprietary side. The feuds that had plagued the Anglican congregations in Philadelphia in the past continued to plague them. Peters's return to the pastorate after resigning the Secretaryship of the colony did not improve Anglican harmony. Some Churchmen were close friends of Franklin, some feared the rise of the Presbyterians more than they despised the Quakers, and a good number thought that the Church would benefit under royal government. Allen estimated that about half of the Anglicans in Philadelphia would vote for the Old Party, but a significant number were also active for the proprietary.

The proprietary leaders had made an effort in the charity schools to cultivate the interest of the Germans and especially of the Lutheran and Reformed churches. Although the schools had failed in their aim to anglicize the Germans, a friendly relationship had been established between the clergy of both denominations and the proprietary government. And in 1764 Penn found that a sizable number of Lutheran and Reformed clergymen were willing to work for the Proprietary Party, first in advising their congregations to vote against the Old Party, and then in collecting signatures on petitions against an appeal for royal government.

Both Lutheran and Reformed leaders had been unhappy with the alliance of the Moravians and other sects with the Quakers. On both religious and political grounds they desired that the Germans should be better organized, educated, and led; the sects and the Quakers blocked all of these efforts. In the West, many Germans who were not pacifists responded like their Scotch-Irish neighbors to the problems of defense, Indians, and representation in the Assembly. And many feared that a victory for the Old Party and a change of government would endanger their rights and liberties. In return for their support, or to ensure it, proprietary politicians tried for the first time to attract the German vote by placing German candidates on the election ticket. Pamphleteers for the government party also used Franklin's disparaging remarks about the boorish qualities of the German herd to good effect.[18]

Although the Lutheran and Reformed clergy gave Penn considerable help, and many of their parishioners voted for proprietary candidates, most of the Germans were not yet ready to break with the long tradition of Quaker and Sect domination in Lancaster, Bucks, and Chester counties. The traditional charges against the Proprietor worked once again, and the Old Party candidates switched the facts around in telling the Germans that if the regular representation in the Assembly were changed, *that* would change the government of the colony!

As the election approached, it was apparent that Franklin and the Old Party faced a real challenge in Philadelphia and in the under-represented western counties. But party organization, tradition, and well-established candidates in the three major counties almost guaranteed an Old Party victory no matter what the opposition might do. The proprietary could not overcome this handicap or the fact that it was not a real party but only a loose collection of alliances and Philadelphia-centered factions.[19] As in the past, the coalition was still rent by personal rivalries, ambitions, and jealousies.[20] Young men were challenging the old leaders for patronage and influence: Peters was back in the Church, and Hamilton was threatened with cancer. In their place, Benjamin Chew and the young Edward and Joseph Shippen were rising to power in proprietary councils. This rivalry and conflict centered around the recently arrived Governor, John Penn. He was inclined to dispense with the old men and turn to the new for advice. When he appointed his friends to proprietary places without the advice and consent of Allen, the Chief Justice threatened to withdraw from politics. Allen had done this before when displeased, and his sulking inactivity had hurt several proprietary candidates in previous elections. In 1764 only Thomas Penn's frantic mediation and appeasement prevented the dispute from splitting the proprietary forces just before the election.[21]

In the midst of the charges and abuse being hurled on all sides, Thomas Penn displayed his moderation and good will toward the colony in a letter of advice to John:

You are much in the right to increase the number of our Friends if you can, but avoid as much as you can imprudent People that will be always proving we are in the right and the Assembly in the wrong. Mr Allen has no private pique but wishes the peace of the Country, and that they may live long under our Government as he thinks they will be less likely to be oppressed while there is a Family to stand between them and the Crown. This is seeing the Affair in a rational light, and the only one for which they can wish to continue under a Proprietor.[22]

Real though the divisions in the proprietary ranks were, the great danger from Franklin held the rivals together long enough to fight the election.

Penn's moderation did not extend to Franklin. When he obtained copies of the "nemine contradicente" resolves from the Assembly, Penn took action to get Franklin removed from the deputy postmaster's position. He found that the Secretary of State, Halifax, agreed that Franklin had misbehaved. "His Lordship said he thought it a kind of Rebellion against his Majesty's Government, and that Mr Franklin must be turned out, if he does not alter his conduct . . . of this opinion was also Lord Hyde, the first Post Master General, to whom I gave a full account."[23] Lord Hyde promised to write Franklin "to tell him all the Officers of the Crown are expected to assist Government, whether in the hands of the Crown or of Proprietarys, and if he does not, he will be displaced; however desirous the Government here are to get the Government of Pennsylvania into their hands, there is not one of them has so little honour, as to favour a Person who shall imbroil Government, to force us to a resignation."[24]

Lord Hyde did write to Franklin as he promised Penn. News of the letter caused some excitement in Philadelphia, and when Franklin was questioned about it he reportedly replied, "Whatever the other party might think, he was not to be *Hyde Bound*."[25] The letter, however, should have suggested to him that the Ministry took a dim view of his methods and would likely ignore the petition to the Crown.

The name of John Dickinson first appears in important political affairs in 1764. He had formerly been a partisan of the Assembly, but in 1764 he published a pamphlet in which he precisely analyzed the state of affairs in Pennsylvania and the value of royal government.[26] At times very critical of proprietary rule, he nevertheless totally rejected the alternative Franklin and Galloway offered the colony. He logically pointed out that neither the Ministry nor Parliament seemed at all disposed to treat colonial rights and legislatures with any especial regard, and, agreeing with

Penn, declared that whatever its failings, proprietary government did offer a buffer between Pennsylvania and the Ministry's
plans for reform. His shrewd assessment of the problem carried
considerable weight, especially in Philadelphia.[27]

It was known in Pennsylvania that the Ministry was contem-
plating some important reforms in colonial policy, and taxation
would probably be one measure for early consideration in Parliament. Although opposition to taxation was not yet organized or
vocal, many in the colony were suspicious and hesitant about rushing off in pursuit of royal government.[28] The English Quakers
who were close to the situation had early realized the danger and
urged Pennsylvania to protect the Charter and even proprietary
government if necessary. Dickinson's pamphlet, perfectly timed
to catch this feeling of uneasiness in Pennsylvania, was a solid
blow against Franklin.

Penn was grateful for Dickinson's work, despite its open criticism of him. He wrote John Penn, "Mr Dickinson's Speech no
doubt opened the Eyes of many People, and the more as he did
not appear by it to pay any regard to us but confined himself to
the only point for the People to consider, whether they would be
most happy under the one or the other Government. Your argument that the People of the Church of England would have
gained nothing by a change of Government is well founded."[29]

In past elections for the Assembly the question of who could
vote or how many voted had had little real bearing on the results.
An examination of a list of voters or of property qualifications and
other limitations on the franchise would not tell much about
democracy or the lack of it in Pennsylvania. In most elections in
the counties, the issue was really settled before the polls opened,
and the voter received a list of candidates whose acceptability to
the county leaders, proprietary or Old Party, was already determined. Ordinarily a single ticket containing a few more names
than the number to be chosen, the slate usually represented a

careful preliminary estimation of the relative power of the Old
Party and its rivals in a given area. Because they had had little
success in the past in most of the counties, it was not uncommon
for proprietary men to refuse to contest elections. Knowing they
would probably be defeated, the gentlemen from Philadelphia
and from the country would not accept the trouble and humilia-
tion of making a futile challenge to the Old Party. Consequently,
the voter was often presented with a ticket that represented only
one interest, and who was elected depended largely on personali-
ties and on the number of friends a candidate had and got to
the polls.

Col. James Burd of Lancaster County described how this selection process worked among the Presbyterians—a process typical of county contests throughout Pennsylvania:

Previous to our Borrough Election we had an Interview with the People
whom we call Old Side. That was on Monday and we endeavoured at this
Interview to settle a Ticket with them in General for the County to prevent
partys, we made several overtures to them . . . we should propose Six men
to them out of which they should Choose one, and they should Name Six men
to us out of which we should choose One . . . which should be the Ticket.
We accordingly Nam'd one out of their Six but they declined taking one
of ours.[30]

This refusal to join in the selection of candidates, to prevent
"partys," was so contrary to the "Custom of this County" that
Burd and his friends tried desperately at the last moment to work
out a settlement. "But those Gentlemen of the Old Side kept
themselves so private that we could not find them." Thoroughly
upset by the unsportsmanlike behavior of the opposition, the New
Side men found that they had to act for themselves on the day of
the election—"We Resolved to stand upon our own Bottom and
form a Ticket for ourselves which we did accordingly."[31]

Because it had so long been in control, the Old Party had the
added advantage of supervision over local election procedures.
Sheriffs, coroners, and even magistrates followed the orders of

the political bosses in the counties. These officials could "influence" voters to appear at the polls or stay away, and as a last
resort could seize the stairs to the voting place and regulate the
hours when the polls would be open, and thereby ensure the election of approved candidates. As William Peters complained to
Penn, "By your having always given the Preference to the
Quakers in the Commissions of Peace and every Favour you could
bestow on them they have obtain'd great Influence in the Country
which they have always and now especially so ungratefully make
use of against you."[32]

With these disadvantages against them, the proprietary leaders
were awakening to the need for revising the election procedure.
In the western counties they circulated a warning that the Presbyterians would "thrash" any sheriff or county official who tried to
prevent qualified men from voting. New attention was given to
the selection of candidates, reflecting a greater awareness of local
conditions. Samuel Purviance, Jr., described the attempt to attract
the Germans and Scotch-Irish to the proprietary: "The design is
by putting in two Germans to draw such a Party of them as will
turn the scale in our Favor. . . . I would be equally agreeable if
Mr Ross came in place of any of the Irish, but as their Interest
must be much Stronger than his, it would be imprudent to offend
them by rejecting one of their proposing."[33] This was a radical
departure from the aloof, aristocratic attitude of the proprietary
leaders in the past elections. But even now the newer political
methods were not wholly accepted by the gentlemen.[34]

Despite improved methods and the help of some Scotch-Irish
and Germans, the proprietary candidates still had little chance to
gain a majority of the seats in the Assembly. The election resulted
in the continued supremacy of the Old Party—Bucks and Chester
counties together returned sixteen of its candidates, and Philadelphia and Lancaster counties gave it most of their seats. The pro-

prietary forces obtained eleven seats, including the county representation from Cumberland, York, and Northampton, and one
seat from Lancaster.[35]

In terms of the past structure of politics in Pennsylvania, the
proprietary accomplishment was remarkable, the more so because
both Franklin and Galloway were defeated in Philadelphia.
There the election had been a reasonably fair test of strength;
both Franklin and the Proprietary Party were strongest in the
City. Year after year, Franklin's election had been automatic,
even while he was in England, and just his removal from the Assembly was a great personal triumph for Penn.[36]

Although the Old Party again won a majority in the legislature, the election had registered a strong protest against its traditional domination, leaders, and policies. Yet after the election,
Franklin continued to direct the business of the Assembly, though
he no longer held a seat there. His allies in the House could not
desert him, because he was their most able and influential leader
and their best insurance against a further rise in proprietary
power. Franklin immediately demanded and received the Assembly's approval of the petition for royal government and the appointment to present it in England. He was also commissioned
with the task of representing, with Jackson, Pennsylvania's opposition to the proposed schemes for colonial taxation.

The Assembly approved the petition as Franklin wished, but
instructed him not to do anything that would prejudice the rights
and liberties of the province. All of the advantages of the Charter
of 1701 were to be preserved if royal government should be
obtained. These instructions, in effect, nullified the petition, and
expressed the growing doubt in the Assembly that royal government was either necessary or desirable.

Penn was fully prepared to block Franklin's efforts in England.
To the Assembly's petition he could now offer numerous counter-

petitions from Pennsylvania. During 1764, and on into 1765, friends of the proprietary government sought statements from all parts of the colony supporting the existing government and repudiating the Assembly and Franklin. The German and Presbyterian clergy solicited signatures from their congregations, and they got many.[37]

Even before Franklin reached England, there was evidence that the Ministry would not attempt to remove the Proprietor without much greater cause than the discontent of a rebellious Assembly. To do so would only confirm the previously rejected claims of the legislature to virtual independent power in the provincial government. In addition, Penn would have to be well paid for relinquishing the government and lands of Pennsylvania. For his part, he was determined not to surrender to any pressure from the Assembly, Franklin, or the Ministry.[38]

Pennsylvania was not the only colony involved in the petition for royal government. Franklin's efforts to oust Penn were copied by anti-proprietary men in Maryland, and New Jersey was engaged in Pennsylvania's troubles by its royal governor, William Franklin. John Penn reported to his uncle:

I have been inform'd that the Assembly of Maryland in Imitation of ours, intend to prefer a Petition to the King for a Change of Government. They are governed by Franklin, and if they do take this Step, it is entirely owing to him. A Gentleman of Credit told me that no business was transacted in their Assembly without consulting him . . . so that I think Lord Baltimore is equally interested with yourself in Crushing this Demagogue. I must not omit mentioning to you that Governor Franklin was very busy at the Election, and left his own Government to keep open house at German Town in favor of his father, and Mr Galloway. He was several days there Canvassing among the Germans.[39]

Involving other provinces in the campaign against proprietary government was not likely to enhance Franklin's standing in England. It smacked too much of a rebellious, self-interested plot against *any* authority outside the control of the Franklinists.

LAST ATTACK ON PENN

There was an appropriate irony, not immediately appreciated in Pennsylvania, in the coincidence of the petition for royal government and the passage of the Stamp Act. From their limited perspective, Pennsylvanians could see only a continuation of the violent political fighting of 1764. The Old Party, now committed to a climactic test of strength with the Proprietor and absolutely determined to win, turned, as it had in 1757, to England for a decision. Although both parties hoped to end the anarchic instability one way or another, past history suggested that this was simply one more step in the long struggle between the executive and the legislature. In fact, however, 1765 marked the closing of the old conflict, but not in the way or for the reasons that Pennsylvanians might have imagined.

No matter how hard the politicians tried after 1765, they could not make provincial politics turn on the question of proprietary rule. The Ministry's intention to raise a revenue in the colonies through taxation rendered the dispute obsolete, and in a matter of months the issues that had dominated politics since the founding of the colony were submerged beneath the greater problems of the imperial crisis. Few in the province recognized this; those who cheered Franklin as he departed for England gave their attention to local disputes, not yet aware that the policies of the

King's Ministers would make a petition for royal government inappropriate and unwise.

Although the Stamp Act was to destroy the long-established focus of provincial politics, it did not change the habits of the politicians or the durable structure of politics. Traditional alignments and antipathies, election procedures, and the entrenched power of the heads of factions all remained, and all resisted the changes demanded by the emerging imperial conflict. Unaccustomed to thinking in transatlantic or intercolonial terms and preoccupied with local matters, most Pennsylvanians were unable to see the Stamp Act as an entirely new proposition, requiring something more than a party reaction. Indeed, it was as a party matter that the politicians assessed and reacted to the tax. Pennsylvanians could instinctively oppose it and other rumored changes in imperial management, but in the beginning the form and degree of their opposition were conditioned by local political considerations. The larger questions of colonial rights—the power of Parliament to lay taxes and the status of American legislatures—came later. According to Carl Becker's well-known statement, the American Revolution had two aspects: "Home rule and who should rule at home." To men like Franklin, the Stamp Act was chiefly concerned with the second aspect.

There was no lack of knowledge in Pennsylvania of the Ministry's plans to tax the colonies. Party leaders had already expressed opposition, but there had been little alarm or excitement. Rather, as Franklin said later, there was almost a feeling that, unfortunate though such a scheme might be, it was inevitable. While Thomas Penn quietly worked among members of the Ministry to delay or stop the measure, he was not optimistic. As early as February 1764 he had written, "There is talk of laying a stamp Duty in all the Colonys and Islands, on Bonds, Deeds, Writs, &ct, this I suppose the People will think hard, and I believe it will be opposed, as an internal Taxation, rather to be done by Act of Assembly, but this [is] in embryo at Present."[1]

If Pennsylvanians were politically astigmatic, it was because they were still intensely preoccupied with the results and meaning of the election of 1764. And that election provided a ready-made framework into which the stamp tax could be fit. By making royal government the overriding question, the Old Party had already put the proprietary in opposition to royal interference in Pennsylvania. The two Franklins, Galloway, Hughes, Thomas Wharton, James Logan, George Ashbridge, and other Old Party propagandists exaggerated proprietary weaknesses and iniquities to contrast with the presumed goodness of the Crown.

Forced to answer, the proprietary leaders defended the Charter and charged that royal government would exchange Pennsylvania's liberties for ministerial meddling and placemen accompanied by troops and taxes. Thus the colony would pay heavily to gratify the "inveterate malice of the Franklinists."[2] Penn's spokesmen also declared that if the Ministry thought it necessary to reform imperial administration—and to raise a revenue to do so—it was largely because of legislative misbehavior in America. One of the objects of the new policy was to establish effective limits upon the overweaning ambitions of the local legislatures and simultaneously to strengthen the executive. Opinion in England, Penn warned, held that colonial legislatures must be curbed or "the constitution will be changed to a perfect Democracy, which must not be, the most considerable Members of both Houses much censure the Democratical spirit that actuates our Assemblys."[3]

Driven to a strongly anti-royal position in their attack upon the petition, proprietary politicians were thus prepared in 1764 to use any changes in English colonial policy to support their contention that Pennsylvania was much safer and much better governed under the Charter and the Proprietor. The Old Party went in the opposite direction: it praised the Crown and the Ministry to strike at Penn.

The election of 1764 had been embarrassing for Franklin but

not politically fatal. Despite the loss of five seats including the places of its two captains, the Old Party remained much stronger than the opposition. Alarming though proprietary gains were, past history indicated that Penn's sudden-built patchwork of alliances would fall apart soon after the election. And with the Assembly safely in its hands, the Old Party still followed the direction of its leaders. Chew wrote to Penn, "Franklin, Galloway & others tho' excluded have had the entire direction of Matters within doors. The measure & plan of each day's proceeding being settled by them every Evening at private meetings & cabals held with their Friends in the house."[4]

Although many in the Old Party feared Franklin's intentions, they were obliged to support him—at least in public. The recent election defeats had actually strengthened him, because there was now indisputable evidence of the rise of proprietary and Presbyterian power. Although royal government might be distasteful or dangerous, it was less so than the menace of Presbyterian ascendancy. A popular interpretation held that those Quakers, Anglicans, and Germans who had defected to the opposition must reconsider and reunite or lose their power forever. Properly exploited, the coalition of the proprietary and the "Oliverian spirit" of the Presbyterians could serve to keep the Old Party in line and frighten Quakers and Anglicans in England into supporting the petition. Believing (mistakenly, as it turned out) that the Friends in England must act this time, Franklin declared, "For the Quakers, who, to show their moderation with Regard to the Proprietors, have (of themselves) undertaken to persuade them to reasonable Measures, will, on finding them obstinate, join their whole Force and weight to procure a happy Event to the Petition, especially as they dread nothing more than what they see otherwise inevitable, their Friends in Pennsylvania falling under the Domination totally of Presbyterians."[5] For English consumption, Franklin emphasized that opposition to the petition came from a

minority conspiracy of secret republicans who were disloyal to the
Crown, criminals who murdered Indians and enlisted mobs to
help them in politics, and a clique of proprietary officials who were
so weak and venal that Pennsylvania was left to anarchy, and
"neither lives nor property are safe."

In Pennsylvania, Galloway and the other Old Party leaders
soothed the worriers with assurances that the colony would lose
nothing and gain a great deal through the change of government.
Franklin's instructions, drawn up at his own and Galloway's
direction, declared that if the Crown took over, Pennsylvania
must retain all of its rights under the Charter, and, if possible, get
concessions easing trade and paper-money regulations. Franklin
was also advised to represent the colony's opposition to "loading
this province with undue Taxes at the next Session of Parliament" and to oppose any other measure that might be inimical to
the interests of the province.[6] These were, however, general instructions, and they allowed him considerable leeway in bargain-
ing with the Ministry. Some Pennsylvanians thought he intended
to proceed without much regard for his instructions. William
Allen told Penn that "The leaders, or rather they who think themselves much of the Party opposed to you, have told me frequently
that they never intended the petition should be presented, but
only kept as a rod to hang over you to bring you to agree to their
measures. But Franklin, though he told them he was of the same
sentiments is making dupes of them, and fully intends to have it
presented."[7] These suspicions were to prove correct.

The glamor of Franklin's emergence as an imperial statesman
and his dramatic work for the repeal of the Stamp Act have
obscured the question of his purpose in going to England in 1765.
It is clear that opposition to the tax was not the reason—that was
at best incidental. Nor is it likely that his hatred for Penn was the
reason, although it was constantly on his mind: "All Hopes of
Happiness under a Proprietary Government are at an End . . .

Our only Hopes are, that the Crown will see the Necessity of taking the Government into its own Hands, without which we shall soon have no government at all."[8] Private revenge was, however, costly and hazardous. It meant a stay in England for an unknown length of time, a disruption of his private affairs in Pennsylvania, and the possibility that he might die without seeing his family and friends in the colony again; he was 58 years old. It also meant another bitter conflict, a prospect he had professed to loathe on his earlier mission.

He left no direct statement about his plans, but other evidence suggests that he had a grand design in mind that included the petition for royal government and, if necessary, a revenue for the Mother Country. In the larger context, his fight against the proprietary was part of a long-range campaign whose ultimate end was the reformation of the Empire. He was thinking in terms of a decisive campaign when he wrote Strahan that proprietary attacks upon him "will ere long either demolish me or I them. If the former happens, as possibly it may Behold me a Londoner for the rest of my Days."[9] If he could defeat Penn and change the existing government of Pennsylvania, he would be in a position to help enlightened, well-intentioned Ministers in England to remodel the imperial structure. Thus the prospect of imperial reform did not alarm him at all. Since 1751, he had been developing various ideas for just such improvements—colonial union, representation for America in Parliament, better management of Indian relations—all of which were necessary, he thought, for the future glory and prosperity of the Empire. On his first trip to England, he had found the Ministry little inclined to take action on any of these ideas. Now, in 1765, attitudes seemed to have changed. If the Ministry was ready to put a new policy into effect, an obvious first step was to remove proprietary governments and establish a unified system of royal administration. Franklin expected that both England and the colonies would have to make concessions: America must stop or be stopped from illegal trade and smuggling, and England must find some way to give American interests formal recognition in Parliament or even in the Ministry. In this momentous undertaking, which Franklin confidently believed would ensure the future of the Empire and the happiness of its people, the Ministry needed information and guidance. Would not this be a priceless opportunity for an able, far-seeing American spokesman?

To accomplish his objectives, Franklin expected that the Old Party leaders in Pennsylvania, under the direction of Galloway, would assist him by keeping up the attack upon the Proprietary Party. It must be made to appear in England that the majority of Pennsylvanians were desperate for a change of government. Then, if the English Quakers added their voices to the clamor for royal government, and if he exerted all of his influence and writing skill upon important men inclined to oppose proprietary governments, his mission could not fail. Hence Franklin expected victory over Penn in 1765. Nevertheless, he was shrewd enough to realize that there were two obstacles to be overcome: the certain opposition of the Proprietor, and the timidity of those in the government who had opposed the Assembly's case in 1760. He knew that Penn would delay, and that many of the Ministers would try to evade an unpleasant contest; it was necessary, therefore, to show patience and, most of all, a willingness to cooperate. He must demonstrate to reasonable men in England that he had the best interests of the Empire in view, and that its development would be furthered if it opposed the narrow, personal interests of the proprietary. As a petitioner and a salesman, Franklin could not afford to be an obstructionist.

When he arrived in England, the protest against the proposed stamp tax was already under way. He immediately joined with the other colonial agents in expressing opposition to the plan, but his own opposition was temperate and circumspect. Grenville's arguments were convincing: England needed financial relief, and improved colonial defense and administration would cost money.[10]

Grenville's mode of raising a revenue might be improper, but the need was obvious. Naturally, Franklin came up with a better scheme. He and Thomas Pownall, who was now an adviser on American affairs to the Grenville Ministry, proposed a plan that would benefit both England and the colonies:

We have taken the Liberty to enclose and beg leave to submit to your consideration, a measure calculated for supplying the colonies with a Paper Currency, become absolutely necessary to their Circumstances, by which measure a certain and very considerable Revenue will arise to the crown. . . . We are from our experience and having been employed in the Public Service in America, entirely confident and certain of the effect of this measure; and if we shall be so happy as to see it adopted, we are ready to explain the manner of carrying it into Execution—& beg Leave to offer our Services in the Administration and Execution of it.[11]

Here was the proper alternative to the Stamp Act. Franklin and Pownall held out the inducement that they were spokesmen for America and competent to put such a measure into effect "on such Terms as Government upon consideration shall find most conducive to the Public benefit."[12]

But once it became evident that the Ministry was determined to impose a stamp tax, Franklin advised his friends in Pennsylvania to accept it. He promised that it would be accompanied with benefits: "The Parliament will however ease us in some Particulars relating to our Commerce, and a Scheme is under Consideration to furnish us a Currency, without which we can neither pay Debts nor Duties."[13] Penn suspected that Franklin had a hand in setting the stamp rates: "Those for Public house Lycences [are] rated extremely high, which may possibly have been suggested by him, as you know those Houses are one of the Complaints [of the Assembly]."[14]

Because the petition was his first consideration and Grenville's support promised to be invaluable, Franklin cooperated. His cooperation was rewarded and further encouraged by the promise of patronage under the Act. When he nominated Hughes to be the stamp agent in Pennsylvania, he accomplished two objectives. First, he rewarded a personal friend and a leader of the Old Party for his loyalty, and showed Pennsylvania what came from loyalty to Franklin and the Crown. Second, he deliberately affronted Penn, who should have been consulted on or offered such patronage. A short time later, Penn gladly disclaimed any part in the appointment: "I find a story has been raised, as if there was a contest about the appointment of Hughes to the office he holds of dispenser of Stamps, which is quite untrue for he was appointed and his Deputation signed several Days before I knew he had been recommended."[15] He also told Dr. Smith, "I did not make any application or care to concern myself about it." This denial came after Pennsylvania had reacted against both the stamp tax and Hughes. At the time the bill was passed, Franklin correctly believed he had scored a victory against Penn. Franklin's devoted supporters likewise saw the implications in this sign of ministerial favor. Nicholas Waln, one of his many correspondents in Pennsylvania, requested, "In all probability there will be Offices of Proffit in the Disposition of the Crown, to any one of which I should be obliged to you for your Recommendation."[16]

There can be little doubt that Franklin saw the Stamp Act as a minor matter, a necessary price for royal government and other reforms. His acceptance of it was an earnest expression of his willingness to assist the government at home. The greater rewards from the Crown would far outweigh the small cost. Thinking of his grand design, Franklin wrote Hughes,

If it continues, your undertaking to execute it may make you unpopular for a Time, but your acting with Coolness and Steadiness, and with every Circumstance in your Power of Favour to the People, will by degrees reconcile them. In the mean time, a firm Loyalty to the Crown & faithful Adherence to the Government of this Nation, which it is the Safety as well as the Honour of the Colonies to be connected with, will always be the wisest Course for you and I to take, whatever may be the Madness of the Populace or their blind Leaders.[17]

Before Franklin left Pennsylvania, Thomas Penn had begun preparations to deal with him and the petition. While he did not relish another protracted battle with Franklin, he had no choice. Whatever reasons might have inclined him to give up the government, which had brought him so much trouble, were set aside; he would not surrender. "Your account of the Governor gives me very great satisfaction and I believe you are under no Danger of having him turned out to make room for Mr. Franklin, and the People in general may be assured I will use all the means in my power to prevent it, which they may be pretty well assured cannot be effected without my consent."[18] Although the Proprietors were charged with being interested only in profits, Thomas Penn rejected the opportunity to maintain his land income while getting rid of the burden of government. His love for Pennsylvania, his sense of duty, and his outrage at what he considered the unconstitutional actions of the Old Party and Franklin demanded that he defend his rights and the rights of the colony under the Charter.

Penn's advantages in the struggle were great—far greater than Franklin calculated. It was difficult to be an avowed enemy of Franklin and the Old Party leadership while Franklin was in Philadelphia, but many worked openly or secretly against the petition. Penn got enough counterstatements from the province to show the Ministry that the colony's support for the petition was far from unanimous. In England the Quakers privately told him that they would not support Franklin, especially if Penn would enter into negotiations leading to some concessions, including weak Governors and limits on proprietary incomes.[19] Fothergill sponsored attempts to reach such an agreement with the Proprietor, hoping thereby to forestall Quaker support in the Assembly for the petition.[20] Richard Jackson, who was considered to be one of Franklin's most important allies in England and a means of access to prominent men, advised the English Quakers that he was opposed to a change in Pennsylvania. And former

Governor Hamilton and William Allen had both been in England, and had used their considerable prestige and influence to undermine Franklin's reputation and block his work. Allen indicated what should be done: "I flatter myself you [Penn] will have given the Ministry and your friends proper impressions of him. Was his true Character known to them they surely would not consider him as a person who deserved credit, or any favor, but rather a severe Censure."[21] The proprietary accused Franklin and his Assembly allies of subverting the government and acting against the Proprietor for private gain and personal malice.

The effect of these efforts in England was significant; Franklin was, as he had been on his earlier mission, suspect. Influential men might receive him and listen attentively to his proposals. They might also like him and profess their inclination to "do him every Service." But most refused to act in his behalf. Although his letters showed that he was received and consulted by the highest people—"I am excessively hurried, being, every hour that I am awake, either abroad to speak with members of Parliament, or taken up with people coming to me at home concerning our American affairs"—he mistook this reception for support.[22] Master politicians that they were, His Majesty's Ministers were adept at dissimulation and capable of masking their intentions behind a façade of friendliness and outward attentiveness. Many petitioners and many ambitious men came their way; it was prudent to listen without making any real commitments.

One obstacle above all others thwarted Franklin's efforts and ensured proprietary victory. No Ministry during the 1760's was strong enough to attempt, against opposition in England, an attack upon proprietary charters. If Penn refused to give up the government voluntarily, nothing but a long, drawn-out legal battle could have forced him out. Even Lord Shelburne, one of the most ardent advocates of reformed colonial administration and a person on whom Franklin counted to support the petition, refused to make it a political issue. Penn told Peters in 1769, "Lord Shelburne, and every other minister, no doubt wish to persuade us to resign our Government, and would agree to give us terms very different from those offered our Father, but he has no thought of forcing us, or [the] opinion that it can be done."[23] Since the Revolution of 1688, charters had been politically untouchable. Penn realized this; Franklin did not. "I am never questioned about any of Franklin's Schemes here, and am confident he can never procure his adherants what they want. We have too much said about East India Charters for Government to make any attempt upon others, and no Minister has ever hinted to me anything more, than that, if we would part with ours, we should have a very valuable consideration for it."[24] Therefore, when Franklin did present the petition to the Privy Council, it was "by his Majesty's order postponed, *sine die,* that is (to use my Lord President's own expression) for ever & ever; this is the most easy way of rejecting, and which they make use of when any considerable bodys of People Petition."[25]

Although Franklin was "much shock'd when he was informed of it," he refused to believe that the Council's action was final. Until 1769 he continued to report to Pennsylvania that favorable action would be taken just as soon as some of his friends came into power. Before 1769, however, Pennsylvania had all but forgotten its war with the Penns and its former desperate need for the salvation of royal government. People in England continued to humor Franklin's obsession; Lord Hillsborough, on taking office as Secretary of State in 1768, put off his plea to revive the petition by saying "he would inquire into the matter, and would talk with me farther upon it."[26]

The news that the Stamp Act had been passed produced an explosive reaction throughout the colonies. But in Pennsylvania, perhaps more than elsewhere, the passage of the Act coincided perfectly with the local political conflict. It was a political disaster

for the Old Party and a heaven-sent weapon for proprietary use
against Franklin. The proprietary leaders were delighted to use
evidence of ministerial intentions and of England's tender regard
for colonial rights to proclaim the advantages of proprietary rule
and the security that lay in the old Charter. They denounced
Franklin and Galloway for being parties to the tax, and Thomas
Penn hoped that "this will convince them also that they ought to
prize the Government they live under."[27]

Because opposition to the Stamp Act suited the political interests
of the proprietary-Presbyterian leadership, they took command
of the protest movement, directing their fire simultaneously at
the Act and at the Old Party. They had some evidence and a great
many more suspicions of Franklin's perfunctory work against the
tax and his subsequent acceptance of it. Their most telling accusation was that he had collaborated with the Ministry to get royal
government and with it rewards for himself and his friends in
Pennsylvania. Joseph Shippen declared,

The People in general here are now pretty well convinced that Mr. Franklin
has more interested Views than himself or his adherents pretend he has. His
not doing the least Service to the province during his present Agency in
England, but on the Contrary his yielding to the late Measures of imposing
Taxes & Burthens on the Colonies, and his Acceptance of Posts for his Friends
to execute the Stamp Act, the very thing he was instructed to oppose, are
Matters which serve to open the Eyes of many that were before blinded in
his Favor.[28]

Other reports from England added support to the charges that
he had sold out the interests of Pennsylvania and America to gain
ministerial favor in his war with Penn and to "gain his own ends,
which were to be made Governor here & to bestow all the places
of profit upon Galloway, & some more of his adherents."[29]

The case against Franklin was ably exploited in Pennsylvania,
and it convinced many that, at best, he had not acted prudently.
But Franklin was in England, and because they did not have control over the Assembly, proprietary men could not get him re-

called. Hence they turned their attention to Hughes. He became the scapegoat of those who hated the tax, disliked Franklin, or sought to pull down the Quakers and the Old Party. David Hall, who had been a partner of Franklin's on the *Pennsylvania Gazette,* wrote that he would fear for Franklin's safety if he were in Philadelphia, because people were so violent against anyone connected with the Act, and "people believe you had a hand in it which has occasioned you many Enemies."[30] Hughes's refusal to give up his appointment and his and Galloway's defense of the Act tended to brand the Old Party leadership as traitors to America. Galloway lost popularity in 1765, but Hughes was the prime target. For a short time in 1765 it seemed that the proprietary forces had finally found an issue to destroy the power of Franklin and his allies. Under this onslaught many of the Old Party were seriously embarrassed and confused. They faced the difficult choice of continuing to support Franklin and the petition or joining the opposition to the tax, thereby giving aid to the proprietary and dividing the Old Party. It was an awkward situation; a few immediately swung over to strong opposition to the tax, whatever the political cost. Others, perhaps the majority in and around Philadelphia, tried to avoid a clear commitment, attempting to minimize the real significance of the tax while remaining loyal to the Party. A minority, led by Galloway and Hughes, stood firm on England's right to tax the colonies and resisted Pennsylvania's participation in the Stamp Act Congress and in the non-importation agreements. These "traitors" were a minority, but they were enough to verify proprietary charges of Old Party complicity in the tax and attempts to profit from it.

Yet the Stamp Act could not long remain simply a local partisan issue in Pennsylvania. As soon as the Pennsylvanians heard about the organized reaction to the tax in other colonies, the issue was lifted above party interests and became an intercolonial, American concern. And once the Pennsylvanians became aware that they were part of this larger protest movement, proprietary success in exploiting the Act for their political benefit declined. Denunciation of the tax and efforts to place blame on one side or the other was the first reaction; the next stage was the general colonial demand for the Act's repeal. At this level, Quakers and Presbyterians, merchants and mechanics could participate in a united movement above party. By late 1765, with attention in Pennsylvania moving to secure repeal of the tax, party divisions began to blur.

Local political considerations did not entirely disappear, of course. The problem of Franklin remained. He was a liability for the Old Party in 1765, but he was also a key part of its leadership. His friends in Pennsylvania anxiously urged him to explain his actions and prove his ardent opposition to the tax. One minor politician, Casper Krible, asked ponderously

if Mr. F friends, Messers Galloway, Fox and others . . . would be Pleased to remind and encourage him . . . That he will to the Utmost of his power at all Opportunities Contribute to the Repeal of the Stamp Acts; And that over and above all this for the sake of his own Credit, to Solicit this and every other matter Touching his Embassy, either by himself or some other Eminent Patrons; and that the same might be made unexceptionably to Appear here. This or such like open and public demonstration of his Utmost endeavours for the Utility and happiness of this Province, would very likely produce good Effects, to the Confusion of all his & his friends Enemies and Slanderers.[31]

Despite the Old Party's desperate attempt to defend Franklin, many were convinced of his complicity in the tax. By agitating for repeal, the Party could help him redeem himself and try to recover its political balance. Thus "repeal" was the theme: everyone must join in this undertaking regardless of party; the Stamp Act had been a mistake, and all America, united in protest, would turn to educate its friends in England and secure an end to the tax.

The Old Party's recovery required some sacrifices. Hughes was abandoned by his former friends and left to the mob, led by the Allens. The petition for royal government was quietly and unofficially dropped. A few of Franklin's closest associates, including Thomas Wharton, continued to press for it. Wharton wrote in

December 1765, "We . . . have the utmost Confidence in thee, & doubt not thy having laid such a Foundation on which thou'l be able to rear this noble structure: a change from the Shackles of a Prop-y Governm-t, to the Freedom of a Royal one."[32] But to most Pennsylvanians, the Stamp Act revealed how insignificant, even artificial, the grievances against the Proprietor had been.

The news from Pennsylvania soon awakened Franklin to his mistake. He complied with the demands of his friends in the colony and wrote letters explaining his conduct. He also got supporting letters from others in England. Fothergill wrote, "From my own Knowledge, I can safely aver that Benjamin Franklin did all in his power to prevent the Stamp Act from passing, that he waited upon the Ministry that then was to inform them fully of its mischievous Tendency, and that he has uniformly opposed it to the utmost of his Abilities."[33] These testimonials made it appear that Franklin had worked against the Act from the moment he arrived in England, but had been helpless in the face of the Ministry's determination to have its way. Such an interpretation was a rather loose treatment of the facts, but the letters helped restore his tarnished reputation in 1766.

The leaders of the Old Party now presented Franklin as a great asset to the colony and to America. They declared that his reputation and his many friends and connections in England could be used to influence the Ministry. Important men in the Mother Country would listen to him, especially if he received the proper support. Franklin used this argument himself, and even his enemies had to admit that he was America's best-known representative at home. The fall of the Grenville Ministry and the assumption of power by the Rockingham group was also a stroke of good fortune. There were supposed to be "friends of America" in the new government, and Franklin declared that he knew and could work with them.

Although Franklin would later be credited with exerting a decisive influence upon the members of the Rockingham government, the degree of his influence was questionable. The leaders based their decision to repeal the Act upon a number of considerations—political expediency, the attitude of the merchants and the King, and complicated party maneuvers. Many people in England contributed to repeal—not the least of whom was Penn.[34] He got little credit for his work, but his connections were just as important as Franklin's. Penn wrote about the change in the Ministry in 1765, declaring that "If Mr. Franklin valued himself on his Interest with the former Ministry he must have that to make again, as nothing countenanced by Lord Bute is to be kept in, both the Secretarys of the Treasury, on whom he availed himself, are removed and no doubt Mr. Jackson must lose his place, as Mr. Dowdeswell* will have some Person he knows better, to be his Secretary."[35] Both Franklin and Penn found that the new Ministry was more inclined to listen to colonial protests and more receptive to American interests.

Franklin was useful in 1766 to a Ministry that had already made its decision. However, the uproar in America and the actions of mobs made its task difficult, because the opposition could claim that England was bowing to lawlessness and disobedience. What was needed was a face-saving scheme that would effect repeal upon the basis of new information and a "reconsideration" of colonial claims and English interests. A well-known American might serve this purpose. Thus the stage was set for Parliament's carefully planned interview of Franklin. This show gave the Ministry the opportunity to ask him the appropriate questions and receive the appropriate answers. He played his part to perfection, and his masterful presentation earned him most of the glory for repeal and established him in England and America as *the* spokesman for the colonies and as a great imperial statesman. It also helped him to re-establish his reputation in Pennsylvania. Full accounts of it went to the province, where his friends broadcast the story of his success. News of repeal united Pennsylvanians in a joyous cele-

* William Dowdeswell was Chancellor of the Exchequer in the Rockingham Ministry.

bration. Once again Franklin was "their great Patriot," and he was lionized along with Pitt, Rockingham, the King, and the other friends of America. Good luck and quick work had given him the chance to recover from the blunder of assisting Grenville. Nevertheless, his mistake cost him a substantial amount of influence in provincial politics.

Franklin had served the Ministry, and it had served him. He was supremely confident that his first interest, the petition, would go forward together with various other improvements in English-colonial relations. Ezra Stiles, a leading figure in Connecticut politics, wrote that he hoped Rockingham would honor Franklin with a knighthood.[36] Some such reward was not far from Franklin's own expectations.

After a fast start in exploiting the Stamp Act for political advantage, the proprietary leaders had found themselves involved in an unexpected and frightening excess of popular response. Affairs in Pennsylvania had quickly got out of hand, and mob violence, numerous public committees and meetings, and impassioned press campaigns caused the leaders to pull back. Many of the "better sort" shared Penn's reaction: "We are very uneasy at the disturbances occasioned by the Stamps, and fear there has been some violent proceedings in Pennsylvania, of which I hope you will give us timely notices."[37] He urged his friends in the colony to suppress violence and reduce party conflict.

Penn's reaction was matched by Franklin's, although for different reasons. Aghast at the news from Pennsylvania, Franklin deplored "what we have lately heard of your Mobs, one cannot say that any Property or Possession is Safe *certainly*,"[38] adding later, "The Outrages continually committed by those misguided people, will doubtless tend to convince all the considerate on your side of the water, of the weakness of our present Government."[39] Although tempted to use provincial reaction to the Stamp Act as further evidence of Penn's incapacity to govern, Franklin was forced to retreat from such purely party exploitation of mob action in order to work for repeal. Penn was plainly worried that Franklin would capitalize on Proprietary Party leadership of the stamp protest, and therefore requested information from Pennsylvania in "answering the charges Mr. Hughes and Mr. Franklin very probably have made against us and our Friends."[40] Likely Franklinist charges of proprietary disloyalty and rebellion seemed to Penn uncomfortably close to the truth.

Once the movement for repeal began, the proprietary lost its opportunity to defeat the Old Party and Franklin. Looking to the future, Penn saw that former disputes might be put aside once the petition was disposed of. Shortly after repeal he gave recognition to Franklin's work and what it might promise for politics in the colony: "We have all been so fully employed on an affair of much greater consequence, *and on the same side,* in which we have nobly succeeded, that I think there is a possibility of burying the former Contests, and living in Peace, at least this is what I wish, and what we should all endeavour may be the case, if it can be on honorable conditions."[41] Penn's hopes for a restoration of harmony and order and a resumption of traditional direction in politics reflected his fear that popular passions endangered the colony and must be calmed. With this Franklin fully agreed.

TO 1776

The political crises that arose between 1764 and 1766 taught Pennslyvania's leaders the hard lesson that they would risk a great deal if they continued to fight each other as they had in the past. What looked at first to be a decisive battle between Penn and Franklin had again ended in a draw. Franklin could not remove Penn, Penn could not destroy Franklin and the Old Party, and neither could expect this situation to change without help from the government at home, which was now suspect because of the Stamp Tax. Faced with mounting restlessness among the people, the politicians agreed (if on nothing else) that they and the regular government must regain control over internal public affairs.

The lessons of the preceding two years were especially impressed upon the Old Party: should future issues arise between England and the colonies, it would not be caught in the embarrassing position of defending an attack upon American rights. With other patriots the leaders would "sniff tyranny on every breeze"—but they were equally determined to keep the direction of provincial protest in the Assembly. They realized, moreover, that if in some future crisis there were to be intercolonial meetings, petitions to the Crown, economic reprisals, and other forms of reaction, the House must prevent the radical firebrands of Philadelphia from exciting and exploiting popular passions for their own ends. Many in the Proprietary Party tacitly agreed to this policy, even if they individually supported a strong whiggish response from the Assembly. What was learned in 1765 was not forgotten in the years that followed, and the Assembly did maintain its supremacy until 1776.

For their own reasons, most of the leaders in both parties wanted peace in politics. Galloway, who was now the undisputed boss of the Old Party, feared mobs, Westerners, and the overturning of the political order more than he hated the proprietary. On the other side, Governor John Penn and his uncle Thomas, who were likewise alarmed at the disorder and at the prospect of continued warfare with the Assembly, were willing to stop pressing the legislature with rigid instructions on every issue. Exhausted and somewhat frightened by the results of the long conflict, many undoubtedly hoped that Governor Penn's report was true—"The Quakers, some of them, profess to be a little tired of their past politicks . . . they are for removing some of the firebrands from the Assembly."[1]

From 1766 onward, both sides made concessions and showed a reluctance to allow internal disputes to go too far. The result was a period of remarkable harmony in legislative-executive relations. There were still sharp fights, of course, over many of the traditional issues, notably finance and frontier lawlessness, but the politicians were much less inclined to make violent assertions of rights and threats of implacable resistance. Thus while imperial relations grew more strained, provincial government enjoyed an increasing measure of peace and cooperation. If proprietary government worked reasonably well in the last decade before the Revolution, it did so, in part, because many people discovered the advantages in it that factional conflict had hitherto obscured.

The armistice between the parties—at least at the top—and the suppression of some of the sharpest points of dispute meant inevitably that the Old Party again won provincial elections. The strength of the proprietary had developed in the conflicts of 1764, and its cohesion had depended upon the threat of the petition. Only these exceptional conditions had forced proprietary leaders to seek out Scotch-Irish and German help—the sort of enterprise described by Samuel Purviance. He had ventured into Quaker territory seeking help against "our dangerous enemy Franklin," and had "met some of our Friends at Chester court & there concerted some measures for dividing the Quaker Interest in that County. . . . I went lately up to Bucks Court in order to concert measures for their Election in pursuance of which we have appointed a considerable meeting of Germans, Baptists & Presbyterians . . . to attempt a general confederacy of the three Societies in opposition to the ruling Party."[2] Efforts of this sort would not be common after 1765. And with the removal of the threat of the petition and the stamp tax, the proprietary coalition fell apart in 1766.

The proprietary leaders, who had never really wished to create a popular party, returned to their old ways—even if this meant losing elections again. For it was and had been the nature of politics that unless there were some great issue to stir the people—accompanied by a deliberate effort to mobilize and use popular support—the conditions that limited political activity and power to the few would prevail. The door had been opened in 1764 and 1765 with alarming results; thereafter the bosses guarded the entrance and admitted as few new men as possible. Thomas Penn, in a declaration of policy, advised, "I hope People will not be long stigmatiz'd with the name of Quaker and Presbyterian faction . . . and I must again recommend it to you to watch all opportunitys when you find any of the opposite Party seem better disposed, to shew them some countenance in order to reconcile Partys, for when a Man acts as if he was sensible he had acted a wrong part, I think it becomes a man of honour to make use of it."[3] He added, "I am pleased with the changes in the Politicks of the Quakers and wish the opposite party would not insist on too great a change of members [in the Assembly]. If they do they will not carry it."[4] With Penn urging reconciliation and a limited election campaign on his followers, the election of 1766 was no contest. In Philadelphia and Philadelphia County the proprietary put up only two candidates to challenge for ten seats. An even greater sign of proprietary decline was the election of Israel Pemberton's brother James to represent the City—a center of proprietary strength and anti-stamp fervor.

On internal questions the gentlemen of both parties were conservatives. Although they could never wipe out the personal and party animosities of the past, and would individually differ greatly on how far to go in supporting colonial resistance to English policies, they did agree that minority rule should be preserved. They chose the candidates and restricted the opportunities to vote, thereby making the results predictable. In 1770 the *Pennsylvania Gazette* complained: "It has been customary for a certain Company of leading men to nominate Persons, and settle the ticket, for Assembly—men, commissioners, assessors, etc. without ever permitting the affirmative or negative Voice of a mechanic to interfere, and when they have concluded, expect the Tradesmen will give a sanction thereto by passing the Ticket."[5] This political structure was not changed until 1776. For in spite of all of the turmoil and crises during the decade before the Revolution, the government of Pennsylvania remained in the hands of those who had long held power. Assembly seats were held by the same men or by their sons, nephews, and cousins year after year, and as a result most of the places were never really contested. Sickness and death were more likely to remove a well-established member than the electorate.

Before the small expansion in representation in 1771, the proprietary might expect to take approximately seven seats and the Old Party from twenty-three to twenty-six. Three to six might be open to contest in any given election. Excluding Franklin, there were seventeen men in the House in 1775 who had been there in 1767, and several other members were in and out in the 1760's and 1770's. Eight of the sixteen members from Bucks and Chester counties, three of the eight from Philadelphia, both from Cumberland, and two of the four from Lancaster were regularly re-elected in these years. In addition, six others replaced retiring or deceased relatives. This meant continuity and stability in the representation of both parties. Purviance again provides a description of the intimate, personal management of elections. His account of the 1766 contest in Philadelphia might have been written with a few changes in particulars in 1756 or 1775:

After the publication of Hughes' & Galloway's Letters the whole City was in the greatest ferment, & Numbers of Quakers who had been strongly against us formerly, began to declaim with great Violence against their own Leaders & made Overtures to our people of joining them in a Ticket; our best Politicians thout it woud be their best Way not to interfer in the Election, but suffer the Quakers who were split amongst themselves to combat one another & Quarrel effectually, but those who revolted to our people pressd them to an Opposition after having stood out till within a few Days of the Election when they agreed on their plan. By that time they were quite too late to prepare Matters & make an Interest thro' the Country which requires time & great Pains, & the other Party who had fix'd their Ticket long before had a great Advantage.[6]

Everything depended upon the leaders' "taking Pains" to form an Interest and manage the Ticket.

New men did come into politics in the 1760's, but if they were to achieve much success before 1775 and outside of Philadelphia, they had to do so within the existing parties. John Dickinson, Edward Biddle, and Michael Hillegas were among the foremost new leaders in politics and in the Assembly. They were, however, a privileged minority; they joined rather than disturbed the political order. Most of the radical revolutionary leaders—those who would manage Pennsylvania after Independence was declared

—did not sit in the House. A few, such as George Bryan, Daniel Roberdeau, Charles Thomson, and Anthony Wayne, sat for the City or County of Philadelphia for a short time, but they were not at home in the Assembly. There was a tendency for new men, if they were ardent whigs or representatives of rising minorities, to be associated with the Proprietary Party because it stood in opposition to the Old Party and the Quakers. Yet even in the Proprietary Party, ambitious newcomers could not challenge the power of William Allen, Chew, Joseph Shippen, James Allen, Charles Humphreys, or Dickinson. How could they attack a man like William Allen, who was an ardent defender of American rights (until Independence) but a traditionalist in local politics?

Before 1776 the effect of the imperial crisis upon internal politics was limited. Despite its rather ponderous conservatism, the Assembly did contain representation from the moderates and the radical whigs. With the help of the radicals in the City, the whigs could push and prod the Assembly along. Pennsylvania's response was never in the forefront. The conservatives, led by Galloway, proceeded cautiously and loyally, doing just enough to keep Pennsylvania in line with the general reaction of other colonies. Radical whig power and propaganda in Philadelphia was undoubtedly effective in assisting whigs in the House, but Philadelphia was not Pennsylvania.

In the counties the influence of the imperial crisis and radical agitation on local politics was much less significant. Before 1775, few county representatives were chosen or rejected primarily on the basis of their whiggishness. Philadelphia County was naturally more influenced by the City, but even there it was not until 1771 that the mechanics could exert enough pressure to force Galloway out of his seat. The Speaker then merely moved to a safe seat in Bucks County. Thus while the noise and ferment of Philadelphia affected the Assembly in its midst, the counties acted as a conservative balance to stabilize politics and sustain the leadership.

The dispersed rural population was more immune to urban pressure and propaganda; it was also true that county conservatism was supported by the established political structure.

As long as the issue was defense of colonial rights and the presumed rights of all Englishmen in the Empire, a protest against Parliament's violation of these rights, while professing loyalty to England and devout hopes for reconciliation, was not a revolutionary action. As long as the conflict remained within these limits, no radical party could effectively challenge the authority of the Assembly. Pennsylvania's equivalent of the radical whigs of Boston were outsiders who had no substantial power beyond the City. They succeeded in electing whig representatives from the City and outside after 1770, but they were unable to dominate the House. Galloway spoke for the House, and he well represented the colony's essential loyalty to the Mother Country and its hope for preserving the connection.

Loyalty and conservatism were not, however, the result of any exceptional love for England and the Crown. They drew from the same sources that had long kept the Quakers and the Old Party in power. A colony of minorities, Pennsylvania's diverse population may have been more cosmopolitan than that of other colonies, but it was little affected by any melting pot. The differences in background and the conflict of interests among its inhabitants had permitted a minority to rule because that minority had presented the least threat to the interests of other minorities. The hates and fears that divided particular groups allowed and indeed demanded that no major change be made in the political structure. The fear of Presbyterian ascendancy, of German ascendancy, of one German group's imposing its religion on another, and of Anglican attempts to secure a bishop and impose an episcopal tyranny on dissenters all acted to fragment Pennsylvania society. The imperial crisis only added to these fears and to the obvious danger that if the existing political and social balance were upset, anarchy would result.

These fears and dangers grew in the decade before 1776, acting against the counterforces that might have led to a reorganization of politics. They especially served to thwart the formation of any radical whig party. There were common resentments against the traditional rule—on questions of representation, defense, election practices, and so forth—but they were not enough to overcome real or imagined divisions. Pennsylvanians looked to what they had; they clung to the Charter and accepted what existed rather than risk internal or external revolution. It was not only the gentlemen who resisted change and were conservative; the common people were also reluctant to accept changes that might deprive them of their liberties and establish some dangerous rival group in power. Until the last moment before Independence was declared, these conservatives exasperated the radicals inside and outside Pennsylvania by remaining loyal to the old government and expressing their fears in petitions for the Charter and against a final separation from the Mother Country.

The events of 1774 and 1775 pushed the Assembly along the route of protest and resistance laid out by the Continental Congress. Reluctantly, the legislators accepted the need to defend the colony and raise and equip a militia; they recognized the establishment of associators, which enforced the non-importation and non-consumption policy of Congress at the local level, and of the Committee of Public Safety, but drew the line at any proposals that might make the breach with England permanent. Their instructions for the delegates to Congress declared in November 1775, "We strictly enjoin you, that you, in Behalf of this Colony, dissent from, and utterly reject, any Propositions, should such be made, that may cause, or lead to, a Separation from our Mother Country, or a Change of the Form of this Government." The Assembly would follow to this point and no further.

Some men saw the likely result of events and withdrew from the House. Galloway, abhorring radicalism and the threat of separation, left in 1775. On the other side, radicals like Joseph Reed and Charles Thomson abandoned the House as too conservative. Pressure thus came from both sides—from the radical and tory extremes. Early in 1776 the radicals openly turned the emergency organizations, the militia, the associators, and the Committees of Correspondence and Public Safety into agencies to displace or overthrow the authority of the Assembly. Yet even then the radicals were unable to capture the House. They failed in the election of October 1775 and again in the special election decreed in March 1776 and held May 1. This latter election was the result of the Assembly's belated attempt to win broader support by substantially increasing the representation for the West and for Philadelphia. Bowing to intense pressure from the radicals in Philadelphia and from leading men in Congress, the House sought an expression from the people on the question of Independence. The election was clearly on this issue, and it was bitterly contested. Despite the radicals' advantages in local associations and militia units and their willingness to use coercion, the conservatives won a majority of the new seats. The electorate, at least, again rallied to the Charter and to the existing government, and a majority of Assemblymen remained opposed to Independence. Whether the election truly represented the will of the people is a matter for conjecture. It is evident, however, that in this last election, the voters rejected the opportunity to throw out the old regime and turn the Assembly over to the proponents of independence and internal revolution.

The radicals finally found a way around the obstinacy of the Assembly and the electorate. By resorting to coercion, threats, and intimidation, they "persuaded" certain members to absent themselves from the House and prevented a quorum from meeting. Unable to conduct its business, the Assembly tottered on and then expired in September 1776. Ironically, one of its last acts was to appropriate £500 for the support of Governor John Penn. Never overthrown by the electorate, the conservative leadership and the traditional structure of political power had prevailed until Independence was a fact. Only the combined forces of the radical minority in Pennsylvania, the power of Congress, and the course of events beyond Pennsylvania brought down the legal government. Perhaps most extraordinary of all, it was not the proprietary executive whom the radicals fought but the representative Assembly.

After 1766, Franklin's influence in provincial politics declined sharply. This loss of influence, which was partly a penalty for his mistaken assessment of the Stamp Act and his campaign for royal government, was compensated for by his new position as an American spokesman in England. Although he became more and more involved in the problems of the Empire, he still tried, until 1769, to push forward the change of government in Pennsylvania. But the failure of his plans to reform the imperial structure, form a colonial union or obtain colonial representation in Parliament, and win support for a more generous paper-money policy and for improved western, Indian, commercial, and defense measures—plus his own private scheme for a grant in the Ohio country—gradually awakened him to the doubtful wisdom of a switch. He wrote to John Ross in May 1768, "I have urged over and over the necessity of the change we desire; but this country itself being at present in a situation very little better, weakens our argument that a royal government would be better managed, and safer to live under than that of a proprietary."[8]

The change in his thinking was slow in coming. Almost any opinion about the future of the Empire, from the most optimistic to the most gloomy, can be found in his writings between 1766 and 1774. A clue to his thinking at any given time is revealed in his changing relationships with leading figures in the government. If Ministers seemed to be favorable to him and his ideas, his reports to friends in Pennsylvania were usually optimistic. His basic principle of political action—a belief in men—remained constant. If he could inform, guide, and persuade important men in England, then all might turn out well—notwithstanding theories, institutions, and abstract rights. Franklin looked hopefully to each change in the composition of the ever-changing ministries, measuring what he might accomplish by the apparent character and attitude of each new officeholder. He expected great things from men like Shelburne, Hillsborough, and Dartmouth. His hopes reached a peak in 1768, when he got hints that he might be appointed to some office—possibly as under-secretary to Lord Hillsborough, the Secretary of State for the Colonies. Although Franklin pretended an off-handed attitude to whether "We may be either promoted, or discarded," his energetic pursuit of the Duke of Grafton's attention betrayed his interest. Ministry leader Grafton was, he wrote, a "nobleman, to whom I could, from sincere respect for his great abilities and amiable qualities, so cordially attach myself, or to whom I should so willingly be obliged for the provision he mentioned . . . if his Grace should think I could, in any station where he might place me, be serviceable to him and to the public."[9]

The failure of his hopes and the failure of the English politicians to act as he thought they should added to his growing despair and disillusionment. However, the fault was not wholly theirs. Always in the background of Franklin's work in England was his long history of lobbying and politicking in behalf of causes not as evidently noble as American liberties. For he was suspected by many, and clearly disliked by some, influential men in England. In 1773, for instance, he wrote that he was not on good terms with Lord North, and attributed this and other signs of coolness to the fact that he "was too much an American." A more likely reason was his long conflict with Penn and the damage that Penn and other proprietary leaders had done to his political credibility and personal reputation. Although none of the people involved said so at the time, the sharp reaction to Franklin's part in obtaining and transmitting Governor Thomas Hutchinson's letters undoubtedly owed a great deal to the long proprietary campaign against him. The Hutchinson affair was seeming confirmation that Franklin was a sly, conniving, unprincipled opportunist, too clever for his or England's good.[10] Thus Solicitor General Alexander Wedderburn's violent personal attack on Franklin was not simply inexplicable bad manners and political stupidity; it was the expression of long pent-up suspicions of Franklin's duplicity and lack of principles—accusations repeatedly made by Penn and the proprietary.

In fairness to the much-maligned politicians in England, it must be pointed out that they could not know of Franklin's future greatness, and could not regard his embassy in England as the labor of an unblemished, disinterested philosopher-statesman devoted to nothing more than the harmonious solution of imperial problems. Franklin was known as the agent and lobbyist for the Assembly and the chief agitator against the legitimate executive in Pennsylvania, interested in patronage for himself and his friends, in western lands, and in faction and party advantage. After Wedderburn's attack and the subsequent loss of his place in the post office, Franklin finally came to the conclusion that, barring a miracle, he could not expect much success in further application to individual leaders in England. There is a certain similarity between the events of 1774 and of 1755—in both cases differences of opinion became personal threats to his position and honor. Both clashes led Franklin to seek revenge by pulling down what the offenders —Penn, Wedderburn, et al.—represented: proprietary and royal government.

After 1766, Franklin was increasingly out of touch with political conditions in Pennsylvania. What he knew of local affairs came from newspapers and from his official and private correspondence. Throughout the period, until his return in 1775, his closest advisers and correspondents were his son, William, and Galloway. From both he received a narrow, partisan, increasingly conservative interpretation of affairs in the province. As time went on, he commiserated with Galloway about the sad state of political morality in Pennsylvania, and urged him to remain steadfast to his principles and his place in the Assembly regardless of what the opposition did to slander his reputation.

Franklin continued to think in terms of politics before 1765; those who attacked Galloway in the 1770's were still, he believed, the dirty supporters of Penn. He wrote his old friend Abel James late in 1772, "It must be very discouraging to our Friend Galloway, to see his long and faithful Services repaid with Abuse and Ingratitude; but let him persevere in well-doing and all will end well, and to his final Satisfaction."[11] He added, "I do not at this Distance understand the Politics of your last Election."[12] He was scarcely aware that the issue in politics was no longer the quarrel with the Proprietor. Until he returned to Pennsylvania in 1775, Franklin remained an Old Party politician in exile, trusting his friends and staunchly believing in their policies. In 1774 he wrote Galloway how much he looked forward to visiting him: "I long to be with you & to converse with you on these important Heads. A few months I hope will bring us together."[13] His ties with the Old Party leaders remained. One wonders whether he, like so many of his associates, would have become a loyalist if he had been in Pennsylvania between 1765 and 1775.

By the time Franklin returned to Pennsylvania, he was ready to plunge into the resistance movement against the English threat. The reports of his mistreatment in the Privy Council had preceded him and lent an air of martyrdom to his embassy, and, with the news he brought from England of ministerial intentions, he was a valuable addition to the radical organization in Philadelphia. He was a hero who had seen the menace at first hand, he was well known in the colony, and with his prestige he was immediately useful to the desperate radicals, who were endeavoring to overcome the conservatism of the Assembly and the lack of patriotic enthusiasm in the hinterland.

Franklin joined the radicals, but he did not take command of them. He found a developed organization already in the hands of the future leaders of the revolution in Pennsylvania. These men had been growing up inside or outside the political order during the decade he had been away. Many of these new leaders remembered him as an associate of Galloway and a leader of the Old Party—now the enemy. Some, like Dickinson, George Bryan, and Michael Hillegas, had been associated with the Proprietary Party, and were naturally suspicious of him. These ambitious men, grasping for power, were not likely to surrender the leadership of the movement to Franklin. He was a useful figurehead to be kept in the Assembly as long as something might be accomplished there (Franklin remained until late February, 1776) or placed in the Pennsylvania delegation to the Continental Congress.

Perhaps Franklin sensed the situation and realized that his own interest and future were best found on the larger scene—in Congress or in the search for foreign assistance. In any event, the power of the new leadership and Franklin's own opinions about his usefulness combined in 1775 and 1776 to keep him out of the direct management of the revolution in Pennsylvania. He assisted it from the outside, letting new men take command of the state in June and July 1776 to create a new constitution and government.[14]

As long as the Empire remained intact, the old regime in Pennsylvania was a durable though brittle structure. Despite rapidly changing conditions, the colony had changed little in the two decades immediately preceding the Revolution. Political conflict had not derived from internal change; rather, it was a jousting at the top among the gentlemen rulers and their factions. The prize was a power advantage for one of them. If possible, it was to be kept within the narrow confines of the established order. A few new combatants were added from time to time, but they entered under the established rules of the game.

After the events of 1765–66, extreme forms of combat between the Old Party and the proprietary ceased. This change was brought about by the removal of Franklin as a direct irritant and by the fear that the people and the Crown might both upset the power of the leaders. But despite their essential similarity of attitude toward the people's place in politics, the Proprietary Party and the Old Party were deeply divided in other ways. The disputes, rivalries, and animosities of the past had been only thinly covered over. To these were added the imperial crisis and the fundamental differences developed in response to it. Until late 1775, the politicians could believe that they were disputing over the means of persuading England to reverse its policy. They could agree that whatever their differences in methods of protest, the Empire would be and must be saved—anything else was unthinkable. And as long as the imperial tie remained, the basic structure of Pennsylvania's government would also be preserved. Many Pennsylvanians apparently believed in this conceptual framework. To them there was a meaningful unity in a government that reached from the county offices up through the provincial parts of government and then to the Crown. Within this ordered relationship was the Charter of 1701 and the stability and safety provided for all individuals and groups in the colony.

Independence shattered this structure and removed the order and protection that had justified the old regime. In this ultimate crisis the gentlemen were incapable of united action. The old leaders could not lead Pennsylvania into the Revolution and guide it in the formation of a new government. No matter how much Israel Pemberton, William Allen, Galloway, and Dickinson might deplore Independence, they were unable either to work together in harmony and mutual trust to prevent it—if they could—or to

form a conservative party to hedge on radicalism after Independence. Faced with extreme pressure from the radical minority in
Pennsylvania and its allies in Congress, and with the destruction
of the Assembly, the proprietary government, and the relationship with England within which they had safely ruled (and quarreled), the leaders of the old regime found themselves at the moment of greatest crisis still imprisoned in the factional and party
divisions of the past. Conservative though most of them were,
they were unable to unite, and thus were swept away.

Once the Assembly was incapacitated, internal revolution was
swift and thorough. Coming between May and August 1776, it
resulted in the emergence of a new group of men hardly known
in Pennsylvania. Few had heard of Timothy Matlack, James Cannon, David Rittenhouse, or Benjamin Rush. These were the men
who had been kept outside of government and politics. They owed
little or nothing to the old leaders or institutions; they represented new interests and conditions that had been suppressed, ignored,
and excluded from polite political society; they were, not surprisingly, inexperienced in government.

There was little political continuity between pre-Revolutionary
and Revolutionary Pennsylvania. Radicalism was a natural product of this disjuncture and the inexperience of the men who suddenly seized the opportunity to create a new government for the
state. The old leaders were, with few exceptions, pushed aside—
the price of a static, unchanging regime that had allowed little
opportunity for gradual change and the training of new leaders
identified with new conditions.

Franklin was wholly a part of this old regime. He had been in
England when the conflict between the executive and the legislature disappeared after 1766, and had lost touch with politics in the
province. The new men who rose to power in 1776 knew him as
a venerable scientist, philosopher, and colonial representative in
London. Some also saw him as an enemy and as a former leader of

the Old Party. Presbyterians, Germans, Westerners, and young men in Philadelphia had not looked to him for leadership in the late 1760's when they were trying to break into the political structure. To gain a share of power, they had struck at the Assembly and the Party of which he was so much a part.

Franklin had done nothing to change the political order; he had sponsored no basic reform other than a change from proprietary to royal government; he had introduced no new group to politics other than his faction in Philadelphia. Intending to act above faction and dispute, he had become the leader of a faction whose politics was especially turbulent and narrowly self-interested. He had started with friendly and profitable relations with the proprietary government and then spent over ten years in a personal, vindictive campaign to overthrow it. He denounced the depravity of Penn's government, yet when he left the province in 1765, Pennsylvanians managed to live in greater peace with the Penns than ever before. He feared the "barbarians" in the western parts of the colony and the danger of Presbyterian power, and both became powerful in 1776. A champion of the British Empire and one of its most devoted sons, Franklin had brought forth plans for its improvement and future glory, only to turn his hand against it and assist in its destruction. Justifying his part in the violent conflicts of Pennsylvania politics on the grounds that he was trying to reform the government, he had closely associated himself with the Party and a portion of the government most resistant to change and reform. Almost without enemies in 1750, he had many in 1776. The internal revolution in politics came therefore not from Franklin's work or under his leadership or the leadership of his party. It was the accomplishment of others.

Yet it was Franklin's luck, his courage, and his vision that ultimately redeemed this disastrous part of his political career. A jump into the hazards of revolution and his great achievements in winning Independence and establishing the Nation—in the more spacious arena of transatlantic affairs, where he was always more comfortable—more than made up for the unrewarding years he had spent in the service of local politics. And Pennsylvania, too, benefited from the work of Franklin the Founding Father and American statesman, even if she had gained little from his labors as an old regime politician.

NOTES

The following abbreviations are used in the Notes:

HSP   Historical Society of Pennsylvania
APS   American Philosophical Society
POC   Penn Official Correspondence (HSP)
PLB   Penn Letter Books (HSP)
INLB   Isaac Norris Letter Books (HSP)
Yale MSS   Papers in the Franklin Collection at
            Yale University

CHAPTER I

1. This and subsequent chapters draw upon the standard body of works, both old and recent, devoted to the political and social history of colonial Pennsylvania. Those of particular significance for this study are individually discussed in the Bibliographical Note.

2. Winifred T. Root, *The Relations of Pennsylvania with the British Government, 1696–1765* (Philadelphia, 1912), pp. 296–97. Root declares, "The Quaker Assembly voted money . . . but in so doing insisted upon the sole right to judge for itself as well as the people of the utility and propriety of all laws without any outside direction from Crown or proprietors. Indeed, the Assembly held the constitutional issue of far more importance than the security of the province or the welfare of the Empire."

3. Thomas Penn to Richard Peters, Feb. 24, 1751, PLB, III.

4. Governor George Thomas to John Penn, May 14, 1741, POC, III. Thomas declared that the Assembly was so powerful that the Governor was reduced to a "cypher or no more than nominal."

5. Thomas Penn to T. Jackson, 1740, Franklin Manuscripts, X (University of Pennsylvania). Penn wrote, "At the Yearly Meeting at Burlington . . . instead of making use of those meetings for regulating Religious Affairs of the Society they are become Councils for the Government."

6. Control of the sheriffs, coroners, inspectors, and other local officials was one of the most important factors in county politics. With such control, elections and voting qualifications could be regulated to serve the dominant faction. The Quakers in the eastern counties maintained their power through these local leaders until 1776.

7. Major figures in the London Quaker community included Elias Bland, David Barclay, John Hunt, Hinton Brown, and Dr. John Fothergill.

8. Although Richard and Thomas Penn were together "the Proprietaries," Thomas managed the family interests and especially the political concerns in Pennsylvania. Unless otherwise noted, he is the Proprietor in this study.

9. James Hamilton to Thomas Penn, July 7, 1753, POC, VI; Richard Hockley to Penn, Aug. 22, 1755, Penn Manuscripts: Correspondence of the Penn Family, 1732–67 (HSP). The vast correspondence of Thomas Penn concerning Pennsylvania is itself the best evidence of his conscientious attention to the government and welfare of the colony. He wrote James Logan in July 1752, "We have nothing in view but what is for the real Interest of the country. It is that alone which inclines us to increase the influence of the Executive part of the Government, by no means to gratify a thurst for Power, and I would not have so much that, should it come into bad hands, it may be made use of to the prejudice of the People" (PLB, III).

10. Penn to Peters, Feb. 20, 1748, and Oct. 9, 1749, PLB, II. Penn declared that until recently he had been unable to help the proposed academy in Pennsylvania because he lacked money.

11. William R. Shepherd, *History of Proprietary Government in Pennsylvania* (New York, 1896), pp. 61–62. The first comprehensive attempt to manage the land business in Pennsylvania came in 1759, when the Assembly announced that it would henceforth treat the Proprietors as mere private landlords.

12. Penn to Peters, Oct. 25, 1755, Penn Manuscripts: Supplementary Proceedings (HSP).

13. Peters to Penn, Apr. 29, 1749, Peters Letter Book (HSP).

14. John Smith to Elizabeth Hudson, Aug. 10, 1750, John Smith Manuscripts (Library Company). Smith, a Quaker leader, declared that the recent election in Philadelphia County was "carried on without opposition from what we used to call The Other Party."

15. Shepherd, *Proprietary Government*, pp. 74–75. Shepherd suggests that Penn's opposition to the granting of large amounts of land to speculators and wealthy men in the colony was a real advantage to the ordinary settler. Great land monopolies in the hands of a few Pennsylvanians were prevented —Penn's monopoly was easier on the people.

16. Isaac Norris to Charles Norris, Apr. 29, 1755, INLB, 1719–56.

CHAPTER II

1. Beginning with the *Autobiography*, Franklin's place in history has been measured and evaluated in a large number of works, including full-scale biographies and individual studies of his "many facets." All are based primarily on Franklin's abundant papers. These papers remain a fundamental, if one-sided, source, revealing on each examination something more about their ex-

traordinary author. Until Yale University and the American Philosophical Society began a new publication of this enormous body of material, the volumes edited by Albert H. Smyth, *The Writings of Benjamin Franklin* (New York, 1905–1907) were the most complete if not the most accurate compilation. A reading of the published and manuscript papers and relevant secondary studies has provided the background for this chapter.

2. Smyth, *Writings of Benjamin Franklin*, II, 363.

3. Franklin's tentative first step into political affairs in the defense crisis of 1747 may best be understood in the context of his innumerable other plans and ideas of the mid-1740's. For a good discussion, see Carl Van Doren, *Benjamin Franklin* (New York, 1938).

4. Penn to Peters, Mar. 30 and Aug. 31, 1748, PLB, II.

5. Peters to Penn, June 16, 1748, Sparks Transcripts (APS); Penn to Peters, June 9, 1748, PLB, II.

CHAPTER III

1. William Logan to James Pemberton, Sept. 25, 1748, Library Company Manuscripts, 1600–1885 (Library Company, Philadelphia). Logan wrote, "People are determined to show him all the Respect in their Power by a Magnificent Reception."

2. Hamilton to Penn, May 5, 1750, POC, V; Penn to Hamilton, July 31, 1749, PLB, II; Penn to Peters, Aug. 2, 1749, Penn Manuscripts: Saunders Coates (HSP). Penn agreed that one hundred thousand pounds was not too great a sum of paper money for the Assembly to issue. He worked to convince men in England that Pennsylvania's money was well managed. One of his converts was Sir John Barnard, an M.P. and an authority on financial matters, who had previously been "an enemy to all colonial paper currency."

3. Hamilton to Penn, Feb. 22, 1750/51, POC, V.

4. Penn to Peters, Mar. 31, 1750, PLB, III.

5. Penn to Hamilton, Aug. 10, 1763, PLB, VII.

6. Penn to Peters, Mar. 31, 1750, Sept. 28, 1751, PLB, III.

7. Hamilton to Penn, Feb. 3, 1750, POC, V.

8. Peters to Penn, Jan. 30, 1750/51, POC, V.

9. Hamilton to Penn, Feb. 3, 1750, POC; *Pennsylvania Colonial Records, Minutes of the Provincial Council, 1683–1776*, Samuel Hazard, ed., VI (Philadelphia, 1852–53), 4 (hereafter cited as *Colonial Records*); Hamilton to Penn, Apr. 30, 1751, POC, V.

10. Penn to Hamilton, Mar. 9, 1752, PLB, III.

11. Hamilton to Penn, Sept. 14, 1751; Peters to Penn, Nov. 17, 1750, POC, V.

12. Penn to Hamilton, Feb. 25, 1750, PLB, III.

13. *Ibid.*, Dec. 12, 1753, POC, VI; Shepherd, *Proprietary Government,* p. 427.

14. Hamilton to Penn, Mar. 18, 1752, POC, V.

15. Penn to Peters, July 17, 1752, Peters Manuscripts, III (HSP); Penn to Hamilton, July 20, 1751, PLB, III. Penn told Hamilton, "There is nothing but the power of appropriating the publick money that can give those People any weight."

16. Penn to Peters, Oct. 17, 1754, PLB, IV.

17. Hamilton to Penn, Mar. 17, 1752, POC, V.

18. *Ibid.*, Feb. 22, 1750/51, POC, V.

19. Peters to Penn, Dec. 5, 1752, POC, V.

20. *Ibid.*, Nov. 17, 1750, POC, V.

21. *Ibid.*, Jan. 30, 1750/51, POC, V.

22. Graeme to Penn, Nov. 6, 1750, POC, V; Penn to Hamilton, Feb. 25, 1750, PLB, III.

23. Graeme to Penn, Nov. 6, 1750, POC, V.

24. All of the proprietary leaders officially deplored the unequal representation in the Assembly, chiefly because the system strongly favored the Quakers (Penn to Robert Morris, Mar. 22, 1756, PLB, IV).

25. Peters to Penn, June 12, 1752, POC, V.

26. Penn to Peters, Mar. 18, 1752, PLB, III. Proprietary leaders on both sides of the Atlantic detested and feared Israel Pemberton more than any other person in Pennsylvania. Hamilton wrote, "Well knowing the violence and rudeness of his temper . . . nothing was capable of satisfying Mr. Pemberton" (Hamilton to Penn, Sept. 14, 1751, POC, V).

27. Smyth, *Writings of Benjamin Franklin,* III, 241-43. In a letter to Peter Collinson on Dec. 29, 1754, Franklin declared, "But in my Opinion great Men are not always best serv'd by such as show on all Occasions a blind Attachment to them. An Appearance of Impartiality in general gives a Man sometimes much more Weight—when he would serve in particular Instances."

28. *Ibid.*, III, 262-65.

29. Penn to Peters, Jan. 9, 1753, Peters MSS, VIII (HSP).

30. Franklin to Collinson, June 26, 1753, Yale MSS, Box 2, 1751-53.

CHAPTER IV

1. Robert Morris to Penn, Oct. 2, 1754, POC, VI. After Hamilton left the government, Allen continued to press the Governor on the danger of the battle, claiming that it would take twelve years, and that in the meantime the

Assembly would be "encouraging associations for the not [sic] payment of Quit rent."

2. Of the Governors from 1750 to 1765, only William Denny responded to the Assembly's threat to cut off his support. The others—Hamilton, Morris, and John Penn—refused to give way.

3. Peters to Penn, Feb. 2, 1753, POC, VI. Peters echoed the local fears: "Will it not . . . be proper to acquaint the Lord President or Lord Halifax with the State of the Province? . . . to the Assembly's having the sole Disposal of the Money; for they dare not disoblige the People thro' fear of losing their Seats in the Assembly."

4. Hamilton to Penn, July 7, 1753, POC, VI.

5. Penn to Peters, June 29, 1753, PLB, III; *Votes and Proceedings of the House of Representatives, 1683–1776* (Pennsylvania Archives, Gertrude MacKinney, ed., Harrisburg, 1931–35), 8th Series, IV, 284, 311, 312 (hereafter cited as *Votes*); Penn to Peters, Oct. 31, 1753, PLB, III.

6. Penn to Peters, Oct. 31, 1753, PLB, III.

7. Isaac Norris to Charles Norris, May 31, 1754, INLB.

8. Robert Morris to Penn, Oct. 2, 1754, POC, VI. Morris reported that leaders in the Assembly had declared that "They will fight the Proprietarys to the last, rather than part with what they call a most valuable privilege, and having upwards of twenty thousand pounds in hand they talk of dealing it out very sparingly that they may hold out the longer, and make no doubt of getting the better in the end."

9. Isaac Norris to Charles Norris, Oct. 7, 1754, INLB. Norris was worried about English opinion and cautioned, "The great care is to act so as to give no just offence to our Superiors on your side of the waters."

10. *Ibid.*, May 31, 1754, INLB.

11. Penn to Peters, June 10, 1754, PLB, III; Richard Hockley to Penn, Aug. 4, 1754, Correspondence of the Penn Family (HSP).

12. Morris to Penn, Oct. 2, 1754, POC, VI; *Votes*, IV, 343–47.

13. Isaac Norris to Charles Norris, Dec. 21, 1754, INLB.

14. Penn to Peters, Nov. 7, 1754, PLB, IV. Penn believed that "Every Person here is of the opinion, that the Money should not be taken on their Terms."

15. Isaac Norris to Charles Norris, Apr. 19, 1754, INLB.

16. Robinson to Morris, July 5 and Oct. 26, 1754, POC, VI.

17. Isaac Norris to Charles Norris, Dec. 21, 1754, INLB.

18. Richard Hockley to Penn, Aug. 5, 1754, Correspondence of the Penn Family (HSP).

19. See Robert L. D. Davidson, *War Comes to Quaker Pennsylvania, 1682–1756* (New York, 1957), pp. 64–90, and Anthony F. C. Wallace, *King of the Delawares: Teedyuscung 1700–1763* (Philadelphia, 1949).

20. Peters to Penn, Nov. 6, 1753, POC, VI.

21. Penn to Hamilton, Mar. 9, 1752, PLB, III; Peters to Penn, Aug. 2, 1753, POC, VI.

22. Isaac Norris to Charles Norris, Apr. 19, 1754, INLB.

23. *Ibid.*, Dec. 21, 1754, INLB.

24. *Ibid.*, May 31, 1754, INLB.

25. *Ibid.*, Oct. 7, 1754, INLB.

26. Morris to Penn, Oct. 2, 1754, POC, VI.

27. Franklin to Smith, Apr. 18, 1754, Yale MSS, Box 1754–56; Penn to Peters, Mar. 9, 1754, PLB, III.

28. Arthur D. Graeff, *The Relations Between the Pennsylvania Germans and the British Authorities 1750–1776* (Norristown, Pa., 1939), p. 47.

29. Smyth, *Writings of Benjamin Franklin*, III, 139.

30. *Ibid.*, III, 48–50, 132–33.

31. Penn to Peters, Feb. 1, 1754, PLB, III.

32. Peters to Penn, Nov. 6, 1753, POC, VI.

33. Franklin to Penn, May 30, 1754, Yale MSS.

34. Penn to Peters, Feb. 1, 1754, PLB, III; Peters to Penn, Nov. 7, 1753, POC, VI. Peters declared, "My hand should have been burnt rather than sign [such] a Paper."

35. Peters to Penn, Nov. 27, 1753, POC, VI.

36. Penn to Peters, Feb. 1, 1754, PLB, III. The "Boston Method" mentioned by Penn refers to Franklin's request for information about regulations of the Indian trade in other colonies which he sent to Governor Shirley and Cadwallader Colden, a member of the Governor's Council in New York.

37. Some of the compromises Franklin accepted in the final draft of the Albany Plan were not to his liking. He told Collinson, "Some Things in the Plan may perhaps appear of too popular a Turn, the Commissioners from the 2 popular Governments, having considerable Weight at the Board" (Smyth, *Writings of Benjamin Franklin*, III, 243).

38. The recently published fifth volume of *The Papers of Benjamin Franklin* (Leonard Labaree, ed. [New Haven, 1962], pp. 397–417) presents a thorough discussion of the origin and development of the Albany Plan. This authoritative analysis supports Franklin's claim to primary responsibility for the ideas and form of the Plan.

39. *Franklin Papers*, V, 414, 409.

40. *Ibid.*, V, 411.

41. *Ibid.*, V, 427. Italics mine.

42. *Ibid.*, V, 405.

43. *Ibid.*, V, 400.

44. Smyth, *Writings of Benjamin Franklin*, III, 40–45.

CHAPTER V

1. Shepherd, *Proprietary Government*, p. 426; William Smith to Penn, 1755, POC, VII. Smith believed that "Surely it is high Time for the British Parliament to interfere, and ascertain the particular powers both of Governors and Assemblies, that now at last we may enjoy some Respite from those eternal quarrels that distract us, and have thrown us almost into the Hands of the Enemy."

2. Penn to Morris, Feb. 26, 1755, PLB, IV.

3. Wells to John Smith, June 20, 1755, Smith MSS (Library Company, Phila.), IV.

4. Penn to Peters, Oct. 4, 1755, Penn MSS: Saunders Coates (HSP).

5. Isaac Norris to Charles Norris, Apr. 29, 1755, and Isaac Norris to John Fothergill, May 25, 1755, INLB.

6. Penn to Morris, Aug. 13, 1755, PLB, IV. Penn reported increasing opposition to the tactics of the Assembly: "The Friends here do not approve of the behavior of their brethren in the Assembly."

7. Peters to the Proprietors, May 17, 1755, Peters MSS, III (HSP); Israel Pemberton to John Fothergill, 755, Etting Collection, Pemberton Papers, II (HSP).

8. William Smith to Penn, 1755, POC, VII.

9. Richard Hockley to Penn, Aug. 25, 1755, Correspondence of the Penn Family (HSP).

10. William Smith to Penn, 1755, POC, VII.

11. *Ibid.*, 1755, POC, VII. Italics mine.

12. Pemberton to John Fothergill, July 19, 1755, Pemberton Papers, II (HSP).

13. Franklin's quarrel with Penn and the proprietary faction developed very quickly. As late as June 26, 1755, he wrote to Collinson, "Our Friend Smith will be very serviceable here."

14. William Peters (brother of Richard Peters) to Penn, Jan. 4, 1756, POC, VIII.

15. Richard Peters to the Proprietors, June 26, 1756, Peters MSS 1755–57 (HSP).

16. Governor Shirley to Governor Morris, May 14, 1755, Yale MSS, Box 3, 1754–56.

17. Morris to Braddock, June 4, 1755, POC, VII. Morris implied that Franklin acted only as his agent: "Mr. Franklin, who I have employed to procure the waggons . . . tells me I may depend on having them."

18. Penn to Peters, July 3, 1755, Penn MSS: Saunders Coates (HSP); Penn to Morris, Sept. 19, 1755, PLB, IV.

19. Penn to Peters, Aug. 13, 1755, Manuscript Letters 1752–72 (HSP).

20. *Ibid.*, July 3, 1755, PLB, IV. "I believe I shall write to Mr. Franklin after I have seen Sir Everard Falconer, but I cannot court a man who has acted the part he has done."

21. William Smith to Penn, 1755, POC, VII.

22. Penn to Peters, Oct. 9, 1756, PLB, V. Penn stated, "I do not know that I have spoke against Mr. Franklin to anyone except mentioning that I thought it wrong he should print the Secretary of States Letters, who is of the same opinion."

23. *Ibid.*, Aug. 13, 1756, PLB, IV.

24. Hockley to Penn, Dec. 24, 1755, POC, VII.

25. Morris to Thomas Penn, 1756, Gratz Collection—French and Indian Wars 1756, Case 15, Box 18 (HSP).

CHAPTER VI

1. Smith to Penn, 1755, POC, VII. Italics in the original.

2. Penn to Peters, Feb. 21, 1755, PLB, IV.

3. Shepherd, *Proprietary Government*, p. 447.

4. Isaac Norris and William Callender to Richard Partridge and Robert Charles, Jan. 12, 1755, INLB.

5. Penn to Peters, Feb. 21, 1755, PLB, IV.

6. *Ibid.*, Feb. 21, 1755, PLB, IV.

7. *Ibid.*, Feb. 21, 1755, and May 8, 1756, PLB, IV.

8. *Ibid.*, June 11, 1755, PLB, IV.

9. *Ibid.*, Apr. 7, 1756, PLB, IV.

10. Isaac Norris to Charles Norris, June 16, 1756, Norris MSS—Copybook, 1756 (HSP). Norris refers to his "intimacy and real friendship for that Gentleman and frequent opportunity of Knowing his Disposition."

11. Penn to Peters, Apr. 20, 1756, PLB, IV; Penn to Morris, Sept. 10, 1756, PLB, IV.

12. *Votes*, IV, 524; Proprietors to Morris, Oct. 5, 1755, PLB, IV. English opinion was largely responsible for Penn's gift of £5,000 for defense. Penn wrote, "I desire you [Morris] will not insist on the appropriation of the remainder, for the times are critical and everybody's eyes are on us; I have visited Sir Thomas Robinson this morning, who says he has heard several People express a dislike of your refusing, on our part, to assist the Publick at such a time as this."

13. Peters to Penn, Oct. 30, 1756, POC, VIII. Peters had information from the Assembly that Isaac Norris was prepared to offer "a good Militia Act and to Accommodate all Differences with the Proprietaries and it will be done if it does not receive an Opposition from B F which it will" (Norris to Fothergill, May 25, 1755, INLB).

14. William Smith, *A Brief State of the Province of Pennsylvania* . . . (Yale University Manuscript); William Allen to Penn, Oct. 20, 1755, POC, VII.

15. Penn to Morris, Mar. 13, 1756, PLB, IV.

16. Pemberton to John Fothergill, n.d., Pemberton Papers, HSP, II.

17. Fothergill to Pemberton, Mar. 16, 1756, Pemberton Papers, HSP, II.

18. Penn to Morris, Mar. 13, 1756, PLB, IV.

19. Penn to Peters, Aug. 13, 1756, PLB, IV. Halifax asked Penn "whether I should not like a Quaker better than a Presbyterian Assembly."

CHAPTER VII

1. Isaac Norris to Charles Norris, Apr. 29, 1755, INLB.

2. *Ibid.*, Oct. 5, 1755, INLB.

3. Peters to Penn, 1756, POC, VIII.

4. *Ibid.*

5. *Ibid.*, June 1, 1756, POC, VIII.

6. Peters to the Proprietaries, Apr. 25, 1756, POC, VIII. "The Church People in general are so poysoned by Franklin that they may prove even worse Enemies to the Proprietaries than the Quakers."

7. Pemberton to Fothergill, May 1756, Pemberton Papers, II (HSP).

8. Theodore Thayer, *Israel Pemberton: King of the Quakers* (Philadelphia, 1943), pp. 115, 121.

9. Thayer, *Pemberton*, pp. 117–18.

10. Penn reported that Samuel Fothergill and "Twenty Friends" presented an "Address from the Meeting to us—they press one of us coming over and living among them, declare their desire to support our just rights and that they will chearfully contribute towards restoring Harmony" (Penn to Peters, May 8, 1756, PLB, IV).

11. Penn to Morris, Aug. 13, 1755, PLB, IV.

12. Peters to Penn, Jan. 4, 1756, POC, VIII.

13. Wallace, *Teedyuscung*, pp. 144–50. Discontent with land sales was not a major cause of the Indian war.

14. Smyth, *Writings of Benjamin Franklin*, III, 341–42.

15. Penn to Morris, May 6, 1756, PLB, IV; Smyth, *Writings of Benjamin Franklin*, III, 307–20.

16. Smyth, *Writings of Benjamin Franklin*, III, 268–302.

17. Penn to Morris, Jan. 27, 1756, PLB, IV.

18. Pemberton frequently expressed his opposition to the militia and to Franklin: "The Great Patriot Franklin who hath the principal direction of forming the bills has discovered very little regard for Tender Consciences."

(Pemberton to Samuel Fothergill, November 1756, Fothergill Letters, Vol. 34 [HSP]).

19. Penn to Peters, May 10, 1755, Penn MSS: Saunders Coates (HSP).

20. Peters to Penn, Jan. 5, 1756, POC, VIII.

21. Morris to William Alexander, Oct. 10, 1756, POC, VIII.

22. William Smith to Penn, 1755, POC, VII. Smith protested "the wicked Insinuation that the Germans would perhaps be obliged sometime to plough the Lord Proprietor's Manors, as in Germany."

23. Peters to Penn, Sept. 22, 1756, POC, VIII.

24. *Ibid.* Isaac Norris led the winning candidates with 1758 votes. John Smith Manuscripts, 1756 (HSP).

26. Edward Shippen to Joseph Shippen, Jr., 1756, Shippen Correspondence, II (HSP).

27. William Peters to Penn, Jan. 4, 1756, POC, VIII.

28. Penn to Richard Peters, Oct. 25, 1755, PLB, IV.

29. Morris to [?] Penn, Oct. 8, 1756, POC, VIII.

CHAPTER VIII

1. Franklin to Joseph Galloway, June 10, 1758, Yale MSS. He told Galloway, "I find myself engag'd in an Affair that will take much more time than I expected. God knows when we shall see it finished."

2. John Kearsley, a Philadelphia physician, was one of the most outspoken in his dislike of Franklin. He wrote, "They talk of sending the Electrician home . . . I am told his office [is] shaky, however, he would not go but to support this falling interest of his own" (Kearsley to Morris, 1757, Yale MSS, Box 1757–58).

3. Peters to Penn, Jan. 31, 1757, Penn MSS, Peters to the Proprietor, 1755–57 (HSP).

4. Morris to Peters, Apr. 6, 1757, Peters MSS, 1755–Nov. 1757 (HSP).

5. Pemberton to Fothergill, July 4, 1757, Pemberton-Fothergill Letters (HSP); William Allen to Dr. Chandler, Feb. 4, 1757, POC, V. Allen declared, "Our Assembly is still chiefly composed of Quakers, and some low people, chosen by their influence; of those that profess Quakerism, there are now in the House fourteen, and one Dutch Menanist [sic]."

6. Franklin to Norris, Jan. 19, 1758, Yale MSS. Franklin informed Norris that "the House will see, that if they propose to continue Treating with the Proprietor, it will be necessary to recall me and appoint another Person or Persons."

7. William Franklin to Joseph Galloway, Dec. 28, 1759, Yale MSS.

8. "Extracts from Lord Loudoun's Diary," June 25, 1757, Yale MSS, Box 1757–58.

9. Earl of Loudoun to the Duke of Cumberland, Oct. 7, 1757, Letterbook of the Duke of Cumberland (Huntington Library).

10. Peters to Penn, Jan. 27, 1757, POC, VIII.

11. Penn to Peters, Apr. 9, 1757, Peters MSS, IV (HSP).

12. Ibid., Apr. 9, 1757, PLB, V.

13. Ibid., July 5, 1758, Penn MSS: Saunders Coates (HSP). Penn reported that Franklin and the Quakers had attempted to see Pitt about the Indian charges. Pitt sent word that the matter should be settled with Lord Halifax and Penn.

14. Fothergill to Pemberton, Sept. 25, 1758, Etting Collection, Dr. John Fothergill Letters to Israel Pemberton (HSP).

15. Ibid.

16. It was the proprietary faction which charged that the Quakers opposed Penn because he had become an Anglican. Franklin told Pemberton that this was part of proprietary strategy in England (Franklin to Pemberton, Mar. 19, 1759 [Smyth, Writings of Benjamin Franklin, III, 472]).

17. Franklin to Galloway, Apr. 7, 1759, Yale MSS.

18. Ibid., Apr. 1, 1759, Yale MSS. Italics in the original.

19. Penn to Peters, July 5, 1758, Sparks MSS (Harvard) on microfilm in the APS; Penn to Peters, June 9, 1760, PLB, VI.

20. Ibid., July 5, 1758, PLB, V.

21. Franklin to Isaac Norris, June 9, 1758, Yale MSS.

22. Franklin to Galloway, Feb. 17, 1758, Yale MSS.

23. Ibid., Apr. 7, 1758, Yale MSS.

24. The work was dedicated to the Speaker of the House of Commons, Arthur Onslow (Franklin to Isaac Norris, Mar. 19, 1758, Yale MSS).

25. Fothergill to Pemberton, June 12, 1758, Etting Collection, Dr. John Fothergill Letters to Israel Pemberton (HSP).

26. Penn to Peters, May 14, 1757, PLB, V.

27. Franklin to Galloway, Feb. 17, 1758, Yale MSS; Franklin to Isaac Norris, Jan. 19, 1759.

28. Thomas and Richard Penn to William Denny, Jan. 28, 1758, PLB, V. Penn ascribed the long delay in the study of the "Heads of Complaint" of the Assembly to the busy schedule of the Attorney General and the Solicitor General.

29. Jackson, "Private Sentiments," 1758, Yale MSS. This work has not been included in books published by either Carl Van Doren or Smyth. Franklin quoted from it in his letter to Galloway, June 10, 1758, Yale MSS.

30. Jackson, "Private Sentiments," Yale MSS.

31. Franklin to Galloway, Apr. 7, 1759, Yale MSS.

32. Ibid., Dec. 28, 1759, Yale MSS.

33. Franklin to [?], Sept. 16, 1758, Stevens Collections, Miscellaneous, I (HSP).

34. Franklin to Galloway, June 10, 1758, Yale MSS.

35. Roberts to Franklin, June 1, 1758, Smith MSS, II (HSP); Memorandum for Mr. Penn," Penn Manuscripts, Smith and Moore vs. Assembly, 1758-59 (HSP).

36. Franklin to Thomas Leech, May 13, 1758, Yale MSS.

37. "The Opinion of Attorney General Pratt and Solicitor General Yorke," June 2, 1759, Penn MSS, Smith and Moore vs. Assembly, 1758-59 (HSP).

38. Jacob Duché to Peters, May 11, 1758, Peters MSS, V (HSP).

39. Franklin to Galloway, Sept. 16, 1758, Yale MSS. Franklin considered the Smith case "an open Declaration of War" by the Proprietor, "and having no longer any Hopes of an Accommodation, I have never since desired an Audience of them."

40. Ibid., Apr. 7, 1759, Yale MSS.

41. Penn to Hamilton, June 27, 1760, PLB, VI.

42. Penn to Peters, May 10, 1760, PLB, VI.

43. Penn to Hamilton, May 24, 1760, PLB, VI.

44. Ibid., June 13, 1761, and Aug. 30, 1760, PLB, VI.

CHAPTER IX

1. Penn to Hamilton, Aug. 30, 1760, PLB, VI.

2. Penn to Peters, Oct. 19, 1760, Sparks MSS (Harvard).

3. Penn to the Rev. Mr. Barton, 1761, PLB, VII.

4. Penn to Peters, Feb. 2, 1758, Yale MSS, Box 4, 1757-59.

5. Franklin to Isaac Norris, Jan. 19, 1759, Yale MSS.

6. Peters to Penn, Jan. 13, 1761, Penn MSS: Saunders Coates (HSP).

7. Thomas Penn to John Penn, Feb. 10, 1764, PLB, VIII.

8. Penn to Hamilton, May 24, 1760, PLB, VI.

9. Ibid., Oct. 18, 1760, PLB, VI. Penn expected that no further money would be needed from the Assembly "as Mr. Amherst has taken possession of Canada."

10. Franklin to Collinson, Dec. 19, 1763, Yale MSS.

11. Thomas Penn to John Penn, Dec. 10, 1763, PLB, VIII.

12. Penn to Hamilton, Apr. 13, 1761, PLB, VII.

13. Logan to Smith, Feb. 20, 1761, Smith MSS (HSP). Logan, a devout Quaker, visited Penn and his wife in England. His remarks suggest that the Proprietor's religion [Anglican] was not an issue in Pennsylvania politics. Of Lady Juliana Penn he wrote in the same letter, "She bears a Universal Good Character and I take her to be more of a Friend than himself. I observe she is very careful in the Education of her Children and I was told by a Sober Friend that She highly Esteems Old William Penn's Writings."

14. Penn to Peters, Dec. 8, 1759, PLB, VI.

15. Franklin to Pennington, May 9, 1761, Society Collection, Benjamin Franklin (HSP).

16. Hamilton to Penn, Nov. 21, 1762, POC, IX.

17. Penn to Hamilton, Feb. 11, 1763, PLB, VII; *Colonial Records*, IX, 62.

18. *Ibid.*, Nov. 11, 1763, PLB, VIII; *Colonial Records*, IX, 156–60.

19. John Harris to Col. Burd, Mar. 1, 1764, Shippen Papers, Correspondence, VI.

20. Even Thomas Penn had a good word for Franklin: "I was very well pleased with a small Pamphlet wrote by Mr. Franklin" (Penn to Peters, Apr. 13, 1764, PLB, VIII).

21. *Colonial Records*, IX, 92–100; *Votes*, V, 293.

22. *Ibid.*, IX, 123–24.

23. *Votes*, V, 413.

24. *Ibid.*, V, 289, 310.

25. *Colonial Records*, IX, 127–28; *Pennsylvania Gazette*, Feb. 9, 1764.

26. "Extract Account of the March of the Paxton Men on Philadelphia from the Journals of H. Melchior Muhlenberg, D.D.," Collections of the HSP, I, 73–77.

27. William Logan to John Smith, Jan. 28, 1764, Smith Correspondence (HSP).

28. James Pemberton to John Fothergill, Mar. 7, 1764, Pemberton Papers, XXXIV (HSP).

CHAPTER X

1. Franklin to Fothergill, Mar. 14, 1764, Yale MSS.

2. Franklin blamed the proprietary government for all of the troubles of the colony in *Cool Thoughts on the Present Situation of Our Public Affairs* (1764) (Smyth, *Writings of Benjamin Franklin*, IV, 226–41).

3. Franklin to Strahan, Mar. 30, 1764, Franklin MSS, Folder 10 (University of Pennsylvania).

4. Franklin to Fothergill, Mar. 14, 1753, Yale MSS.

5. Franklin to Strahan, Sept. 1, 1764, Yale MSS. In discussing his pamphlet *A Narrative of the Late Insurrections*, Franklin told Strahan, "You cannot conceive the number of Bitter Enemies that little Piece has rais'd me among the Irish Presbyterians." He added the remark that he was still at war with the Proprietary Party, "and who will ere long either demolish me or I them. If the former happens, as possibly it may, Behold me a Londoner for the rest of my Days."

6. Thomas Penn had ordered the strongest measures taken against the mur-

derers of the Indians. He stated that he was alarmed at the support given to the "Paxtang People" (Penn to Peters, Apr. 13, 1764, PLB, VIII; Penn to the Rev. Mr. Barton, Apr. 11, 1764, PLB, VIII).

7. Joseph Shippen reported to his father that "Messrs. Allinson, Humphreys, William Henry and Johnny Allen" told the Governor that "not only the Presbyterian Congregation of this Town, but the rest throughout the Province are resolved to have no concern with any such Petition" (Joseph Shippen to Edward Shippen, Apr. 11, 1764, Shippen Papers, 1727–83 [Library of Congress]).

8. Collinson to Edward Hyde, Oct. 11, 1764, Collinson-Bartram Papers (APS).

9. Franklin to Cadwallader Evans, July 13, 1765, Franklin Papers, (APS).

10. Allen to Penn, Oct. 21, 1764, POC, IX.

11. Logan to John Smith, Jan. 21, 1764, Smith MSS (HSP).

12. Pemberton to David Barclay, Nov. 6, 1764, Pemberton Papers, XVII (HSP).

13. Barclay to Pemberton, July 5, 1764, Cox, Parrish, Wharton Collection, XI (HSP).

14. Logan to John Smith, Oct. 22, 1764, Smith MSS, VI (Library Company, Phila.).

15. Pemberton and John Hunt convinced the Yearly Meeting to oppose the petition and "influence the Assembly to moderate measures" (Pemberton to Barclay, Nov. 6, 1764, Pemberton Papers, XVII [HSP]).

16. Allen to Penn, Sept. 25, 1764, POC, IX.

17. William Bingham to John Gibson, May 14, 1764, Shippen Papers, Correspondence, VI (HSP).

18. Heinrich Miller, who published *Der Wochentliche Philadelphische Staatsbote*, opposed Franklin and the petition for royal government.

19. See Charles H. Lincoln, *The Revolutionary Movement in Pennsylvania, 1760–1776*, for a different view of Pennsylvania's political development.

20. William Peters to Penn, May 5, 1764, POC, IX; Edward Shippen to Col. Burd, Oct. 25, 1762, Shippen Papers, Correspondence, V (HSP). Shippen recounts his quarrel with Hockley and adds, "I have good reason to believe I shall soon stand as fair with our Proprietarys as ever I did."

21. John Penn to Thomas Penn, June, 1764, POC, IX.

22. Thomas Penn to John Penn, June 8, 1764, PLB, VIII.

23. Thomas Penn to Benjamin Chew, June 8, 1764, PLB, VIII.

24. *Ibid.*

25. John Penn to Thomas Penn, Sept. 22, 1764, POC, IX.

26. William Peters to Thomas Penn, May 5, 1764, POC, IX. The pam-

phlet was entitled *A Speech on a Petition for a Change of Government of the Colony of Pennsylvania.*

27. Edward Shippen to Joseph Shippen, May 29, 1764, Shippen Papers —Correspondence of Edward and Joseph Shippen 1750–78 (APS). Edward declared, "I am pleased with the Governor's Message, and also with Johnny Dickinson's sentiments, and courage . . . and tho' he should lose his seat in the House by it, he will go off with HONOR."

28. Thomas Penn to John Penn, Feb. 10, 1764, PLB, VIII. Penn believed that the proposed stamp duty "will be opposed as an internal Taxation rather to be done by Act of Assembly, but this is in embryo at present."

29. *Ibid.*, Aug. 12, 1764, PLB, VIII.

30. James Burd to Samuel Purviance, Jr., Sept. 17, 1764, Shippen Papers, Correspondence, VI (HSP).

31. *Ibid.*

32. Peters to Penn, June 4, 1764, POC, IX.

33. Purviance to James Burd, Sept. 10, 1764, Shippen Papers, Correspondence, VI (HSP).

34. John Penn to Thomas Penn, May 5, 1764, POC, IX. John Penn expressed his disgust with the efforts of the opposition to collect signatures on Franklin's petition: "Thomas Wharton, Philip Syng and one Knowles, a barber . . . go into All of the houses in Town without distinction . . . they kept open house at a Tavern for all the Blackguards in Town by which means a few Ship Carpenters and some of the lowest sort of people were prevailed upon to sign it."

35. *Votes*, V, 360.

36. George Bryan and John Dickinson replaced Franklin and Galloway.

37. Thomas Penn to Chew, Dec. 7, 1764, PLB, VIII. Penn reported that he had received a petition from Pennsylvania against the proposed change of government "signed by Eight thousand and six hundred People."

38. Penn's determination to resist any pressure put upon him to give up the government was expressed often in his letters. In 1757 he declared, "As to the change of government, I defy them to bring anything of that kind to pass that is disagreeable to me, Ministers have spoke to me upon it, and I know they have mentioned it when together . . . and that full and honourable satisfaction to my liking should be made to us" (Penn to Hamilton, July 7, 1757, PLB, V).

39. John Penn to Thomas Penn, Oct. 19, 1764, POC, IX.

CHAPTER XI

1. Thomas Penn to John Penn, Feb. 10, 1764, PLB, VIII.
2. William Allen to Penn, Mar. 11 and May 19, 1765, POC, IX.

3. Penn to Peters, Feb. 11, 1764, PLB, VIII.

4. Chew to Penn, Nov. 5, 1764, POC, IX.

5. Franklin to John Ross, Feb. 14, 1765, Read Manuscripts (HSP).

6. Chew to Penn, Nov. 5, 1764, POC, IX.

7. Allen to Penn, Mar. 11, 1765, POC, X.

8. Franklin to Fothergill, Mar. 14, 1764, Yale MSS.

9. Franklin to Strahan, Sept. 1, 1764, Yale MSS.

10. Benjamin Franklin to William Franklin, Nov. 9, 1765, C. M. Smith Manuscripts (HSP). Franklin thought it was better to suspend the Act until the colonies were clear of debt "& then drop it on some other decent Pretence, without ever bringing the Question of Right to a Decision."

11. Pownall and Franklin to Grenville, 1765, Yale MSS.

12. *Ibid.*

13. Franklin to John Ross, Feb. 14, 1765, Read MSS (HSP).

14. Penn to William Allen, Feb. 15, 1765, PLB, VIII.

15. Penn to Richard Hockley, Sept. 22, 1765, PLB, VIII; Penn to William Smith, Apr. 11, 1765, PLB, VIII.

16. Waln to Franklin, Oct. 11, 1765, Papers of Dr. Franklin—Miscellaneous, Vol. 75 (APS).

17. Smyth, *Writings of Benjamin Franklin*, IV, 392.

18. Penn to William Smith, Feb. 15, 1765, PLB, VIII.

19. William Logan to John Smith, Oct. 22, 1764, Smith MSS (Library Company, Phila.); Pemberton to David Barclay, June 1764, Pemberton Papers, XVII (HSD).

20. Thomas Penn to John Penn, July 6, 1765, PLB, VIII.

21. Allen to Penn, Mar. 11, 1765, POC, X.

22. Smyth, *Writings of Benjamin Franklin*, IV, 408.

23. Penn to Peters, May 18, 1769, Harvard-Sparks Transcripts (APS microcard).

24. Penn to Allen, May 19, 1767, PLB, IX.

25. Thomas Penn to John Penn, Nov. 30, 1765, PLB, VIII.

26. Smyth, *Writings of Benjamin Franklin*, V, 99.

27. Penn to Edward Shippen, July 16, 1766, PLB, IX.

28. Shippen to Penn, Sept. 25, 1765, POC, X.

29. John Penn to Thomas Penn, Sept. 12, 1766, POC, X.

30. David Hall to Franklin, Sept. 6, 1765, David Hall Letterbook (APS).

31. Casper Krible to David Deshler *et al.*, Oct. 21, 1765, Yale MSS.

32. Wharton to Franklin, Dec. 30, 1765, Yale MSS.

33. Fothergill to James Pemberton, Feb. 27, 1766, POC, X.

34. Penn to Chew, Apr. 1, 1766, PLB, VIII.

35. Penn to Allen, July 13, 1765, PLB, VIII.

36. Stiles to Franklin, Feb. 27, 1766, Yale MSS.
37. Thomas Penn to John Penn, Nov. 9, 1765, PLB, VIII.
38. Franklin to Samuel Rhoads, July 8, 1765, Society Collections—Benjamin Franklin (HSP).
39. Benjamin Franklin to [?], Feb. 27, 1766, Franklin MSS (University of Pennsylvania).
40. Penn to Chew, Apr. 1, 1766, PLB, VIII.
41. Penn to William Smith, Apr. 1, 1766, PLB, VIII. Italics mine.

CHAPTER XII

1. John Penn to Thomas Penn, Sept. 12, 1766, POC, X.
2. Samuel Purviance, Jr., to James Burd, Sept. 20, 1765, Shippen Papers —Correspondence, VII (HSP).
3. Thomas Penn to John Penn, Dec. 14, 1765, PLB, VIII.
4. *Ibid.*, Nov. 8, 1766, PLB, IX.
5. *Pennsylvania Gazette*, September 1770.
6. Samuel Purviance, Jr., to James Burd, 1766, Shippen Papers Correspondence, VII (HSP).
7. *Votes*, VIII, 7353.
8. Franklin to Ross, May 1768, Yale MSS.
9. Smyth, *Writings of Benjamin Franklin*, V, 143–45.
10. For a detailed discussion of this incident, see Carl Van Doren's *Benjamin Franklin* (New York, 1938), pp. 437–78.
11. *Ibid.*, V, 461.
12. *Ibid.*, V, 461.
13. *Ibid.*, VI, 196–97.
14. Franklin's role in the Constitutional Convention of 1776 was more honorary than substantial. There is no evidence to indicate that he had any significant influence on the form of the new government.

BIBLIOGRAPHICAL NOTE

As the Notes to this study indicate, the foundation of my investigation and its conclusions rest on the manuscript sources of Pennsylvania history. Although the Notes pertain, with few exceptions, chiefly to quotations from the sources, I have, of course, consulted the substantial number of secondary works that bear directly or tangentially upon Franklin and the problems of provincial politics. Many of these works are well known to scholars, and discussion of them is unnecessary. I have therefore selected for comment only those works that were of particular value to this study or represent a genre of interpretation.

The fundamental source for all studies of the period is the still only partly explored manuscript resource—a tremendous quantity of material that offers the colonial historian a great opportunity and challenge in all aspects of Pennsylvania history. One may begin, and be tempted to remain, in the manifold collections of the Historical Society of Pennsylvania. The Penn Manuscripts, both official and private, are the most important source of information about government, politics, land management, and the activities of important men in the colony. These are supported on the proprietary side by the papers of Richard Peters, the Shippen Papers, and the Etting Collection. The Shippen Papers, a virtually untouched mine of information, reveal the activities of a major American family—and a delightful, very close-knit family it was. The Quakers are well represented by the papers of their leading families; for politics, I have found the Norris Manuscripts, Pemberton Papers, and John Smith Diaries especially useful. These were supplemented by relevant materials from the Read Manuscripts, the Hughes Papers, the Yeates Papers, and the Gratz Collection.

The American Philosophical Society has a massive collection of Franklin Papers and related materials. It also holds a significant part of the Shippen Papers. I found the pamphlet collection in the library of the University of Pennsylvania valuable as a source of the impassioned expressions of the politicians about major and minor issues, which often reveal more about the writer than the object of his attack or defense. The Franklin project at Yale University has amassed nearly everything pertaining to Franklin, from personal letters to broadsides, and this collection, which includes many hitherto unpublished items, was a vital part of my study.

Two of the most important sources of primary materials are in printed form: the *Pennsylvania Archives. Selected and Arranged from Original Documents in the Office of the Secretary of the Commonwealth, Eighth Series,* 8 vols. (Harrisburg, 1931–35), which is usually referred to as the *Votes and Proceedings of the House of Representatives of the Province of Pennsylvania;* and the *Minutes of the Provincial Council of Pennsylvania, 1683–1776,* 10 vols. (Philadelphia, 1852–53), which is known as the *Colonial Records.* In addition, the *Pennsylvania Magazine of History and Biography (PMHB)* contains a large amount of primary source material as well as articles on Pennsylvania history.

Only one work, William R. Shepherd's *History of Proprietary Government in Pennsylvania* (New York, 1896), has attempted to examine in detail the structure and function of proprietary government. Despite its rather loose organization and difficult style, it remains a first-rate, information-packed study. Although Shepherd does not give enough attention to the period after Thomas Penn assumes power, he does explore some of the problems facing the later Proprietaries, and admits, somewhat reluctantly, worth in Thomas Penn and justice in his case against the Assembly. After Shepherd, the two standard treatments of Pennsylvania political development are Charles L. Lincoln's *The Revolutionary Movement in Pennsylvania 1760–1776* (Philadelphia, 1901) and Robert L. Brunhouse's *The Counter-Revolution in Pennsylvania 1776–1790* (Philadelphia, 1942). Both Lincoln and Brunhouse are ardent supporters of the theme of democratic growth and find it triumphant in the Pennsylvania Constitution of 1776. Both also see an illiberal combination of proprietary leaders, Quakers, merchants, and other tory-minded easterners opposing the will of the people before 1776.

Sister Joan de Lourdes Leonard, C.S.J., has done an interesting and informed study of the rapid expansion of legislative power in her unpublished doctoral dissertation, "The Composition, Organization, and Legislative Procedure of the Pennsylvania Assembly, 1682–1776" (University of Pennsylvania, 1947). She explores this problem in an article derived from the dissertation, "The Organization and Procedure of the Pennsylvania Assembly, 1682–1776" (*PMHB* [1948]).

Two thoughtful and timely works indicate that a re-examination of Pennsylvania politics is under way. David Hawke's *In the Midst of a Revolution* (Philadelphia, 1961) looks again at the critical months before and after Independence and finds that opposition to Independence was widespread among all classes, groups, and sections in the province. Roy N. Lokken's "The Concept of Democracy in Colonial Political Thought," which appeared in the *William and Mary Quarterly (WMQ)* in 1959, restates the fact that democracy had a different meaning in the eighteenth century. While men's actions may have led in a modern, democratic direction, no such direction was apparent to them or had any influence upon their actions.

Most of the numerous works devoted to the Quakers in Pennsylvania emphasize the religious impulse underlying the activities of the Society of Friends and its members. Whatever else may have been true about their places in society, the distinguishing characteristic of these men was their Quaker faith. Typical of the older works concerned with the faith and its ensuing social and political benefits for Pennsylvania are Isaac Sharpless's *A Quaker Experiment in Government* (Philadelphia, 1898) and Sidney Fisher's *The Quaker Colonies* (New Haven, 1921). More recent studies do not stray entirely from this theme, but most do admit that the Quakers had other interests, sometimes as important as their principles. Frederick Tolles, while holding high the torch of Quaker idealism, directs the light into the broader reaches of society in his excellent *Meetinghouse and Countinghouse* (Chapel Hill, 1948) and in *Quakers and the Atlantic Culture* (New York, 1960). In *James Logan and the Culture of Provincial America* (Boston, 1957), he shows in Logan's life a blend of the faith and learning of the Enlightenment. While Tolles does not deal directly with politics, his writings would agree with the view of recent political historians that the essential qualities of the faith could not survive in the rough and tumble of political conflict. Hence, tragically, the Quakers were forced to withdraw from such conflict in 1756 and 1776.

Theodore Thayer's interesting biography, *Israel Pemberton: King of the Quakers* (Philadelphia, 1943), and Robert L. D. Davidson's *War Comes to Quaker Pennsylvania 1682–1756* (New York, 1957) argue that the Quakers surrendered power in 1756 and were not responsible for what ensued in Pennsylvania thereafter. This interpretation rests on the assumption that the Quakers who were interested in preserving their power and acted against the dictates of the Meeting ceased to be Quakers. Such a view puts a narrow interpretation upon an association with a religious denomination. The fact that some Quakers were censured by the Meeting, and were thus not in good standing, did not necessarily destroy their social, political, and personal ties with the secular position of the Society in Pennsylvania. As John Adams discovered to his dismay in 1776, the Quakers remained a powerful force in provincial politics whether they were religiously sound or not.

In a later work, *Pennsylvania Politics and the Growth of Democracy 1740–1776* (Harrisburg, 1953) Thayer restates the standard interpretation that Pennsylvania, under Quaker leadership (to 1756) and afterwards under Franklin, was proceeding in a firmly democratic direction. Edwin B. Bronner's *William Penn's "Holy Experiment": The Founding of Pennsylvania, 1681–1701* (New York, 1962) finds that the settlers were forced to accept power during the colony's early years.

Most of the studies of Franklin that touch upon his political activities see him only as an imperial and national statesman. This deficiency is chargeable in part to Franklin, who directed attention in his writings to those things he found rewarding—and Pennsylvania politics was not among them. Hence his life after 1750 is understood to have been absorbed in science, travel, and imperial and revolutionary affairs. Almost invariably, he is considered an enemy of proprietary government because it was bad government, a partisan of the Assembly because it was representative and reflected local interests, and a defender of American rights against the threat of the Stamp Act and later measures of Parliament.

If used with other corrective sources, Franklin's own writings remain the best source of information about his political attitudes and actions. The standard collection is the inaccurate 10-volume edition edited by Albert H. Smyth, *The Writings of Benjamin Franklin* (New York, 1905–1907), which is now being replaced by the meticulous scholarship of the Yale-American Philosophical Society edition, Leonard Labaree, editor, *The Papers of Benjamin Franklin* (New Haven, 1959–). Until this project is completed, the *Letters and Papers of Benjamin Franklin and Richard Jackson, 1753–1785* (New York, 1945), edited by Carl Van Doren, and *Benjamin Franklin's Letters to the Press, 1758–1775* (Chapel Hill, 1950), edited by Verner Crane, are necessary supplements to the Smyth volumes.

The still great biography by Carl Van Doren, although giving inadequate coverage to Franklin's political career and unswerving in upholding the almost god-like perfection of Franklin's works, presents, nonetheless, the most satisfactory account of the whole complex design of Franklin's life. One may also find much of value in Verner Crane's two pleasantly written studies, *Benjamin Franklin: Englishman and American* (Baltimore, 1936), and *Benjamin Franklin and a Rising People* (Boston, 1954).

Two small studies deal with Franklin's political theories, expressing in both cases his optimism, pragmatism, and humanity rather than the specific theory he applied to individual political problems: Malcolm R. Eiselen's *Franklin's Political Theories* (Garden City, N.Y., 1928) and Clinton Rossiter's "Political Theory of Benjamin Franklin" (*PMHB* [1952]).

Three recent articles have dealt with episodes in Franklin's political activities. In "Benjamin Franklin and the Quaker Party, 1755–1756" (*WMQ* [1960]), John Zimmerman limits his consideration to Franklin's rise in the Assembly in 1755 and 1756 after the exclusion crisis. In "A Scurrilous Colonial Election and Franklin's Reputation" (*WMQ* [1961]), J. Phillip Gleason looks into the heated exchange of pamphlets in the election of 1764. An interesting critique of Franklin's attitude toward the German settlers is contained in Glenn Weaver's "Benjamin Franklin and the Pennsylvania Germans" (*WMQ* [1957]).

Any study of colonial Pennsylvania must consider and profit from the stimulating work of Carl Bridenbaugh in *Cities in Revolt: Urban Life in America 1743–1776* (New York, 1955) and in *Rebels and Gentlemen* (New York, 1942), written with Jessica Bridenbaugh. Both works portray a sophisticated society in Philadelphia containing numerous talented men of several religious and political persuasions.

The best treatment of Pennsylvania's Indian problems appears in

Anthony F. C. Wallace's *King of the Delawares: Teedyuscung, 1700–1763* (Philadelphia, 1949). To this may be added an older but broader work, George A. Cribbs's *The Frontier Policy of Pennsylvania* (Pittsburgh, 1919). Minorities in Pennsylvania have had their share of books and articles, but individual groups need further study. Wayland F. Dunaway's *The Scotch-Irish of Colonial Pennsylvania* (Chapel Hill, 1944) includes a great deal of information about settlements, but its analysis of the Scotch-Irish against the larger background of Pennsylvania society is limited. Useful material about the Germans is offered in Arthur D. Graeff's *The Relations between the Pennsylvania Germans and the British Authorities 1750–1776* (Norristown, 1939) and in Dietmar Rothermund's "The German Problem of Colonial Pennsylvania" (*PMHB* [1960]). There is a lack of information about the western parts of Pennsylvania. Trouble in the West that attracted the attention of government often gives the historian his only glimpse into the society of that area. Brooke Hindle ably exploits one such occasion in his article on "The March of the Paxton Boys" (*WMQ* [1946]).

The Albany Plan and Franklin's part in it have occasioned considerable interest. Verner Crane and Lawrence H. Gipson have exchanged conflicting interpretations about the contributions of Franklin, Thomas Hutchinson, and others to the Plan in the *PMHB* (1950 and 1951). The apparent final word, upholding Franklin's primary claim, may be found in the fifth volume of the *Papers of Benjamin Franklin,* previously noted. A further contribution to an understanding of the Albany Plan is Alison G. Olson's "The British Government and Colonial Union, 1754" (*WMQ* [1960]), which shows the views and hand of the Board of Trade in plans for colonial cooperation. David C. Jacobson's "John Dickinson's Fight Against Royal Government, 1764" (*WMQ* [1962]) presents Dickinson's arguments against the Old Party's petition for royal government. For a generally sympathetic view of Franklin's role in the Stamp Act crisis, Edmund S. and Helen M. Morgan's *The Stamp Act Crisis* (New York, 1953) is the standard work.

Other than anecdotal "life and times" and brief sketches such as E. H. Baldwin's "Joseph Galloway, the Loyalist Politician" (*PMHB* [1902]), few biographies of the major figures in pre-Revolutionary Pennsylvania are available. Modern writers are more likely to turn their attention to men whose importance lies in the Revolution or after-wards. One of the best studies of this type is Charles Page Smith's *James Wilson: Founding Father 1742–1798* (Chapel Hill, 1956). Of the few that portray colonial worthies, Nicholas B. Wainwright's *George Croghan: Wilderness Diplomat* (Chapel Hill, 1959) and "William Denny in Pennsylvania, 1756–1757" (*PMHB* [1957]) are both excellent. The Provincial Secretary, Richard Peters, was the subject of an informal study in Hubertis Cummings's *Richard Peters* (Philadelphia, 1944). In addition to Tolles's *Logan* and Thayer's *Pemberton,* Roy N. Lokken's *David Lloyd, Colonial Lawmaker* (Seattle, 1959) deals with a major Quaker leader. Thomas Penn, William Allen, and Isaac Norris all await the study of historians and biographers.

INDEX

Albany Congress, 63, 73–76. *See
also* Plan of Union
Allen, James, 193
Allen, William: and chancery courts,
38; Chief Justice, 45; and Franklin, 48–49, 69–70, 83–84, 177;
and proprietary policy, 54; and
Israel Pemberton, 107; and politics, 114–15, 158–60, 162, 210–
11; attacked, 157; in England,
179, 193; and the Quakers, 216
Amherst, Jeffrey, 141, 149, 151
*An Historical Review of the Consti-
tution and Government of Pennsylvania*, 128–30, 132
Andrews, Peter, 98
Armstrong, Col. John, 150
Ashbridge, George, 171
Assembly: composition, 3; powers,
5–6; conflict with Thomas Penn,
17; Indian policy, 38–39; and
paper money, 40–43; and excise,
42; and suspending clause, 57–
59; quarrel with Governor Morris, 59–61; appeals to England,
60–61; Franklin's role in, 71,
90–91, 99–104, 114, 172–73;
war tactics, 77–80; expectations
in 1757, 118; and Smith-Moore

case, 134–37; Privy Council report against, 137–39; changes in
tactics, 144–45; and Indian menace, 150–52; and crisis of 1764,
154–57, 159–60; Galloway's role
in, 172–73; political supremacy,
189, 191–95; and election of
1776, 196. *See also* Old Party;
Penn, Thomas; Proprietary Party; Quakers
Autobiography, 117–18, 208–9

Barnard, Sir John, 209
Biddle, Edward, 192
Board of Trade: on colonial defense,
39; and Thomas Penn, 44–45;
and Indian policy, 63; rejects As-
sembly petition, 78–79; influence
of, 122; report on Pennsylvania
legislation, 137–39
Bouquet, Henry, 149
Brown, Hinton, 61
Bryan, George, 193, 201
Burd, Col. James, 165
Bute, Lord, 147–48, 185

Carlisle Conference, 63
Chancery courts, 8, 37–38
Charity schools, 67–69